Computer Science with Python

Textbook - XII

(As per CBSE Syllabus CODE 083)

Meenu Kohli

www.bpbonline.com

FIRST EDITION 2022

ISBN: 978-93-5551-170-6

Distributors:

BPB PUBLICATIONS
20, Ansari Road, Darya Ganj
New Delhi-110002
Ph: 23254990/23254991

MICRO MEDIA
Shop No. 5, Mahendra Chambers,
150 DN Rd. Next to Capital Cinema,
V.T. (C.S.T.) Station, MUMBAI-400 001
Ph: 22078296/22078297

DECCAN AGENCIES
4-3-329, Bank Street,
Hyderabad-500195
Ph: 24756967/24756400

BPB BOOK CENTRE
376 Old Lajpat Rai Market,
Delhi-110006
Ph: 23861747

Published by Manish Jain for BPB Publications, 20 Ansari Road, Darya Ganj, New Delhi-110002
and Printed by him at Manipal Technologies Limited, Manipal

www.bpbonline.com

Dedicated to

My two pillars of strength and source of encouragement
RAdm S.M. Sharma, AVSM, VSM (Retd.) and Mrs. Kavita Sharma
Who believed in me when I did not in myself...

About the Author

Meenu Kohli is the author of "Python Interview Questions", "Basic Core Python Programming" and "Advance Core Python Programming". A B.E. (Electronics) from D.Y. Patil College of Engineering, Pune University, she has worked extensively as a Software Developer, Tester, and Trainer in reputed MNCs. She has experience of working on challenging projects across varied development environments such as Python, Java, EJB, C, C++, PHP, JSP, JavaScript, HTML, .NET, R, MySQL, Oracle, DB2. She is a keen observer and passionate learner. In addition to software development, she is also a professionally trained software tester and a certified Six Sigma Green Belt from the National Institute of Industrial Engineering – Mumbai. She has experience of teaching Electronics and Computer Science undergraduate students and has also imparted her knowledge to several software-development courses. She later diversified into writing technical books primarily related to Python.

Acknowledgement

This book is a dream come true for me as I always wanted to write a book for school children. I would like to thank Team BPB for believing in my abilities and giving me this opportunity. I hope that I am able to impart valuable information to the readers and make them fall in love with computer science and Python.

Preface

This book has been designed for Class XII students appearing for CBSE's **Computer Science with Python** (083) board exam. It has been designed as per the new revised syllabus. The book explains all the topics in detail along with examples. It covers all the topics for Term1 and Term 2 class XII board exams. The content of this book is divided into three Units as shown below:

Unit I: Computational Thinking and Programming – 2

Chapter 1 Functions

Chapter 2 Recursion

Chapter 3 Files

Chapter 4 Efficiency Ideas

Chapter 5 Stack and Queues

Unit II: Computer Networks

Chapter 1 Evolution of Networking

Chapter 2 Data Communication Terminologies

Chapter 3 Network Devices

Chapter 4 Network Topologies Types

Chapter 5 Network Protocol

Chapter 6 Mobile Telecommunication Technology

Chapter 7 Introduction to Web Services

Unit III: Database Management

Chapter 1 Database Concepts

Chapter 2 Working with Queries

Chapter 3 Joins

Chapter 4 MySQL for Python

Syllabus

TERM 1:

UNIT I: COMPUTATIONAL THINKING AND PROGRAMMING – 2

Revision of Python topics covered in Class XI.

Functions: types of function (built-in functions, functions defined in module, user defined functions), creating user defined function, arguments and parameters, default parameters, positional parameters, function returning value(s), flow of execution, scope of a variable (global scope, local scope)

Introduction to files, types of files (Text file, Binary file, CSV file), relative and absolute paths

Text file: opening a text file, text file open modes (r, r+, w, w+, a, a+), closing a text file, opening a file using with clause, writing/appending data to a text file using write() and writelines(), reading from a text file using read(), readline() and readlines(), seek and tell methods, manipulation of data in a text file

Binary file: basic operations on a binary file: open using file open modes (rb, rb+, wb, wb+, ab, ab+), close a binary file, import pickle module, dump() and load() method, read, write/create, search, append and update operations in a binary file

CSV file: import csv module, open / close csv file, write into a csv file using csv.writerow() and read from a csv file using csv.reader( ) TERM 2: Unit I: Computational Thinking and Programming – 2

Data Structure: Stack, operations on stack (push & pop), implementation of stack using list.

UNIT II: COMPUTER NETWORKS

- **Evolution of networking:** introduction to computer networks, evolution of networking (ARPANET, NSFNET, INTERNET)
- **Data communication terminologies:** concept of communication, components of data communication (sender,receiver, message, communication media, protocols), measuring capacity of communication media (bandwidth, data transfer rate), IP address, switching techniques (Circuit switching, Packet switching)
- **Transmission media:** Wired communication media (Twisted pair cable, Co-axial cable, Fiber-optic cable), Wireless media (Radio waves, Micro waves, Infrared waves
- Network devices (Modem, Ethernet card, RJ45, Repeater, Hub, Switch, Router, Gateway, WIFI card)
- **Network topologies and Network types:** types of networks (PAN, LAN, MAN, WAN), networking topologies (Bus, Star, Tree)
- **Network protocol:** HTTP, FTP, PPP, SMTP, TCP/IP, POP3, HTTPS, TELNET, VoIP
- **Introduction to web services:** WWW, Hyper Text Markup Language (HTML), Extensible Markup Language (XML), domain names, URL, website, web browser, web servers, web hosting

UNIT III: DATABASE MANAGEMENT

- **Database concepts:** introduction to database concepts and its need
- **Relational data model:** relation, attribute, tuple, domain, degree, cardinality, keys (candidate key, primary key, alternate key, foreign key)
- **Structured Query Language:** introduction, Data Definition Language and Data Manipulation Language, data type (char(n), varchar(n), int, float, date), constraints (not null, unique, primary key), create database, use database, show databases, drop database, show tables, create table, describe table, alter table (add and remove an attribute, add and remove primary key), drop table, insert, delete, select, operators (mathematical, relational and logical), aliasing, distinct clause, where clause, in, between, order by, meaning of null, is null, is not null, like, update command, delete command
- **Aggregate functions (max, min, avg, sum, count), group by, having clause, joins :** Cartesian product on two tables, equi-join and natural join
- **Interface of python with an SQL database:** connecting SQL with Python, performing insert, update, delete queries using cursor, display data by using fetchone(), fetchall(), rowcount, creating database connectivity applications

Code Bundle and Coloured Images

Please follow the link to download the
Code Bundle and the *Coloured Images* of the book:

https://rebrand.ly/001a84

The code bundle for the book is also hosted on GitHub at **https://github.com/bpb-publications/Computer-Science-with-Python-Textbook--XII**. In case there's an update to the code, it will be updated on the existing GitHub repository.

We have code bundles from our rich catalogue of books and videos available at **https://github.com/bpbpublications**. Check them out!

Errata

We take immense pride in our work at BPB Publications and follow best practices to ensure the accuracy of our content to provide with an indulging reading experience to our subscribers. Our readers are our mirrors, and we use their inputs to reflect and improve upon human errors, if any, that may have occurred during the publishing processes involved. To let us maintain the quality and help us reach out to any readers who might be having difficulties due to any unforeseen errors, please write to us at :

errata@bpbonline.com

Your support, suggestions and feedbacks are highly appreciated by the BPB Publications' Family.

Piracy

If you come across any illegal copies of our works in any form on the internet, we would be grateful if you would provide us with the location address or website name. Please contact us at **business@bpbonline.com** with a link to the material.

If you are interested in becoming an author

If there is a topic that you have expertise in, and you are interested in either writing or contributing to a book, please visit **www.bpbonline.com**. We have worked with thousands of developers and tech professionals, just like you, to help them share their insights with the global tech community. You can make a general application, apply for a specific hot topic that we are recruiting an author for, or submit your own idea.

Reviews

Please leave a review. Once you have read and used this book, why not leave a review on the site that you purchased it from? Potential readers can then see and use your unbiased opinion to make purchase decisions. We at BPB can understand what you think about our products, and our authors can see your feedback on their book. Thank you!

For more information about BPB, please visit **www.bpbonline.com**.

Contents

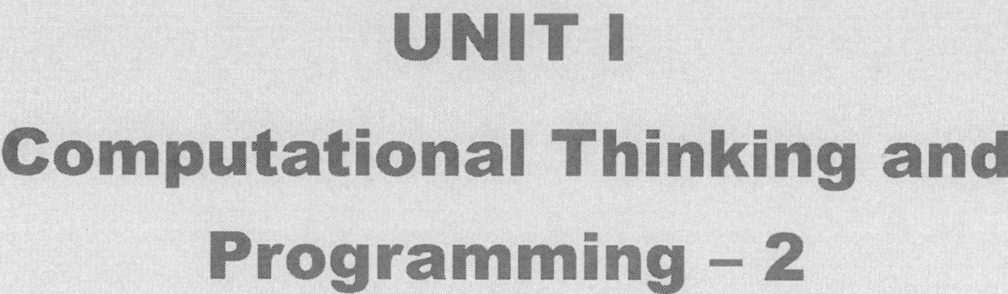

UNIT I

Computational Thinking and Programming – 2

- Functions
- Recursion
- Files
- Efficiency Idea
- Stack and Queue

1 Functions

In this chapter, you will cover:

- **Functions:** Types of function (built-in functions, functions defined in module, user defined functions), creating user defined function, arguments and parameters, default parameters, positional parameters, function returning value(s), flow of execution, scope of a variable (global scope, local scope).
- **Python libraries:** Creating python libraries.

Introduction

You have learnt about Python basics and Python data types and control structure. In this chapter, you will learn how to create functions. A function is block of reusable code that is defined to carry out one particular task.

1.1 What are functions?

In this chapter, you will learn about 'functions' which is the core topic for any object-oriented programming language. Functions form the most important aspect of programming in Python. The time has come to combine and use all the Python concepts that you have learned in class XI to create reusable functions. Functions are organized blocks of reusable code. Functions are important because:

- They provide better readability and modularity*.
- Functions help save time and effort in designing and executing the code.
- Functions reduce duplication of code.
- They make code reusable.
- They Make code easy to maintain.
- With functions it becomes easier to understand how the code works.
- Functions help in dividing complex large problem into smaller simple problems.
- Functions help in information hiding.

Notes

* The act of dividing a program or code into individual independent modules is called modularity.

In Python programming, functions can be classified into two types:

a. **Built-in functions:** Built-in functions are functions that are provided by Python. They are readily available. All the functions that we have worked with till now are all built-in functions such as max(), min(), len(), dir(), slice(), sorted() and so on.

b. **User-defined functions:** This chapter is actually all about user-defined functions. These functions are not provided by Python, but are created by programmers to perform a particular task.

1.2 Creating Functions

In the last section, you learnt about advantages of working with functions. Functions make code reusable. If there is a block of code that you need to execute often, you can put that block of code in a function, and call it whenever the specific task, defined by that block of code is required. There is a software development practice by the acronym 'DRY' that stands for"Don't Repeat Yourself". So, we can say that functions help in keeping the code DRY. This is opposite to another coding acronym called WET, which stands for "Write Everything Twice". So, we can say that we do not want to keep our code WET.

1.2.1 Simple Functions

In this section, you will create your first function.

For creating a function, you will have to follow certain rules regarding:

- How to define a function
- The function body
- Calling a function

1.2.1.1 Definition of a function

1. The definition of a function starts with the 'def' keyword.
2. The `def` keyword is followed by the name of the function.
3. The name of the function is followed by `parenthesis ()`.
4. After the parenthesis comes the colon : which marks the beginning of the function's block of code.

```
def helloWorldFunc():
```

1.2.1.2 Function Body

The block of code that comes after the function definition should be indented one level to the right, which is four spaces as per PEP-8. You may be aware of this rule as you have implemented the same while working with the **if...else** statement, and loops such as the **for** and **while** loop.

```
def hello_world_func():
    '''
    This is my first function.
    I am learning a lot and this looks like fun
    This function just prints a message.
    '''
    print('My first function prints HELLO WORLD!!')
```

1.2.1.3 Calling a function

You can call the function anytime by its name followed by parenthesis.

```
hello_world_func()
```

A function does not execute as long it is called **explicitly**.

Code:

```
def hello_world_func(name):
    '''
    This is my first function.
    I am learning a lot and this looks like fun
    This function just prints a message.
    '''
    print('My first function prints HELLO WORLD!! I am {}'.format(name))

hello_world_func('Meenu')
```

You may recall that strings in triple quotes are used for multi-line commenting, and if placed directly under the definition of the function, module or class it acts as docstring. The multi-line comment in triple quotes is highlighted in bold for your understanding. It is not mandatory, but it can be of great help in understanding complex functions as you will see in a short while.

The function `hello_world_func()` has only one print statement. There are some points, which are not mandatory but are best practices to follow:

1. Use lowercase letters for function name, words can be separated by underscore. Some also prefer to use camel case.
2. It is recommended to have a docstring as the first part of the function. The docstring must emphasize on what the function does, and not on how it does it.
3. Place the code after docstring.

Output:

```
My first function prints HELLO WORLD!!
>>>
```

Now, type the following command on the Python shell:

```
help(hello_world_func())
```

This command will give details about the structure of this function.

```
>>> help(hello_world_func())
My first function prints HELLO WORLD!!
Help on NoneType object:

class NoneType(object)
 |  Methods defined here:
 |
 |  __bool__(self, /)
 |      self != 0
 |
 |  __repr__(self, /)
 |      Return repr(self).
 |
 |  ----------------------------------------------------------------------
 |  Static methods defined here:
 |
 |  __new__(*args, **kwargs) from builtins.type
 |      Create and return a new object.  See help(type) for accurate signature.
```

To view the docstring, print the following command:

```
>>>print(hello_world_func.__doc__)
This is my first function.
I am learning a lot and this looks like fun
This function just prints a message.
>>>
```

1.2.2 Defining functions that take parameter

The code shown in the previous section defines a simple function. In this section, we will modify the same function to take parameter that is the name of a person, and prints the name along with the message.

```
def hello_world_func(name):
   '''
   This is my first function.
   I am learning a lot and this looks like fun
   This function just prints a message.
   '''

   print('My first function prints HELLO WORLD!! I am {}'.format(name))

hello_world_func('Meenu')
```

In the function definition, the parenthesis has a parameter **name**. So, when you call **hello_world_func()**, you have to pass an argument that can be passed on to the function.

```
Output:
My first function prints HELLO WORLD!! I am Meenu
>>>
```

Explanation: To understand how the code works, it is important to first understand the difference between a parameter, and an argument.

```
                    Parameter
def hello_world_func(name):
    '''
This is my first function.
I am learning a lot and this looks like fun
This function just prints a message.
'''
    print('My first function prints HELLO WORLD!! I am {}'.format(name))


hello_world_func(Meenu)
                    Argument
```

Figure 1.1: *Difference between a parameter, and an argument*

Parameters are variables local to function, and are part of definition. Arguments are values that are passed on to the function. So, **name** is the parameter of the function **hello_world_func()** and "**Meenu**" is the argument that is passed on to the function **hello_world_func()** when it is called. When the function **hello_world_func()** is called, parameter **'name'** is mapped with the argument **'Meenu'** and this value is then used for computation purposes.

A function can have more than one parameter, and in that case order in which arguments are passed matters. For example, look at the following code:

```
def hello_world_func(name,age,profession):
    '''
    This is my first function.
    I am learning a lot and this looks like fun
    This function just prints a message.
    '''
    print('I am {} years old.'.format(age))
    print('My name is {}.'.format(name))
    print('I am {} by profession.'.format(profession))
hello_world_func(32,'Architect','Michael')
```

The function **hello_world_func()** takes three parameters in the following order **name**, **age**, **profession**.

The arguments are passed to the function in the order: **32,'Architect','Michael'**.

As a result, the parameter **name** gets mapped to value **32**, **age** gets mapped to **'Architect'** and **profession** gets mapped to **'Michael'**. So, when we execute the code following output is generated:

```
I am Architect years old.
My name is 32.
I am Michael by profession.
```

So, now let's call the function **`hello_world_func()`** and pass the arguments in the right order.

hello_world_func('Michael',32,'Architect')

Output:

```
I am 32 years old.
My name is Michael.
I am Architect by profession.
```

Python programmers often use parameters and arguments interchangeably as both are in a way quite similar but as a Python developer, you should know the difference between the two. Parameters are declared in the function definition, and arguments are passed through as values to a function when it is called.

1.3 Functional arguments

There are three types of functional arguments in Python.

a. Positional arguments
b. Default arguments
c. Keyword arguments

1.3.1 Positional arguments

All the examples that we have used till now are examples of positional arguments, i.e., arguments are assigned to the parameters in the order in which they are passed or their position.

```
def sum_prod(num1,num2):
    num_sum = num1 + num2
    num_prod = num1 * num2
    return num_sum,num_prod
x = int(input('Enter the first number :'))
y = int(input('Enter the second number :'))
print(sum_prod(x,y))
```

Output:

```
Enter the first number :10
Enter the second number :20
(30, 200)
>>>
```

The position argument looks at the position of the parameter where it will be assigned. So, the value of x gets mapped to num1, and value of y gets mapped to num2 and these values are passed on to the function block code.

If you call a function with different number of parameters, an error will be generated.

1.3.2 Default arguments

You have the option of specifying default value of a parameter in the function definition. The positional argument for which a default value is defined, becomes optional and therefore known as default argument.

Code:

```
def sum_prod(num1,num2 =0):
    num_sum = num1 + num2
    num_prod = num1 * num2
    return num_sum,num_prod

print(sum_prod(2,5))
print(sum_prod(2))
```

Output:

```
(7, 10)
(2, 0)
>>>
```

The function shown above can be called with one or two arguments. If you omit the second argument, the function definition will pass on its default value, which is 0.

Let's take a look at another example.

In Python, a non-default argument cannot follow a default argument.

```
def sum_func(num1,num2 =0,num3):
    return num1+num2+num3
```

The preceding function will throw an error because num3 which is a non-default argument follows num2, which is a default argument. So, if you type sum_func(10,20), the interpreter will not understand whether to assign 20 to num2 or continue with the default value. The complexity will increase as the number of default arguments increase.

```
def sum_func(num1,num2 =30,num3=40):
    return num1 + num2 + num3


print(sum_func(10))
print(sum_func(10,20))
print(sum_func(10,20,30))
```

Output:

```
80
70
60
>>>
```

1.3.3 Keyword arguments

Keyword arguments allow you to ignore the order in which the parameters are entered in a function or even skip them when calling a function.

The function with keyword arguments are defined the same way as the function with positional arguments, but the difference is in the way they are called. Have a look at the following code:

```
def sum_func(num1,num2 =30,num3=40):
    print("num1 = ", num1)
    print("num2 = ", num2)
    print("num3 = ", num3)
    return num1 + num2 + num3

print(sum_func(num3 = 10, num1 =20))
```

Output:

```
num1 = 20
num2 = 30
num3 = 10
60
>>>
```

As you can see, the arguments are not passed in the desired order, but while passing the arguments, it is specified which argument belongs to which parameter. Since the default value of num2 is zero, even if it is skipped, it does not matter. We wanted to use the default value of num2. So, the value of num1 and num3 were specified. If that is not done, the output will be incorrect. As you can see in the following code, the value 20 is assigned to num2 and default value of num3 is taken as a result of which the result is completely different.

Code:

```
def sum_func(num1,num2 =30,num3=40):
    print("num1 = ", num1)
    print("num2 = ", num2)
    print("num3 = ", num3)
    return num1 + num2 + num3
print(sum_func(10, 20))
```

Output:

```
num1 = 10
num2 = 20
num3 = 40
70
>>>
```

1.4 The return statement

The **return** statement is used at the end of the function when there is a need to send back the result of the function back to the caller. Software programming is not about printing results all the time. There are some calculations that must be performed behind the scene, hidden from the users. These values are further used in calculations to get the final output that the users desire. The value obtained from the **return** statement can be assigned to a variable and used further for calculations.

Look at the code given in the box below. The function **`adding_numbers()`** adds three numbers and returns the result which is is assigned to variable x. The value of x is then displayed as output.

```
def adding_numbers(num1, num2, num3):
    print('Have to add three numbers')
    print('First Number = {}'.format(num1))
    print('Second Number = {}'.format(num2))
    print('Third Number = {}'.format(num3))
    return num1 + num2 + num3

x = adding_numbers(10, 20, 30)
print('The function returned a value of {}'.format(x))
```

Output:

```
Have to add three numbers
First Number = 10
Second Number = 20
Third Number = 30
The function returned a value of 60
```

So you can say that:

1. A **`return`** statement exits the function. It is the last statement of a function, and any statement coming after that will not be executed.
2. It sends back a value that can be **None**. So, it is said that when a function does not return a value explicitly it returns **`None`** implicitly.
3. If a function has to return more than one value, then all the values will be returned as a tuple.

Example 1.1

Write a function that prompts the user to enter values for list. The function should return back the length of the list.

Answer:

```
def find_len(list1):
    return len(list1)
x = input('Enter the values separated by single space :')
x_list = x.split()
print(find_len(x_list))
```

Output:

Enter the values separated by single space :1 'Gmail' 'Google' 1.09 [2,3,45,9]

5

>>>

Explaination: When you execute the program, you will be prompted to enter valules separated by single space. In this case, five values are passed:

1. 1
2. 'Gmail'
3. 'Google'
4. 1.09
5. [2,3,45,9]

So, the program counts the number of elements passed in as inputs, and displays the result of 5.

Example 1.2

The following code returns the value of sum and product of two numbers.

Code:

```
def sum_prod(num1,num2):
    num_sum = num1 + num2
    num_prod = num1 * num2
    return num_sum,num_prod
```

```
x = int(input('Enter the first number :'))
y = int(input('Enter the second number :'))
print(sum_prod(x,y))
```

Output:

Enter the first number :10

Enter the second number :20

(30, 200)

Example 1.3

Write code to find the HCF of two given numbers.

Answer:

HCF stands for Highest Common Factor or Greatest Common Divisor for two numbers. This means that it is the largest number within the range of 1 to smaller of the two given numbers that divides the two numbers perfectly giving the remainder as zero.

1. **Define a function hcf() that takes two numbers as input.**

```
def hcf(x,y):
```

2. **Find out which of the two numbers is greatest, the other one will be the smallest.**

```
small_num = 0
if x > y:
    small_num = y
else:
    small_num = x
```

Set a for loop for the range **1** to **small_num+1**. (We take the upper limit as **small_num+1** because the **for** loop operates for one number less than the upper limit of the range). In this **for** loop, divide both the numbers with each number in the range, and if any number divides both, perfectly assign that value to **hcf** as shown in the following code:

```
for i in range(1,small_num+1):
    if (x % i == 0) and (y % i == 0):
        hcf = i
```

Suppose, the two numbers are 6 and 24, first both numbers are divisible by 2. So, hcf = 2, then both numbers will be divisible by 3. So, the value of 3 will be assigned to 3. Then, the loop will encounter 6, which will again divide both the numbers equally. So, 6 will be assigned to hcf. Since the upper limit of the range has reached, the function will finally have hcf value of 6.

3. **Return the value of hcf:**

```
return hcf
```

Code:

```
def hcf(x,y):
    small_num = 0
    if x > y:
        small_num = y
    else:
        small_num = x
    for i in range(1,small_num+1):
        if (x % i == 0) and (y % i == 0):
            hcf = i
    return hcf
print(hcf(6,24))
```

Output:

```
6
```

1.5 Scopes and namespace

Namespace is a container that has all the names (**of variables/functions/classes**) that you define. You can define same names in different namespaces. A name or a variable exists in a specific area of the code which defines its scope. The information regarding binding between the variables/objects is stored in the namespace. There are three types of namespaces or scopes.

a. **Built-in Namespace:** These are in-built functions that are available across all files or modules.

b. **Global Namespace:** The global namespace has all the variables, functions, and classes that are available in a single file.

c. **Local Namespace:** The local namespace are variables defined within a function.

The scopes are nested, which means that the local namespace is nested within a global namespace which is nested within built-in namespace. Each scope has its namespace.

1.5.1 Built-in namespace

Built-in namespace are available across all the files, and modules in Python. All functions that you see below print(), tuple(), type() are all built-in function, and belong to this namespace and are available across all files and modules in Python.

```
>>> list1 = [1,2,3,4,5,6]
>>> tup1 = tuple(list1)
>>> type(tup1)
<class 'tuple'>

>>> print("Hi")
Hi
>>>
```

1.5.2 Global namespace

```
Look at the following code:
x = 20
x += y
print(x)
```

When we execute this code, it generates a Name Error:

Output:

```
Traceback (most recent call last):
  File "F:\2020 - BPB\input.py", line 2, in <module>
    x += y
NameError: name 'y' is not defined
>>>
```

This is because Python looks for the name **y** in the global namespace, and fails to find it. It then looks for it in the built-in namespace, and does not find it again. Hence, an error is generated. The following code works fine and does not produce any error because the statement **y = 5** created a global namespace:

```
x = 20
y = 5
x += y
print(x)
```

Output:

```
25
>>>
```

1.5.3 Local namespace

Now, let's look at another example.

Code:

```
x = 20
def print_x():
    x = 10
    print('Local variable x is equal to ',x )

print('Global variable x is equal to ',x )
print_x()
```

Output:

```
Global variable x is  equal to  20
Local variable x is  equal to  10
>>>
```

When a call is made to the function, the Python interpreter tries to locate the local variable called **x**. If that is not available, it will look for **x** at global namespace.

Code:

```
x = 20
def print_x():
    print('Local variable x is equal to ',x )

print('Global variable x is equal to ',x )
print_x()
```

Output:

```
Global variable x is  equal to  20
Local variable x is  equal to  20
>>>
```

Local variables, i.e., the variables within a function are created when a call is made to that function. When a function is called, a new scope is created, and variables are assigned to that scope. Once the function has been executed, its scope also disappears. In the first example, when the function print_x() was called, it was able to find a local variable x = 10 within the local namespace, and used it up. The value of x existed within the function, and vanishes when the function stops executing.

Sometimes, when we want to use the global variable inside our function namespace, we should use global keyword for clarity. Look at the following code:

Code:

```
x = 20
def print_x():
    global x
    x = 10
    print('Local variable x is equal to ',x )

print('Global variable x is equal to ',x )
print_x()
print('Global variable x is equal to ',x )
```

The moment global keyword is used, the function print_x() comes to know that the global variable x will be used. In the next statement x = 10, the value 10 is assigned to x which is a global variable. Therefore, you will see in the output the value of global variable x is 20 before the function is called, and 10 after the function is called. When you are using a **global** keyword with a variable name within a function, Python will not allow you to create another variable with the same name within the same function.

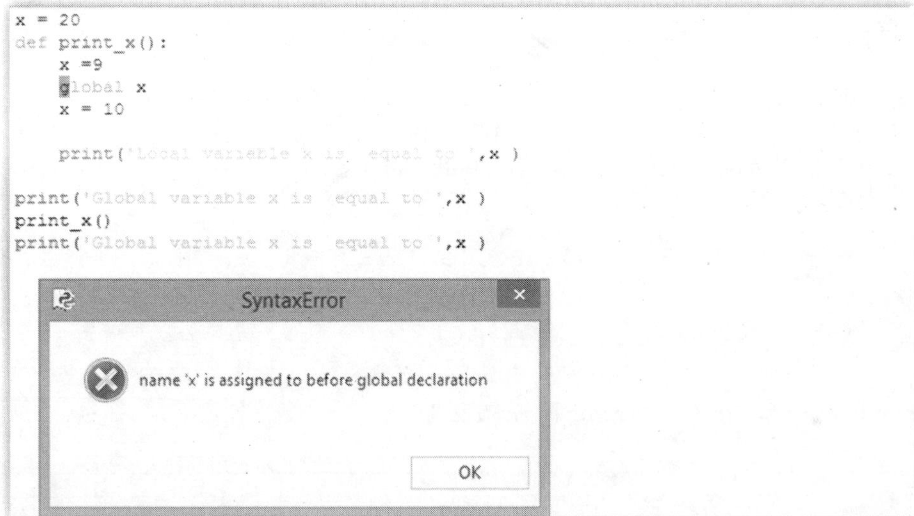

Figure 1.2: *Python does not allow you to create another variable within a function with the same name*

1.6 Using functions in Modules

You can organize your code in Python with the help of modules. Modules can be used to group functions or pieces of related code. This makes it easier to understand and develop programs. Modules can have classes, functions and variables. This section explains how to define functions in modules and use them. Module can be defined as part of code library. It is nothing but a file which contains a set of functions that you want to use in your program.

A module is Python file with .py extension.

Let's create a file: `my_first_module.py`.

Step 1: Write the code for your module.

In this case we have written a small function **`happy_birthday()`** as shown below:

```
def happy_birthday(name):
    print("Happy Birthday dear ", name," !!")
```

Figure 1.3: *happy_birthday() function*

Step 2: Save your file with .py extension in the "Lib" folder in Python directory

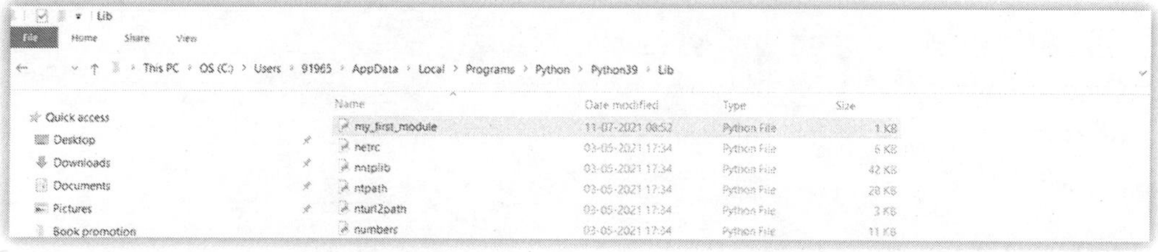

```
Lib
File  Home  Share  View
This PC > OS (C:) > Users > 91965 > AppData > Local > Programs > Python > Python39 > Lib
```

Name	Date modified	Type	Size
my_first_module	11-07-2021 08:52	Python File	1 KB
netrc	03-05-2021 17:34	Python File	6 KB
nntplib	03-05-2021 17:34	Python File	42 KB
ntpath	03-05-2021 17:34	Python File	28 KB
nturl2path	03-05-2021 17:34	Python File	3 KB
numbers	03-05-2021 17:34	Python File	11 KB

Figure 1.4: *Saving file with .py extension in "Lib" folder*

Your module is ready.

```
>>> import my_first_module
>>> my_first_module.happy_birthday("Rajiv")
Happy Birthday dear  Rajiv  !!
>>> 
```

Figure 1.5: *Access Module*

1.7 Python Libraries

We have seen how to create a module. A module is nothing but a Python file that contains functions, variables and classes. A collection of modules is known as a **package** or a **Python library**.

Modules are used to bring in clarity by allowing modularity of code. They are used to group relatable code together and make it reusable. By doing so, it becomes easy to understand code. We can use a module in our code with the help of import statement.

`import module_name`

to check all the functions and other attributes of a module give the following command

`dir(module_name)`

```
>>> import random
>>> dir(random)
['BPF', 'LOG4', 'NV_MAGICCONST', 'RECIP_BPF', 'Random', 'SG_MAGICCONST', 'System
Random', 'TWOPI', '_Sequence', '_Set', '__all__', '__builtins__', '__cached__',
'__doc__', '__file__', '__loader__', '__name__', '__package__', '__spec__', '_ac
cumulate', '_acos', '_bisect', '_ceil', '_cos', '_e', '_exp', '_floor', '_inst',
 '_log', '_os', '_pi', '_random', '_repeat', '_sha512', '_sin', '_sqrt', '_test'
, '_test_generator', '_urandom', '_warn', 'betavariate', 'choice', 'choices', 'e
xpovariate', 'gammavariate', 'gauss', 'getrandbits', 'getstate', 'lognormvariate
', 'normalvariate', 'paretovariate', 'randbytes', 'randint', 'random', 'randrang
e', 'sample', 'seed', 'setstate', 'shuffle', 'triangular', 'uniform', 'vonmisesv
ariate', 'weibullvariate']
```

Figure 1.6: *Accessing* ***random*** *module*

If you want to make use of certain attributes of a module in your code you can do that by using from along with import statement.

from filename import function_name

e.g. **from math import math.sqrt**

To import all names from a module into your code use from *

*from <filename> import**

With the help of dot notation you can use any function of the module.

Example:

From math import*

math.sqrt(21)

Collection of related modules is known as a library. A library also has a **_init_.py** file.

The **__init__.py** file informs the interpreter that a Python module exists in a directory. This file can be blank. It is mandatory to have a **__init__.py** file if want to import modules from another folder into your project.

Creating Python Library is very easy. Here are the steps that you can follow to create a Python library.

Step 1: **Create the structure of your directory:** We are going to create a directory by the name **mygreetinglibrary** as shown in the figure 1.7:

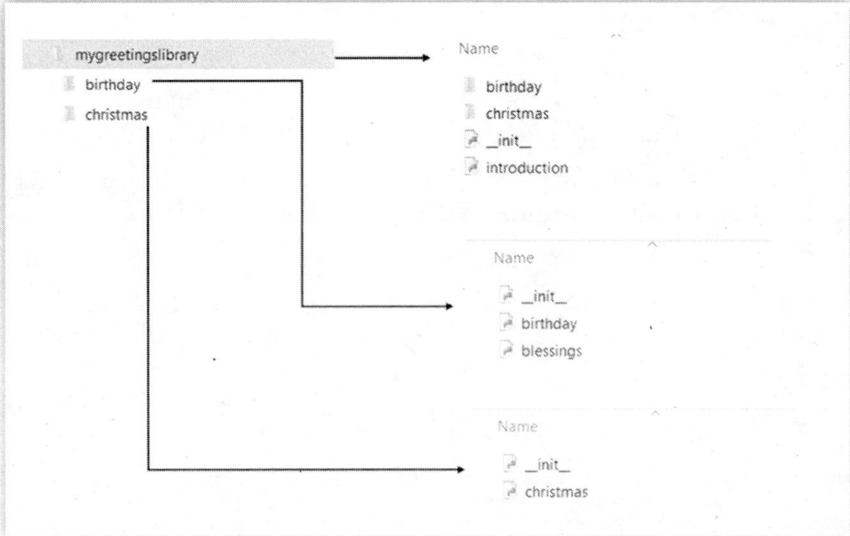

Figure 1.7: *Create structure of directory*

Step 2: **Create your Python files and save it in the right location**: The _init_.py file can be empty but is mandatory.

introduction.py

```
def introduction():
print("HI this is a greetings library")
```

birthday.py

```
def christmas():
print("Merry Christmas")
```

blessings.py

```
def blessings():
print("God bless you")
```

christmas.py

```
def christmas():
print("Merry Christmas")
```

Step 3: **Locate the site-packages folder and paste your package in it:** To use our package it must be place in the site-packages folder of the Python distribution. You can locate the folder as shown in figure 1.8:

```
Python 3.9.5 (tags/v3.9.5:0a7dcbd, May  3 2021, 17:27:52) [MSC v.1928 64 bit (AMD64)] on win32
Type "help", "copyright", "credits" or "license()" for more information.
>>> import sys
>>> print(sys.path)
['', 'C:\\Users\\91965\\AppData\\Local\\Programs\\Python\\Python39\\Lib\\idlelib', 'C:\\Users\\91965\\AppData\\Loca
l\\Programs\\Python\\Python39\\python39.zip', 'C:\\Users\\91965\\AppData\\Local\\Programs\\Python\\Python39\\DLLs',
'C:\\Users\\91965\\AppData\\Local\\Programs\\Python\\Python39\\lib', 'C:\\Users\\91965\\AppData\\Local\\Programs\\P
ython\\Python39', 'C:\\Users\\91965\\AppData\\Local\\Programs\\Python\\Python39\\lib\\site-packages']
>>> |
```

Figure 1.8: *import sys and print sys.path to get the location of site-packages.*

Go to site-packages folder and paste your package there.

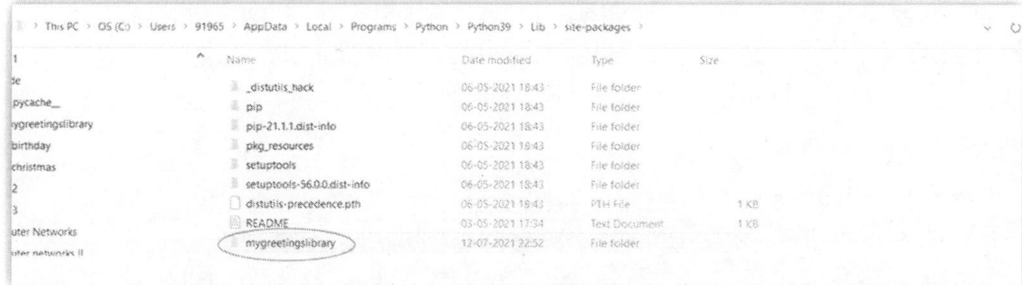

Figure 1.9: *paste your mygreetinglibrary folder in site-packages.*

Step 4: Import your library and use it.

```
>>> import mygreetingslibrary.introduction
>>> mygreetingslibrary.introduction.introduction()
HI this is a greetings library
>>>



>>> import mygreetingslibrary.birthday.blessings
>>> mygreetingslibrary.birthday.blessings.blessings()
God bless you
>>>
```

***Figure 1.10:** importing mygreetingslibrary*

Points to remember

- Functions are organized blocks of reusable code.
- Functions simplify coding, and have many advantages.
- Every function is dedicated to perform single-related action.
- In Python programming functions can be classified as:
  1. Built-in functions that are provided by Python.
  2. User-defined functions that are created using python by programmers to perform a particular task.
- A function block begins with the keyword **def** and is followed by the function name and parenthesis() after which a colon (:) is placed to mark the beginning of the function code block.
- The code block must be properly indented as per PEP-8.
- You can call the function anytime by its name followed by parenthesis.
- The function does not execute as long it is called explicitly.
- You can use docstring for documenting important features of a function
- Functions may or may not take parameters it depends on the function definition.
- Parameters are variables local to function and are part of definition.
- There are three types of functional arguments in Python.
  a. Positional arguments
  b. Default arguments
  c. Keyword arguments
- Return statement is used for exiting a function by passing back an expression to caller.
- It is possible for a program to return nothing(None).
- Namespace is a space that has all the names(of variables/functions/classes) that you define in a program.
- Namespace ensure that the names are unique so that there is no conflict.
- In Python, namespace is implemented in form of dictionary.
- The namespace maintains a name to object mapping where the name acts as a key and objects are values.

- A name or a variable exists in a specific area of the code, which defines its scope. A variable can reach anywhere in the area that is defined by its scope. Three types of namespace or scopes are as follows:
    a. **Built-in Namespace:** These are in-built functions that are available across all files or modules.
    b. **Global Namespace:** The global namespace has all the variables, functions, and classes that are available in inside a single file.
    c. **Local Namespace:** The local namespace are variables defined within a function.

Conclusion

In this chapter, you learnt how to create your own functions. You will learn recursion in Python in the next chapter.

? EXERCISE

Short questions and answers

1. **A named block of code than can be reused and called by its name is called a ________.**

   Answer: Function

2. **Why are functions required?**

Answer: Many times in a program, a certain set of instructions may be called more than once. Instead of repeating the same piece of code, it is better to define a function, and place the code in it. The function can then be called whenever there is a need. This saves time and effort, and the program can be developed easily. Functions help in organizing the code, and testing of code also becomes easy.

3. **What is the difference between passing immutable and mutable objects as argument to a function?**

   Answer: If immutable arguments such as strings, integers, or tuples are passed to a function, the object reference is passed but the value of these parameters cannot be changed. It acts like pass by value call. Mutable objects too are passed by object reference, but their values can be changed.

4. **In- built functions can be used easily by importing the modules in which they are defined in your code.**

   a) True

   b) False

   Answer: False

5. **Functions provide better modularity.**

   a) True

   b) False

   Answer: True

Coding questions and answers

1. **Write code to find all possible palindromic partitions in a string.**

   Answer: The code to find all possible palindromic partitions in a string will involve the following steps:

   1. Create a list of all possible substrings.
   2. Substrings are created by slicing the strings as all possible levels using for loop.
   3. Every subtring is then checked to see whether it is a palindrome.
   4. The substring is converted to a list of single characters.
   5. In the reverse order, the characters from the list are added to a string.
   6. If the resultant string matches the original string, then it is a palindrome.

Code:

```
def create_substrings(x):
    substrings = []
    for i in range(len(x)):
        for j in range(1, len(x)+1):
            if x[i:j] != '':
                substrings.append(x[i:j])
    for i in substrings:
        check_palin(i)

def check_palin(x):
    palin_str = ''
    palin_list = list(x)
    y = len(x)-1
    while y>=0:
        palin_str = palin_str + palin_list[y]
        y = y-1
    if(palin_str == x):
       print("String ", x, "is a palindrome")


#Execution
x = "malayalam"
create_substrings(x)
```

Output:

String m is a palindrome

String malayalam is a palindrome

String a is a palindrome

String ala is a palindrome

String alayala is a palindrome

String l is a palindrome

String layal is a palindrome

```
String  a  is a palindrome
String  aya  is a palindrome
String  y  is a palindrome
String  a  is a palindrome
String  ala  is a palindrome
String  l  is a palindrome
String  a  is a palindrome
String  m  is a palindrome
```

2. What will be the output of the following function?

```
def happyBirthday():
   print("Happy Birthday")
   a = happyBirthday()
   print(a)
```

Answer: Happy Birthday

None

3. What will be the output of the following code?

```
def outerWishes():
    global wishes
    wishes = "Happy New Year"

def innerWishes():
    global wishes
    wishes = "Have a great year ahead"
    print('wishes =', wishes)

wishes = "Happiness and Prosperity Always"
outerWishes()
print('wishes =', wishes)
```

Answer: The output will be as follows:

wishes = Happy New Year

4. What would be the output for the following code?

```
total = 0
def add(a,b):
    total = a+b
    print("inside total = ",total)

add(6,7)
print("outside total = ",total)
```

Answer: inside total = 13

outside total = 0

5. **Write a function that calculates HCF using Euclidean Algorithm, and returns that value.**

   Answer: Figure 1.11 shows two ways to find HCF:

   On the left hand side, you can see the traditional way of finding the HCF. On the right hand side is the implementation of **Euclidean** algorithm to find HCF.

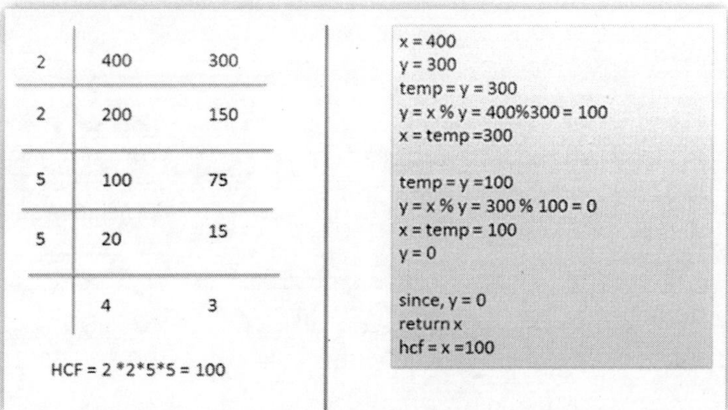

Figure 1.11 *Finding HCF using normal method and Euclidean Algorithm*

Code:

```
def hcf(x,y):
    small_num = 0
    greater_num = 0
    temp = 0
    if x > y:
        small_num = y
        greater_num = x
    else:
        small_num = x
        greater_num = y
    while small_num> 0:
        temp = small_num
        small_num = greater_num % small_num
        greater_num = temp
    return temp

#Execution:
print("HCF of 6 and 24 = ",hcf(6,24))
print("HCF of 400 and 300 = ",hcf(400,300))
```

Output:

HCF of 6 and 24 = 6

HCF of 400 and 300 = 100

6. **A function that does not return explicitly returns implicitly none. Prove.**

Answer:

```
def find_len(list1):
    print("List Recieved")
    print(len(list1))

x = input("Enter the values separated by single space :")
x_list = x.split()
print(find_len(x_list))
```

Output

Enter the values separated by single space :1 'Gmail' 'Google' 1.09 [2,3,45,9]

5

List Recieved

None

>>>

Explaination: The function **find_len()** does not return the length of the list; hence, the print statement displays none. Hence proved that when a function does not return explicitly, it implicitly returns none.

7. **Determine the output of the following:**

```
x = 20
def print_x():
    global x
    x = 10
    return x
print(print_x() )
```

Answer: 10

8. **Determine the output of the following:**

```
x = 20
def function_1():
    global x
    x = 10
    return x
def function_2():
    return x
print(function_2())
```

Answer: 20

9. Write a function to find factorial of a number using for loop.

Answer: The code for finding a factorial using **for l**oop will be as follows:

Code:

```
def factorial(number):
    j = 1
    if number==0|number==1:
        print(j)
    else:
        for i in range (1, number+1):
            print(j, " * ",i, " = ",j*i)
            j = j*i
```

Execution:

```
factorial(5)
```

Output

```
1 * 1 = 1
1 * 2 = 2
2 * 3 = 6
6 * 4 = 24
24 * 5 = 120
120
```

10. Write a function for Fibonacci series using a for loop:

Answer:

Fibonacci series: 0,1,1,2,3,5,8....

We take three variables:

i,j, and k:

- If i = 0, j =0, k =0
- If i =1, j =1, k =0
- If i>1:

```
temp =j
j =j+k
k=temp
```

The calculations are as shown as follows:

I	K	J
0	0	0
1	0	1
2	0	temp = j =1 j = j + k = 1+0 =1 k = temp =1
3	1	temp = j =1 j = j + k = 1+1 =2 k = temp =1
4	1	temp = j =2 j = j + k = 2+1 =3 k = temp =2
5	2	temp = j =3 j = j + k = 3+2 =5 k = temp =3
6	3	temp = j =5 j = j + k = 5+3 =8 k = temp =1

```
def fibonacci_seq(num):
    i = 0
    j = 0
    k = 0
    for i in range(num):
        if i==0:
            print(j)
        elif i == 1:
            j = 1
            print(j)
        else:
            temp = j
            j = j+k
            k = temp
            print(j)

#Execution
fibonacci_seq(10)
```

```
Output
0
1
1
2
3
5
8
13
21
34
```

11. How would you write the following code using a while loop?

```
def test_function(i,j):
        if i == 0:
            return j
        else:
            return test_function(i-1,j+1)
print(test_function(6,7))
```

Answer:

13

12. What will be the output of following code?

```
total = 0
def add(a,b):
        global total
        total = a+b
        print("inside total = ",total)
add(6,7)
print("outside total = ",total)
```

Answer: The output will be as follows:

```
inside total = 13
outside total = 13
```

Descriptive questions and answers

1. **Write a short note on function.**

   Answer: The answer to this question should include:

1. Definition of function.
2. Importance of functions in Python coding.
3. Classification or types of functions in Python programming along with examples.

2. Write a short note on how a function is called?

Answer: The syntax for calling a function is as follows:

```
function_name(arguments)
```

Where, **`function_name`** is the name of the function that you want to call and arguments are the values that the function requires as per its definition, the arguments must be separated by commas and must be enclosed in parenthesis. When the function is called the arguments are mapped to the respective parameters and the block of code is executed accordingly.

3. What is the difference between formal arguments and actual arguments?

Answer: Formal arguments, also known as parameters are used in function definition where they are placed inside the parenthesis. These parameters receive the actual values when a function is called.

Actual arguments are the arguments that exist in the function call. These values are passed on to the function. It is mandatory to pass values as per the function definition. The formal arguments get substituted by the functional arguments when a call is made.

4. What are the different types of functions in Python?

Answer: There are two types of functions in Python:

1. **Built-in functions:** library functions in Python.
2. **User-defined functions:** defined by the developer.

5. What is a function header?

Answer: The first line of function definition that starts with def and ends with a colon(:) is called a function header.

6. When does a function execute?

Answer: A function executes when a call is made to it. It can be called directly from the Python prompt or from another function.

7. What is a parameter? What is the difference between a parameter and argument?

Answer: A parameter is a variable that is defined in a function definition whereas an argument is an actual value that is passed on to the function. The data carried in the argument is passed on to the parameters. An argument can be passed on as a literal or as a name.

```
def function_name(param):
```

In the preceding statement, param is a parameter. Now, take a look at the following statement, it shows how a function is called:

```
function_name(arg):
```

`arg` is the data that we pass on while calling a function. In this statement, **`arg`** is an argument.

So, a parameter is simply a variable in method definition, and an argument is the data passed on the method's parameter when a function is called.

8. What is the difference between a function that prints a value and a function that returns a value.

Answer: When a function returns a value, it sends back a value that can be captured or in other words assigned to a variable, which is not the case with the function that prints the value.

9. What is the use of the return statement?

Answer: The return statement exits function, and hands back value to the function's caller. You can see in the code given below. The function **func()** returns sum of two numbers. This value assigned to "total" and then the value of total is printed.

```
def func(a,b):
    return a+b
total = func(5,9)
print(total)
14
```

10. Local scope is nested within the global scope, which is nested inside the built-in scope. What is the meaning of this statement?

Answer: Scope of a variable can be used to know which program can be used from which section of a code. The scope of a variable can be local or global.

Local variables are defined inside a function, and global functions are defined outside a function. Local variables can be accessed only within the function in which they are defined. Global variable can be accessed throughout the program by all functions.

```
total = 0 # Global variable

def add(a,b):
    sumtotal = a+b #Local variable

    print("inside add() total = ",total)

#Execute:
add(3,4)
```

When a reference is made to a variable, Python will look for that variable first within its own scope, and if it does not find it there, it will search up the chain of all enclosing scope and namespace.

11. What are local and global variables?

Answer: Local Variables are defined and used within a function. The interpreter does not recognize any variable defined within a function outside that function, which means that the variable is recognized only when the function in which it is defined is executed, and its identity is lost the moment the function has finished its task.

A global variable just like its name can be used anywhere in a file. It can be used inside or outside a function without declaring it again.

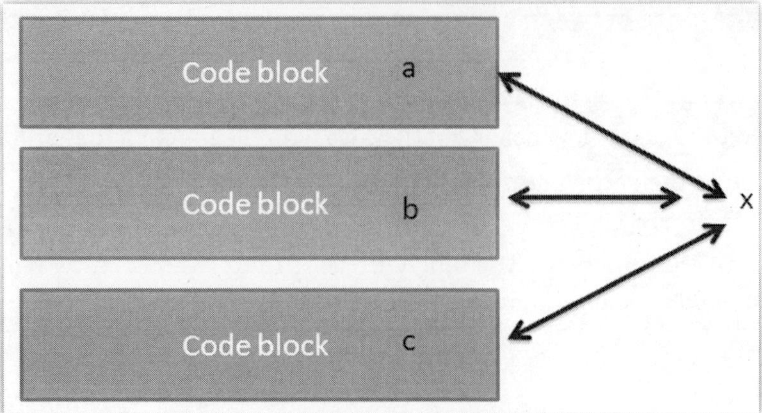

Figure 1.12 *Local and Global variables*

Variable x is a global variable and can be used in any block of code in the file, but that is not the same with variable a, b, and c as they can only be used in the code block in which they are defined. Variables a, b, and c are local variables.

12. What is a default parameter?

Answer: Default parameter is also known as **optional parameter**. While defining a function if a parameter has a default value provided to it, then it is called a **default parameter**. If while calling a function the user does not provide any value for this parameter, then the function will consider the default value assigned to it in the function definition.

13. Define any three types of function arguments in Python along with example?

Answer: The are three types of function arguments in Python:

1. **Default Arguments:** Assumes a default value, if no value is provided by the user.

```
def func(name = "Angel"):
print("Happy Birthday ", name)

func()
Happy Birthday  Angel
```

You can see that the default value for name is "Angel" and since the user has not provided any argument for it, it uses the default value.

2. **Keyword Arguments:** We can call a function, and pass on values irrespective of their positions provided we use the name of the parameter and assign them values while calling the function.

```
def func(name1, name2):
print("Happy Birthday", name1, " and ",name2,"!!!")

func(name2 = "Richard",name1 = "Marlin")

Output:

Happy Birthday Marlin  and  Richard !!!
```

3. **Variable-length Arguments:** If there is an uncertainty about how many arguments might be required for processing a function, we can make use of variable-length arguments. In the function definition, if a single '*' is place d before parameter, then all positional arguments from this point to the end are taken as a tuple. On the other hand if "**" is placed before the parameter name, then all positional arguments from that point to the end are collected as a dictionary.

```
def func(*name, **age):
    print(name)
    print(age)
func("Lucy","Aron","Alex", Lucy = "10",Aron = "15",Alex="12")

Output:
('Lucy', 'Aron', 'Alex')
{'Lucy': '10', 'Aron': '15', 'Alex': '12'}
```

14. What is a fruitful and non-fruitful function?

Answer: Fruitful function is a function that returns a value, and a non-fruitful function does not return a value. Non-fruitful functions are also known as void function.

2 Recursion

In this chapter, you will cover:

- **Recursion:** Simple programs with recursion, sum of first n natural numbers, factorial, fibonacci series.

Once you understand the concept of function, you will learn about scenarios where a problem can be solved by a function making call to itself. This is known as **Recursion**.

Programming is all about solving complex problems, and a good programmer should know that there can be more than one way of solving a problem. He should also be aware of different techniques that can be applied to get the solution problem. In this chapter, you will learn about recursion which is a fundamental technique of computer programming used to resolve a particular type of complex problems.

Recursion in programming can be applied to solve a problem whose solution depends on the solutions to smaller instances of the same problem.

We can therefore say that Recursion refers to a function, which can calculate the right answer by first solving a smaller version of its own self and then using that result along with some more computation to get the final answer. The definition of recursion will become more clear as you go through the examples given in this chapter.

Let's have a look at our first example - finding the factorial of a number.

2.1 Finding factorial of a number using recursion

A factorial of a number is the product of that number and all positive integers below it. So, factorial of 5 or 5! can also be represented as follows:

5! = 5 * 4 * 3 * 2 * 1 ....(1)

Now, look at the preceding statement carefully. Since a factorial of a number is product of that number and all positive numbers below it we can say that 4 * 3 * 2 * 1 = 4!. Hence, statement (1) can be rewritten as:

5! = 5 * 4 * 3* 2 * 1 = 5 * 4! ......(2)

Following the definition of factorial, we can now write (2) as:

5! = 5 * 4 * 3 * 2 * 1 = 5 * 4 * 3! ......(3)

Similarly,

5! = 5 * 4 * 3 * 2 * 1 = 5 * 4 * 3 * 2! ....(4)

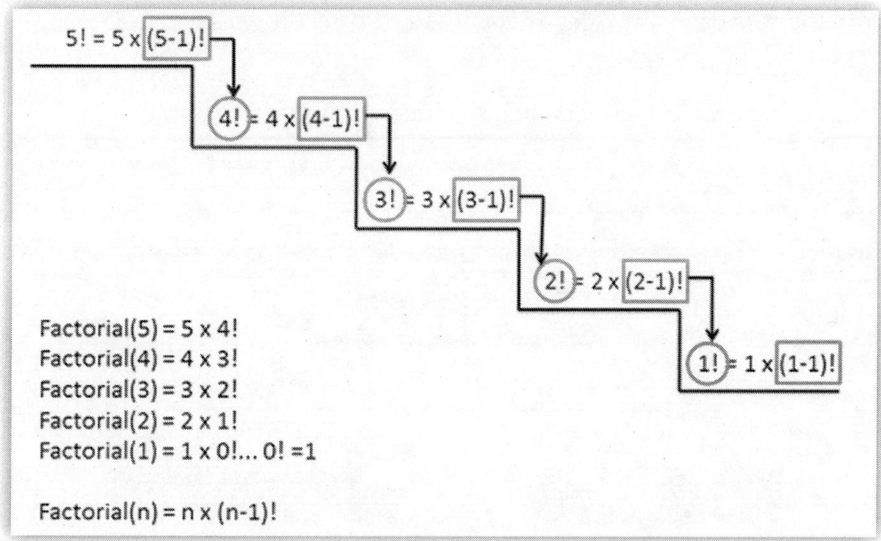

Figure 2.1: *Calculating factorial of a number*

So, if we define a method **find_factorial(n)** to find factorial of number n, it would mean that **find_factorial(n)** is same as **n * find_factorial(n-1)** and **find_factorial(n-1)** is same as **(n-1) * find_factorial(n-2)**, and so on.

Now, let's start writing the code for recursion, the following may seem like the right way to solve the problem. However, the following code is not complete yet.

```
def find_factorial(n):
        return n*find_factorial(n-1)
```

At this point, it is important to understand **base case** or **terminal case**. Every problem in recursion has a **base case**. It is one or more special values for which a function can be evaluated without recursion or it is that part of the recursion problem, which cannot be defined in smaller instances of itself. Without a base case a recursive function will never stop executing. A recursive function makes calls to itself, which step by step takes the function to the base case, and the function then stops executing.

So, the preceding code is not complete because it has no base case.

As per the definition of factorial, we say that factorial of a number is the product of itself with all the positive numbers below it. This means that the last number to be multiplied is always 1. Thus, the function should stop executing when a call is made to it with value ***n*= 1**. This will be the base case for out **find_factorial()** function.

```
def find_factorial(n):
        if(n==1):
                return 1
        return n*find_factorial(n-1)
```

2.2 Algorithm for finding factorial using recursion

Function **find_factorial(n)**

Step1: Read the number n provided for finding factorial.

Step2: Check whether the value provided is equal to 1. If true, return 1.

Step3: Else return value of n*find_factorial(n-1).

Let's learn few more facts about recursion before moving ahead with coding.

2.3 Types of recursion

Recursion can be classified as direct recursion or indirect recursion.

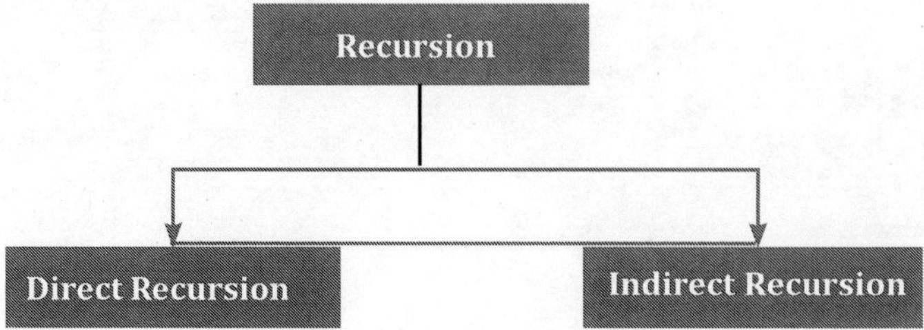

Figure 2.2: *Types of Recursion*

If a function makes a call to itself, then it is an example of direct recursion. For example: in the factorial function, the **find_factorial()** function made a call to itself. Therefore, we can call it an example of direct recursion. However, sometimes there are scenarios where a function **f()** may call another function **f1()**, which in return makes a call back to function **f()**. This is known as **Indirect Recursion**. As an example, have a look at the following code:

```
def happy_new_year(n=1):
    if(n<=0):
        how_many_times()

    for i in range(n):
        print("Happy New Year")

def how_many_times():
    val = input("How many times should I print?:")
    if val=='':
        happy_new_year()
    else:
        happy_new_year(int(val))

how_many_times()
```

In the preceding example, there is a function called **happy_new_year()** that prints the *"Happy New Year"* message as many number of times as you want. If no value is provided, then it takes the default value as 1, and prints the message once. If the value is invalid, that is, 0 or below, if calls a function **how_many_times()** which prompts the user again to provide another value and makes a call back to **happy_new_year()** with the new value. Have a look at the following figure 2.3:

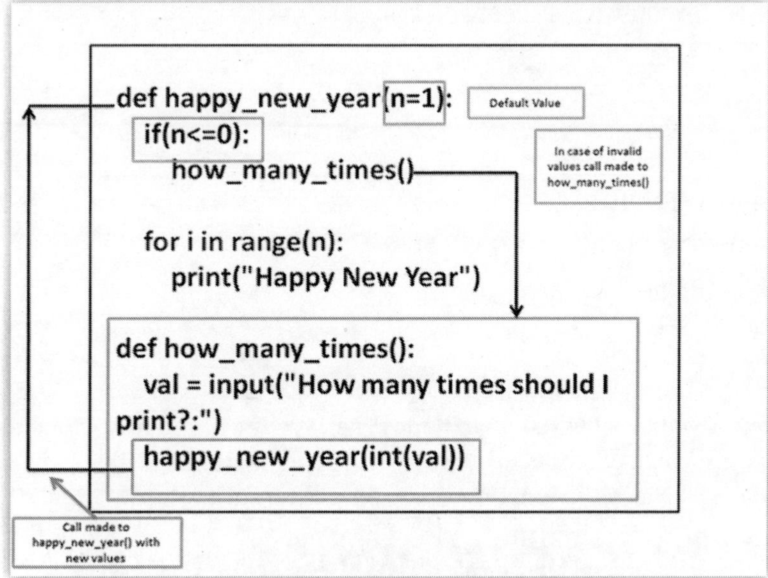

Figure 2.3: *Indirect Recursion*

Let's have a look at some interesting output for this code:

Case 1: Call is made to **`happy_new_year()`** with no input value.

Output:

Happy New Year

Explanation: Since no value was provided the message got printed only once as that is the default value.

Case 2: Callis made to **`happy_new_year()for n=0`**.

Output: Since **`n =0`**, **`how_many_times()`**is called again till a value of n greater than 0 is provided.

```
How many times should I print?:0
How many times should I print?:0
How many times should I print?:7
Happy New Year
Happy New Year
Happy New Year
Happy New Year
Happy New Year
Happy New Year
Happy New Year
>>>
```

Explanation: The user provided n = 0 twice as a result of which the function **`happy_new_year()`** called **`how_many_times()`** backeach time till the user decided to provide a value greater than 0 which in this case is 7. So, for n <=0, the function prompts the user to provide another value, and the function happy_new_year() is called again with the new input value.

Case 3: Call made with invalid values again and again.

Output:
happy_new_year(-2)
How many times should I print?:-3
How many times should I print?:-8
How many times should I print?:0
How many times should I print?:2
Happy New Year
Happy New Year

Explanation: An invalid value is passed on to **`happy_new_year()`** function, which then calls the **`how_many_times()`** function which prompts users to provide a valid number. However, the user continues to provide invalid values so both the functions keep on calling each other till a valid value is provided.

2.4 Advantages and disadvantages of recursion

Let's have a look at advantages and disadvantages of recursion:

Advantages of recursion

- Requires fewer lines of code. The code looks clean.
- Allows you to break a complex task into simpler tasks.

Disadvantages of recursion

- Forming the logic for recursion can sometimes be difficult.
- Debugging a recursive function can be difficult.
- Recursive functions consume more memory and time.

Example 2.1 Recursion for Fibonacci Numbers

Fibonacci series have integers arranged in the following sequence:

0, 1, 1, 2, 3, 5, 8, 13, 21, 34, 55, 89, 144,...........

Before we start writing the code, it is important to understand how the sequence is created. Look at the following illustration:

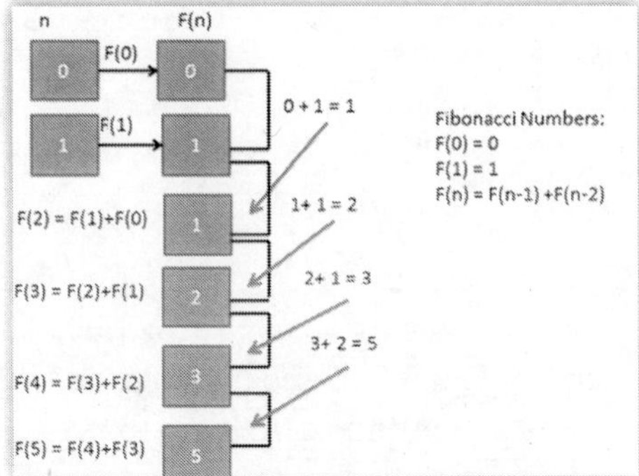

Figure 2.4: *Fibonacci numbers*

From the logic shown in the preceding figure, you can easily calculate that:

F(6) = F(5) + F(4) = 5 + 3 = 8

F(7) = F(6) + F(5) = 8 + 5 = 13

Therefore, *F(n) = F(n-1) + F(n-2)*

So, we need to follow the following steps to create a sequence of Fibonacci numbers:

Function **fib(n)**

Step 1: Read the number n.

Step 2: If n=0, return 0

Step 3: If n=1, return 1

Step 4: Else return fib(n-1)+fib(n-2)

The code for Fibonacci numbers would be as follows:

```
def fib(n):
    if(n==0):
        return 0
    elif(n==1):
        return 1
    else:
        return fib(n-1)+fib(n-2)
```

Points to remember

- Recursion is defining anything in terms of itself. Recursion is when a function makes a call to itself again and again till a base condition is met that stops the function from executing further.
- When a function makes a call to itself, it is called recursion. The same sets of instructions are repeated again and again for new values, and it is important to decide when the recursive call must end.
- Recursion can be of two types: (1) direct and (2) indirect.
- Recursive functions make the code look neat.
- It helps in breaking a complex task into simpler sub-problems.
- It can be easier than implementing iterations.
- It can be little difficult to understand the logic behind recursion.
- Recursion can consume more memory and time and can be hard to debug.
- A recursive function consists of two things:
    1. Base case or terminating case
    2. Recursive case
- Every function that uses recursion can be written using iteration and vice versa.

Coding questions and answers

1. **Write code to find the sum of natural numbers from 0 to the given number using recursion.**

   Answer:

I	Result
0	0
1	1 + 0 = i(1) + i(0) = 1
2	2 + 1 = i+ i(1) = 3
3	3 + 3 = i+ i(2) = 6
4	4 + 6 = i+ i(3) = 10
5	5 + 10 = i + i(4) = 15

   Observe for i = 0, the result is 0, thereafter result = i(n)+i(n-1).

Code:

```
def natural_sum(num):
    if num == 0:
        return 0
    else:
        return (num + natural_sum(num-1))
#Execution:
print(natural_sum(10))
```

Output:

55

2. **Write Fibonacci sequence using recursion.**

   Answer: The Fibonacci sequence = 0,1,2,3,5,8,13.....

i	Result
0	0
1	1
2	1+0 = i(0) + i(1) = 1
3	1+1 = i(2) + i(1) = 2
4	2+1 = i(3) + i(2) = 3
5	3+2 = i(4) + i(3) = 5

   Observe for i = 0, the result is 0 and for i = 1, the result is 1. Thereafter, the value of i(n) = i(n-1) + i(n-2).We implement the same, when we try to find Fibonacci code using recursion.

   - The **`fibonacci_seq(num)`**, takes a number as argument.
   - If **`num`** = 0, result is 0
   - If **`num`** = 1, result is 1
   - Else result is **`fibonacci_seq(num-1) +  Fibonacci_seq(num-2)`**

- If you want to find Fibonacci Sequence for 10 then:
  - For elements 0 to 10
  - Call the **fibonacci_seq()** function
    - *fibonacci_seq(0) = 0*
    - *fibonacci_seq(1) = 1*
    - *fibonacci_seq(2) = fibonacci_seq(1)+ fibonacci_seq(0)*
    - *fibonacci_seq(3) = fibonacci_seq(2)+ fibonacci_seq(3)*

Code:

```
def fibonacci_seq(num):
    if num<0:
        print("Please provide a positive integer value")
    if num == 0:
        return 0
    elif num == 1:
        return 1
    else:
        return (fibonacci_seq(num-1)+fibonacci_seq(num-2))
```

Execution:

```
for i in range(10):
    print(fibonacci_seq(i))
```

Output:

```
0
1
1
2
3
5
8
13
21
34
```

3. **Write a code to find nth power of 3 using recursion.**

   Answer:

   1. Define function n_power(n), it takes the value of power an parameter(n).
   2. If n = 0 then return 1 because any number raise to power 0 is 1.
   3. Else return (n_power(n-1)).

N	n < 0	n == 0	Result
4	No	no	n_power(3)*3
3	No	no	n_power(2)*3*3
2	No	no	n_power(1)*3*3*3
1	No	no	n_power(0)*3*3*3*3
0	No	yes	1*3*3*3*3

Code:

```
def n_power(n):
    if n < 0:
        print("please enter a positive value")
    elif n == 0:
        return 1
    else:
        return n_power(n-1)*3
print(n_power(4))
```

Execution:

```
print(n_power(4))
```

Output:

81

4. **What would be the output of the following code?**

```
def funny(x):
    if (x%2 == 1):
        return x+1
    else:
        return funny(x-1)
print(funny(7))
print(funny(6))
```

Answer:

For x =7

1. x = 7
2. x % 2 is 1
3. return 7 + 1 = 8

For x = 6

1. x =6
2. x%2 = 0
3. Return funny(5)
4. x = 5
5. x%2 =1
6. Return x+1 = 6

5. **What would be the output of the following program?**

```
def test_function(i,j):
    if i == 0:
        return j
    else:
        return test_function(i-1,j+1)
print(test_function(6,7))
```

Answer: 13

Explanation:

i	j	i == 0 ?	Return
6	7	No	test_function(5,8)
5	8	No	test_function(4,9)
4	9	No	test_function(3,10)
3	10	No	test_function(2,11)
2	11	No	test_function(1,12)
1	12	No	test_function(0,13)
0	13	Yes	13

Output:

13.

6. **What will be the output for the following code:**

```
def even(k):
    if k <= 0:
        print("please enter a positive value")
    elif k == 1:
        return 0
    else:
        return even(k-1) + 2
print(even(6))
```

Answer: 10

Explaination:

K	k <= 0	k == 1	Result
6	No	no	even(5)+2
5	No	no	Even(4)+2+2
4	No	no	Even(3)+2+2+2
3	No	no	Even(2)+2+2+2+2
2	No	no	Even(1)+2+2+2+2+2
1	No	yes	0+2+2+2+2+2 = 10

3 Files

In this chapter, you will cover:

- **Text file:** Opening a text file, text file open modes (r, r+, w, w+, a, a+), closing a text file, opening a file using with clause, writing/appending data to a text file using write() and writelines(), reading from a text file using read(), readline() and readlines(), seek and tell methods, manipulation of data in a text file
- **Binary file:** Basic operations on a binary file: open using file open modes (rb, rb+, wb, wb+, ab, ab+), close a binary file, import pickle module, dump() and load() method, read, write/create, search, append and update operations in a binary file
- **CSV file:** import csv module, open / close csv file, write into a csv file using csv.writerow() and read from a csv file using csv.reader( )

Introduction

"File" is a very common name that you may keep on hearing every now and then. Your dad may be maintaining separate files for bank documents, office papers, Car documents, etc. In the same way, you must be maintaining different files for different projects in your school or college. So, basically, you need files for storing important information which is the same in the case of computers also. Important information can be stored in files on your computer. Instead of maintaining hardcopy of a huge amount of data, you can store all the information that you require in a file on your system.

File is contiguous set of bytes that is used to store data. Data can be in a text file or an exe file. However, when the computer has to process these files the information they contain must be converted to binary format. Let's learn more about files.

3.1 Advantages of Storing Data in Files

Before you start working with files, you need to understand the advantages of storing data in files:

1. Data remains stored in the file permanently. i.e., it remains in the system even when you have switched off your computer.
2. You can easily update the file as and when required.
3. Once the data is stored in a computer it can be used by various applications for complex calculations.
4. Files can be used to store any amount of data which may not be possible physically. Also once the data is on a file it can be used for analysis and you can immediately search for any information.

3.2 Directory and File Management with Python

Files have three main parts as shown in figure 3.1.

1. Header
2. Data
3. End of File

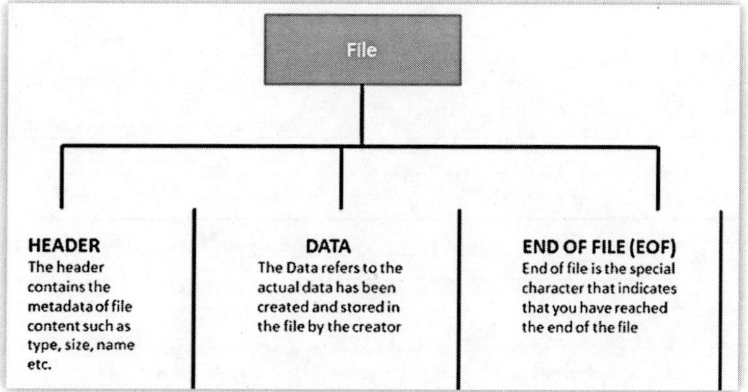

Although we can work with files of any type but for now let's restrict ourselves to .txt and .csv files.

Before we start working on files let's have a look at some important aspects of Python directory and file management. In an operating system, files are organized in a directory. To work with Directory we need to import the **os module**.

```
import os
```

3.3 Retrieve the current working directory using getcwd()

If you want to retrieve the absolute path of current working directory(cwd), you will have to import the os module and call its getcwd() method as shown below:

```
>>>import os
>>>os.getcwd()
'C:\\Users\\MYPC\\AppData\\Local\\Programs\\Python\\Python38-32'
```

To render the directory name using print command give the following command:

```
>>> import os
>>> print(os.getcwd())
C:\Users\MYPC\AppData\Local\Programs\Python\Python38-32
```

3.4 Checking contents of Python directory using listdir()

You can check the contents of the directory with the help of `listdir()` method. This method displays the list of all the contents in the directory in a python list.

```
>>> import os
>>>os.listdir()
['comment.py', 'DLLs', 'Doc', 'include', 'Lib', 'libs', 'LICENSE.txt',
'NEWS.txt', 'python.exe', 'python3.dll', 'python38.dll', 'pythonw.exe',
'Scripts', 'tcl', 'Tools', 'vcruntime140.dll']
```

3.5 Create directory using mkdir()

You can use `mkdir()` to create a directory

So, let's make a folder to keep are python files.

```
>>> import os
>>>os.mkdir("Learning Python")
```

If you give **`listdir()`** command you will see the name of the new folder there:

```
>>>os.listdir()
['comment.py', 'DLLs', 'Doc', 'include', 'Learning Python', 'Lib', 'libs',
'LICENSE.txt', 'NEWS.txt', 'python.exe', 'python3.dll', 'python38.dll',
'pythonw.exe', 'Scripts', 'tcl', 'Tools', 'vcruntime140.dll']
```

You can also check in the window explorer. If you go to the same path in the windows explorer which in this case is 'C:\Users\MYPC\AppData\Local\Programs\Python\Python38-32' then, you will see the newly created folder there: (figure 3.2)

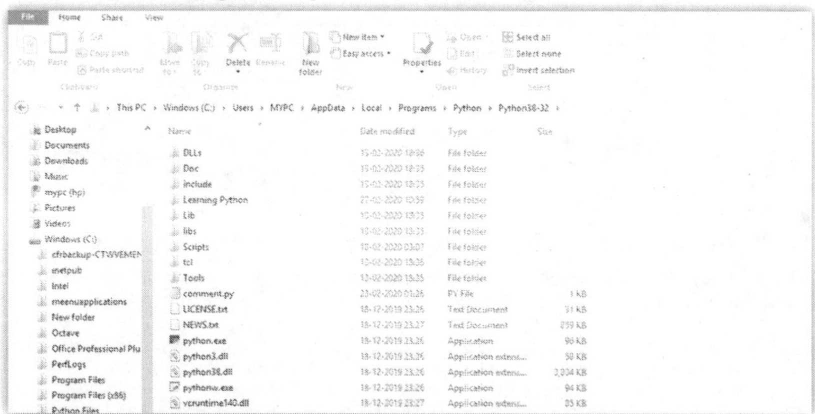

Figure 3.2: *Newly created folder*

3.6 Renaming a directory using rename()

You can rename the folder "Learning Python" to "Understanding Python" by using `rename()` method.

```
>>> import os
>>>os.rename("Learning Python","Understanding Python")
>>>os.listdir()
['comment.py', 'DLLs', 'Doc', 'include', 'Lib', 'libs', 'LICENSE.txt',
'NEWS.txt', 'python.exe', 'python3.dll'', 'python38.dll', 'pythonw.exe',
'Scripts', 'tcl', 'Tools', 'Understanding Python', 'vcruntime140.dll']
```

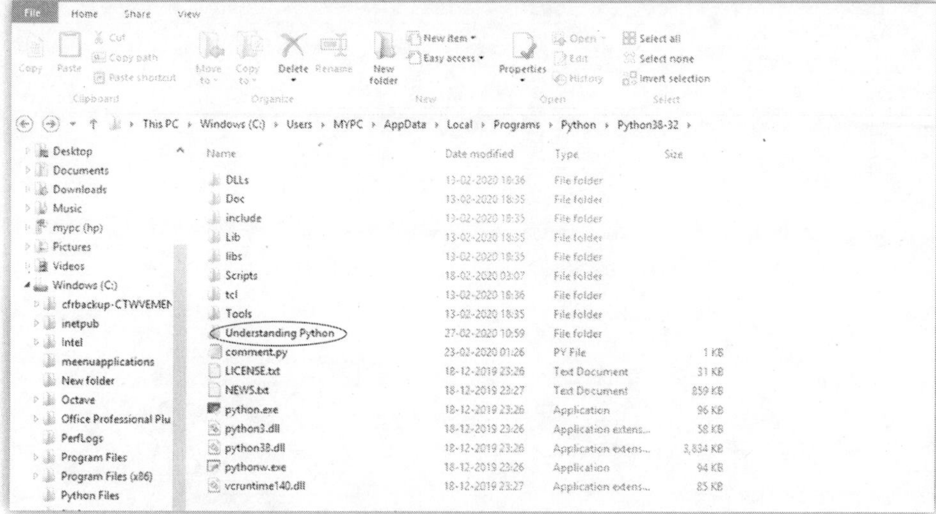

Figure 3.3: *Renaming a directory using rename()*

3.7 Remove a directory using rmdir()

You can remove the directory using **`rmdir()`**

As you can see the directory a new text file by the name **`delete_file.tx`** t was created. (figure 3.4)

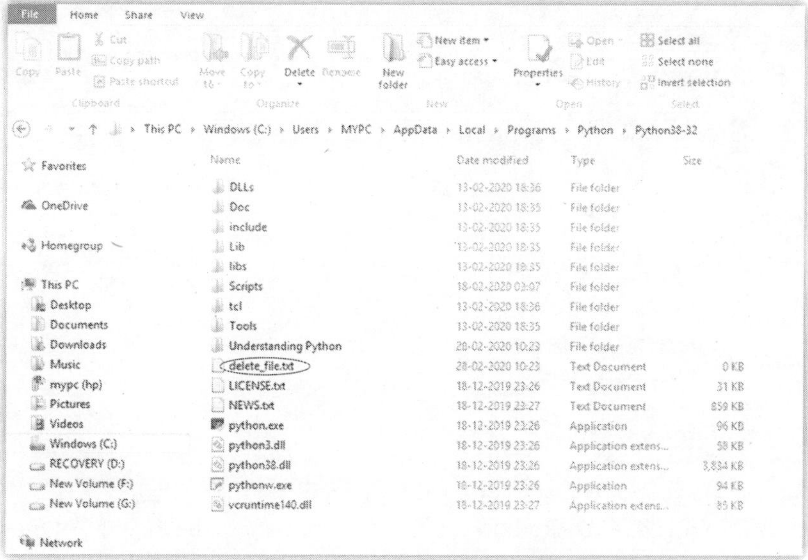

Figure 3.4: *Remove a directory using rmdir()*

Now we will see how to remove this file from the directory.

```
>>> import os
>>>os.remove("delete_file.txt")
```

Once the above command is given, the file will disappear from the directory.

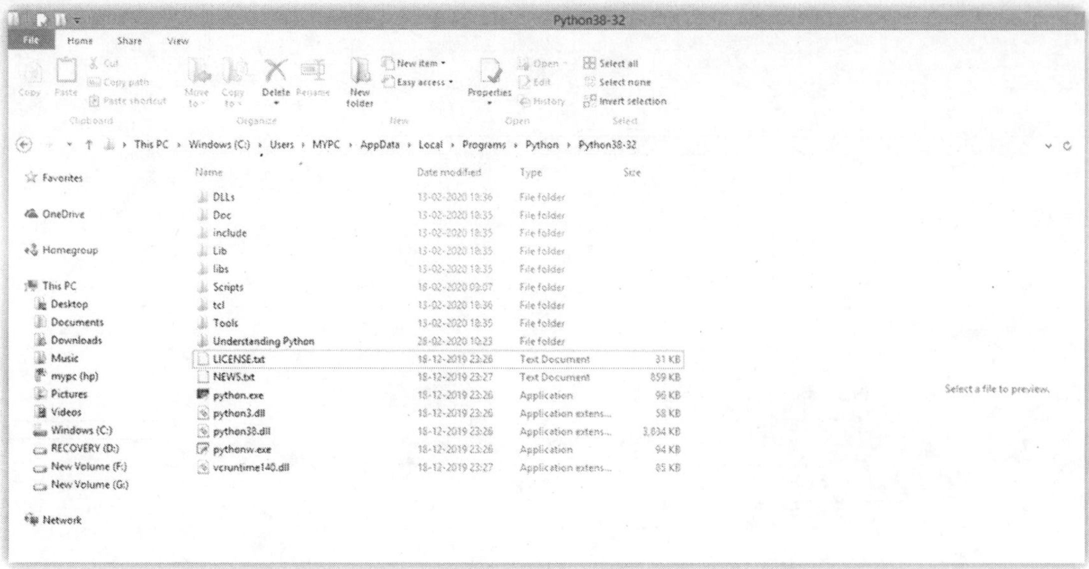

You can use `os.path.exists()` to check if a directory exists.

```
>>> import os
>>>os.path.exists('C:\\Users\\MYPC\\AppData\\Local\\Programs\\Python\\
Python38-32')
True
```

3.8 Working with Files

In this section you will learn how to work with files using Python. In this section you will learn how to:

- Open and close a file
- Use the access mode for writing into a file
- Work with binary files
- Use file attributes

3.8.1 open() and close()

In order to work with a file you will have to open it. So, opening a file will always be the first step while working with files. After you have worked on the file it is important to close it. All files that have been opened must be closed after you have finished working on them.

To demonstrate how we can work with files. A text file "first_file.txt" has been created in the Python directory. (figure 3.6, 3.7)

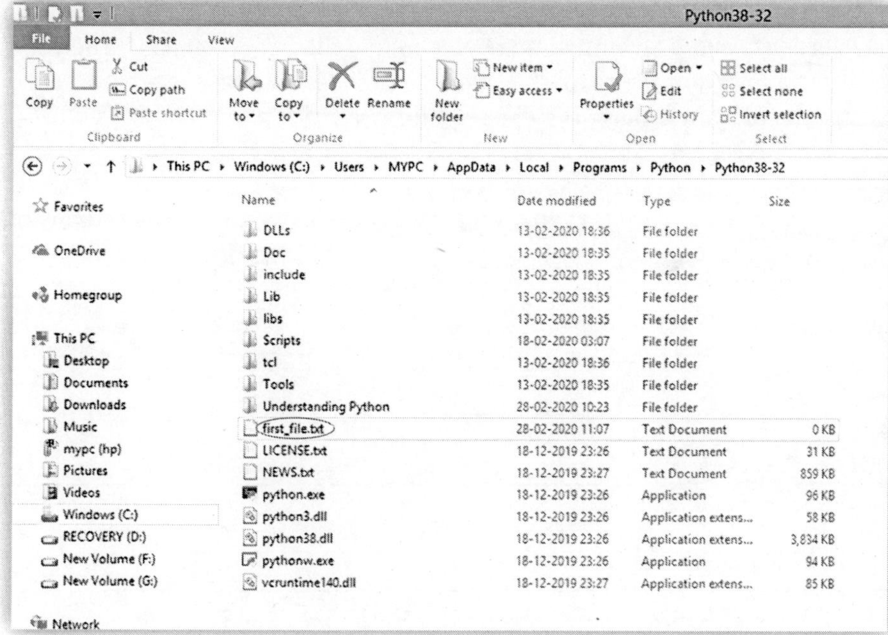

Figure 3.6

The content of the file is as follows:

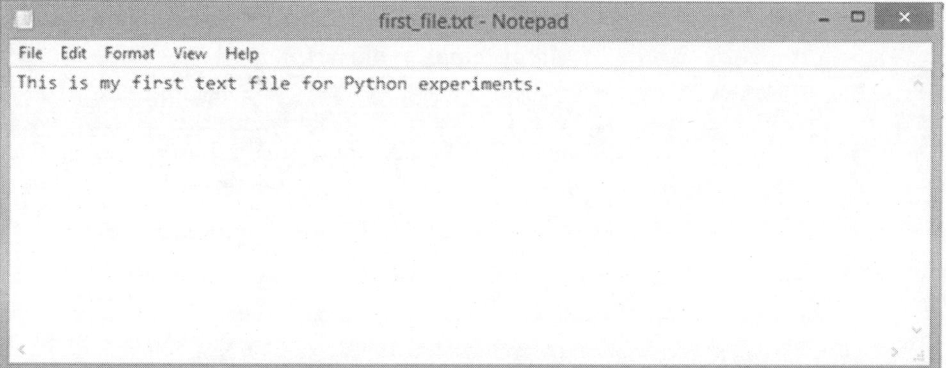

Figure 3.7

To open a file, you can use open() function.

Syntax:

```
file_obj = open(file_name, access_mode,buffering)
```

- **`file_name`** = name of the file that you want to access it is a mandatory parameter.
- **`access_mode`** = optional parameter, default mode is **`read(r)`**. It specifies the mode in which it has to open. We have provided a complete table on various types of access modes.
- **`Buffering`** = optional parameter, 1 means buffering will be performed using the indicated buffer size, any value less than 1 means that the buffer size is the system default.

```
file_handler  = open("first_file.txt")
```

Before we start working with files we should learn how to close a file. Any file that has been opened must be closed in order to avoid any unwanted behaviour. A file left open may or may not cause problems while executing a program. To be on the safe side the file must be closed once you have worked on the file. To close the file you can use the **`close()`** function.

```
file_handler.close()
```

To ensure that a file is properly closed even if there is any error, we can use try-finally block.

```
file_handler  = open("first_file.txt")
try:
#code
   ..........
finally:
file_handler.close()
```

Or

You can use the '*with*' keyword as shown below:

```
>>> with open("first_file.txt") as file_handler:
```

3.8.2 Access Mode in File Writing

We will now be working with "first_file.txt". The file

Table 3.1: *Access mode in file writing*

File Mode	Name	Description
r	Read	The file opens in read mode and the file pointer is placed at the beginning of the file. "r" is also considered as the default mode.

```
# Use read() function to extract all the contents of the file in String format.
>>>file_handle = open("first_file.txt","r")
>>> try:
      file_handle.read()
finally:
      file_handle.close()
```

Output:

"This is my first text file for Python experiments.\nThere is a lot that can be done with files in Python.\nLet's get Started."

OR

```
# Use read() function to extract first few (in this case 10) characters of the file
>>>try:
      file_handle.read(10)
finally:
      file_handle.close()
```

Let's get Started.		
r+	Read and write on existing file	This access mode opens the file for both read and write. The file pointer is placed at the beginning of the file.

(I) **Reading a file using r+ mode:**

```
>>>file_handle = open("first_file.txt","r+")
>>>try:
    file_handle.read()
finally:
    file_handle.close()
```

Output:

"This is my first text file for Python experiments.\nThere is a lot that can be done with files in Python.\nLet's get Started.\n"

(II) **Reading and writing with r+ mode:**

```
file_handle = open("first_file.txt", 'r+')
>>>try:
    file_handle.write("Now I am using r+ mode")
    file_handle.read()
finally:
    file_handle.close()
```

Output:

22

"file for Python experiments.\nThere is a lot that can be done with files in

Python.\nLet's get Started.\n"

If you open the file the content would be as follows:

the number 22 shows that it starts reading at location 22. If you see a total of 22 characters were inserted.

So, you see that "r+" mode inserts the content at the beginning of the file. However, there may be times when you do not desire this. To, insert text at any other position we need to make use of seek() function. The seek() function takes two parameters, the first parameter is the position of the read/writer pointer in the file. The second parameter is optional and defaults to 0 which means beginning of the file. To insert content in the current location the value of second parameter should be changed to 2.

(III) Inserting text at the end of the file

```
>>>file_handle = open("first_file.txt",'r+')
>>>try:
    file_handle.seek(0,2)
```

```
        file_handle.write("\n Now I am using r+ mode. Inserting at the end of file")
        file_handle.read()
    finally:
        file_handle.close()
```

```
This is my first text file for Python experiments.
There is a lot that can be done with files in Python.
Let's get Started.
 Now I am using r+ mode. Inserting at the end of file
```

In order to use "r+" mode it is important for the file to exist on the system. Else , an error will be displayed.

```
>>> file_handle = open("my_file.txt",'r+')
Traceback (most recent call last):
  File "<pyshell#56>", line 1, in <module>
    file_handle = open("my_file.txt",'r+')
FileNotFoundError: [Errno 2] No such file or directory: 'my_file.txt'
>>>
```

w	Write	This access mode opens the file in write mode only. If the file exists then it overwrites the content of the file and if does not exist then a new file is created and contents are written on that file.

```
>>>file_handle = open("first_file.txt", "w")
>>> try:
        file_handle.write("Hi There")
    finally:
        file_handle.close()
```

The above piece of code replaces the content of the file with "Hi There"

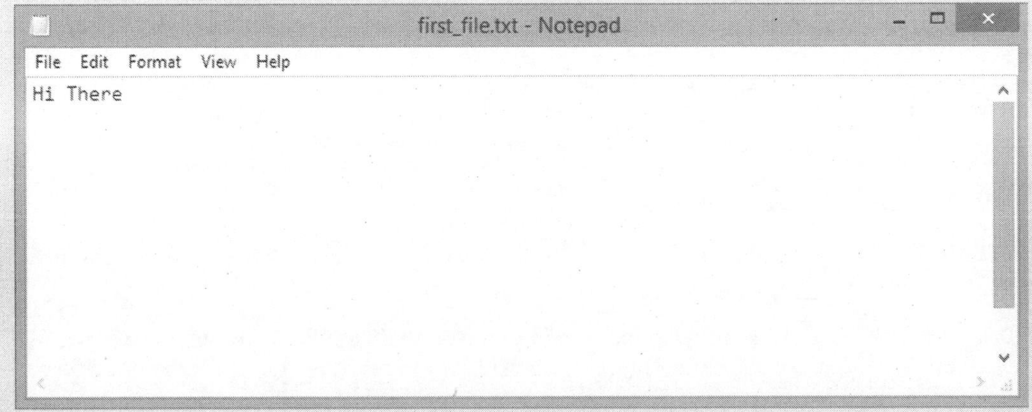

```
first_file.txt - Notepad
File Edit Format View Help
Hi There
```

Figure 3.8

If the file does not exist then a file will be created by the given name and contents will be added.

```
>>>file_handle = open("first_file1.0.txt","w")
>>>try:
        file_handle.write("Hi There")
    finally:
        file_handle.close()
```

Since, no file by the name “first_file1.0.txt” existed, therefre it was immediately created.

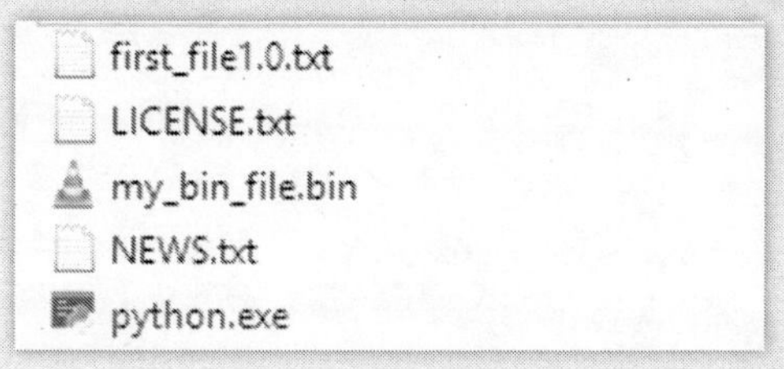

Figure 3.9

The contents of the file were as follows:

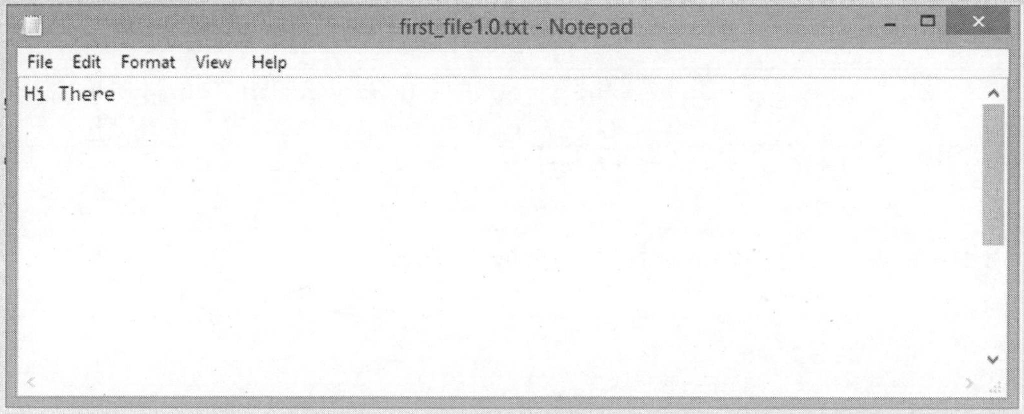

Figure 3.10

When the access mode is “w” you cannot perform any read operations.

```
>>>file_handle = open("first_file.txt","w")
>>>try:
        file_handle.read()
   finally:
        file_handle.close()
```

Traceback (most recent call last):

```
  File "<pyshell#17>", line 2, in <module>
file_handle.read()
io.UnsupportedOperation: not readable
```

w+	Read and write	This opens the file in both read and write mode and if the file does not exist then a new file will be created with the same name for reading and writing

```
>>>file_handle = open("first_file.txt","w+")
>>> try:
        file_handle.write("Hi")
    finally:
        file_handle.close()
```

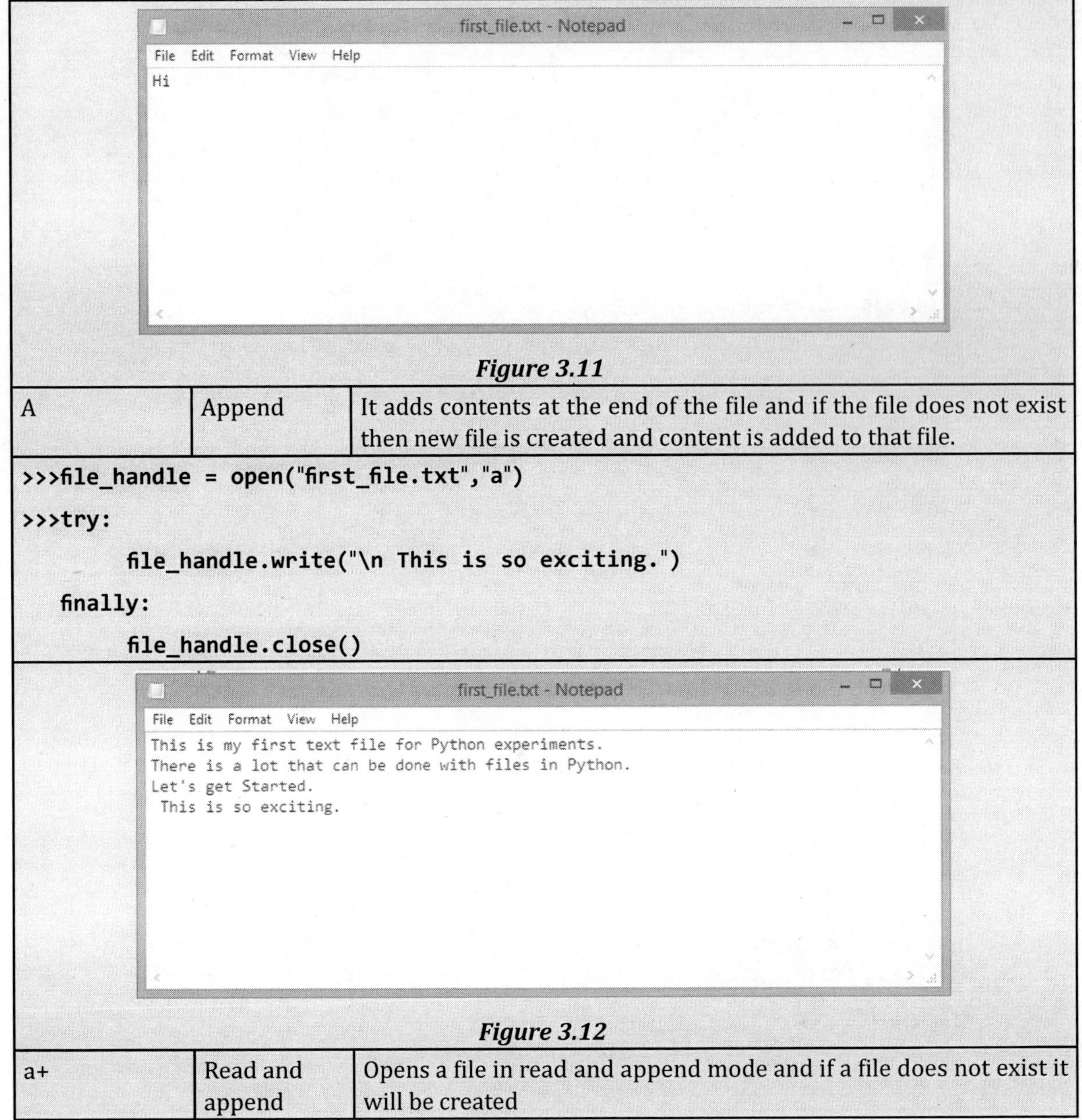

Figure 3.11

A	Append	It adds contents at the end of the file and if the file does not exist then new file is created and content is added to that file.

```
>>>file_handle = open("first_file.txt","a")
>>>try:
        file_handle.write("\n This is so exciting.")
   finally:
        file_handle.close()
```


Figure 3.12

a+	Read and append	Opens a file in read and append mode and if a file does not exist it will be created

3.8.3 Writing to a binary file using "wb" access mode

The code given below explains how you can write to a binary file using "wb" access mode.

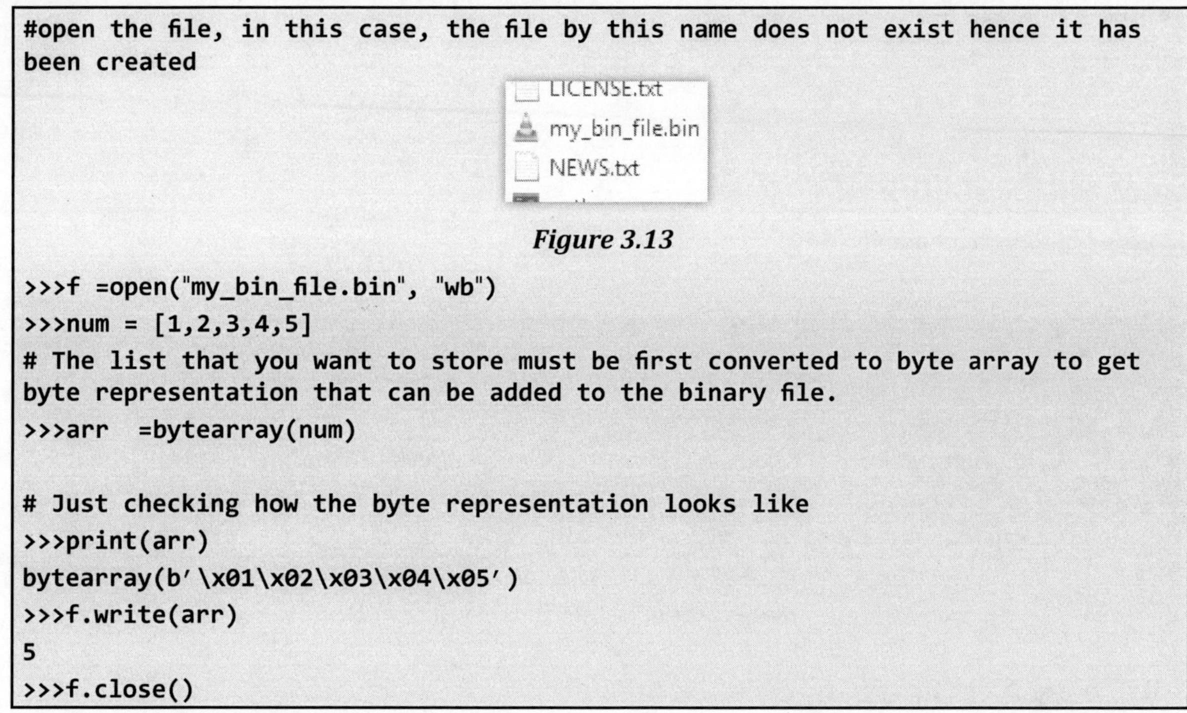

```
#open the file, in this case, the file by this name does not exist hence it has
been created
```


Figure 3.13

```
>>>f =open("my_bin_file.bin", "wb")
>>>num = [1,2,3,4,5]
# The list that you want to store must be first converted to byte array to get
byte representation that can be added to the binary file.
>>>arr  =bytearray(num)

# Just checking how the byte representation looks like
>>>print(arr)
bytearray(b'\x01\x02\x03\x04\x05')
>>>f.write(arr)
5
>>>f.close()
```

3.8.4 Reading the contents of a binary file using "rb" access mode

You can read the contents of a binary file using "rb" access mode

```
>>> f =open("my_bin_file.bin", "rb")
>>> number = list(f.read())
>>> print(number)
[1, 2, 3, 4, 5]
```

3.8.5 Write and Read strings with binary files

To write text to a binary file we open the file in **"wb"** mode. Similarly to read strings from a binary file we open the file in **"rb"** mode. The following piece of code explains how this can achieved.

```
#Writing
file_handle =open("my_bin_file.bin", "wb")
msg = "Hi there"
arr = bytearray(msg.encode())
file_handle.write(arr)
file_handle.close()

#Reading
file_handle = open("my_bin_file.bin","rb")
msg = file_handle.read()
print(msg)
print(msg.decode())
```

Output:

b'Hi there'

Hi there

3.8.6 Other operations on binary file

Table 3.2 displays commands for some more operations that can be executed on a binary file.

Table 3.2

File Mode	Name	Description
rb+	Read and Write on existing file	Allows you to perform read and write operations on an existing binary file.
wb+	Read and write	Allows you to perform read and write operation on a binary file. If the file does not exist then a new file will be created with the same name.
Ab	Append	Appends content to the end of the file
ab+	Read and Append	Read and append a file. New content are added at the end of the file. If the file does not exist then a new file will be created with the same name.

3.8.7 File Attributes

The following code displays how you can use file attributes to check if a file is open or closed, its mode and name.

```
file_handle = open("first_file.txt","w+")
print('Closed or Not - ', file_handle.closed)
print('Mode : ',file_handle.mode)
print('Name : ',file_handle.name)
```

Output:

```
Closed or Not -  False
Mode :  w+
Name :  first_file.txt
```

3.8.8 Various File related methods

The following table lists down various methods available in order to work with files.

Table 3.3

Method	Description
close()	Close the file
flush()	Flush the internal buffer memory
fileno()	Returns the integer
next()	Returns next line from the file
read()	Reads the file
readline()	Reads an entire line

`readlines()`	Returns line by line till the end of ie and then returns a list of lines in the file
`seek()`	To change the position
`tell()`	Tells the file's current position of the file pointer within the file.
`truncate()`	Truncates a file
`write()`	Writes to a file
`writelines()`	Writes sequence of strings to a file

Example 3.1: `read line()`

```
>>>file_handle = open("first_file.txt","r")
>>> try:
        file_handle.readline()
    finally:
        file_handle.close()

'This is my first text file for Python experiments.\n'
```

Example 3.2: `readlines()`

```
File_handle = open("first_file.txt","r")
>>> try:
        file_handle.readlines()
    finally:
        file_handle.close()
['This is my first text file for Python experiments.\n', 'There is a lot that can be done with files in Python.\n', "Let's get Started."]
```

Example 3.3: `writelines()`

```
>>>file_handle = open("first_file.txt","w")
>>> try:
        file_handle.writelines(['Hi\n', 'How are you \n', 'Good to see you :)'])
    finally:
        file_handle.close()
```

3.9 Pickle Module Python

Data Serialization in Python is a process by which Python objects and be converted into a format for storage into file or for transmission over network and then later converted back into the same Python object for further usage. When you are working with Python objects, you may often feel to save the object as it is. Let's suppose you have a dictionary object that has some important data. If you save it on to a text file, it would display an error.

Type the following code:

```
topper_students = {"Ramesh":["Sharma",15,"X"], "Ranjita":["Verma",14,"IX"], "Venkatesh":["Naidu",16,"IX"]}
file_handle = open("picklefile.txt","w")
try:
    file_handle.write(topper_students)
finally:
    file_handle.close()
```

Figure 3.14

Output:

```
Traceback (most recent call last):
  File "C:/Users/91965/OneDrive/Desktop/Meenu Kohli/Computer Science with Python
 - XII/1. Getting the book together/Unit 1/code/working_with_pickle.py", line 4,
 in <module>
    file_handle.write(topper_students)
TypeError: write() argument must be str, not dict
>>>
```

Figure 3.15

The solution to this problem is that we use the Pickle module to encode or serialize the Python object(which in this case is **`topper_students`** dictionary) in a format that can be saved on the disc and later load or decode it into the same Python object.

Pickle is the native Python module for serializing and deserializing Python object structures. This module can be used for encoding Python objects into strings of bytes and then storing the information to a file. It also allows you to deserialize data back to original Python object. Let's see how this is done.

Step 1: Import pickle module

import pickle

Step 2: Define your object. It is a dictionary having the student first name as key and value has a list that has the surname, age and class of the student

topper_students = {"Ramesh":["Sharma",15,"X"], "Ranjita":["Verma",14,"IX"], "Venkatesh":["Naidu",16,"IX"]}

Step 3: Open file in "wb" mode, this will overwrite the file if it exists or else create a new file. You can now **dump()** the object onto the file.

```
import pickle
topper_students = {"Ramesh":["Sharma",15,"X"], "Ranjita":["Verma",14,"IX"], "Venkatesh":["Naidu",16,"IX"]}
file_handle = open("picklefile.txt","wb")
try:
   pickle.dump(topper_students,file_handle)
finally:
   file_handle.close()
```

This will look in the editor as follows:

```
import pickle
topper_students = {"Ramesh":["Sharma",15,"X"], "Ranjita":["Verma",14,"IX"], "Venkatesh":["Naidu",16,"IX"]}
file_handle = open("picklefile.txt","wb")
try:
    pickle.dump(topper_students,file_handle)
finally:
    file_handle.close()
```

Figure 3.16

Step 4: `Deserialize topper_students` using the load() function. This function is used to read the pickled representation of the object and return the Python object in its original form.

```
>>> import pickle
>>> file_handle = open("picklefile.txt","rb")
>>> obj = pickle.load(file_handle)
>>> print(obj)
{'Ramesh': ['Sharma', 15, 'X'], 'Ranjita': ['Verma', 14, 'IX'], 'Venkatesh': ['N
aidu', 16, 'IX']}
```

Figure 3.17

3.9.1 Advantages of pickle module

1. Your programs's state data can be saved to the disk.
2. Pickle module allows you to transfer data over Transmission Control Protocol(TCP) or socket connection.
3. Very useful in working with Machine Learning algorithms.

3.9.2 Disadvantages:

1. Do not use Pickle for exchanging data between different languages, platforms or even different version of Python. It does not guarantee cross-language compatibility.
2. It is possible to construct malicious serialized data. Hence, you should not attempt to deserialize data coming from an untrusted source or data that has been tampered with.

3.9.3 What Python objects can be pickled?

Following Python objects can be pickled

- Booleans
- Integers
- Floats
- Complex numbers
- (normal and Unicode) Strings
- Tuples
- Lists
- Sets and
- Dictionaries

Working with CSV files

Content of items.csv file is as follows:

Item	Quantity	amount
soap	6	42
shampoo	2	350
washing powder	1	150
conditioner	1	75
toilet cleaner	1	95
disinfectant	1	100

Figure 3.18

Reading from a csv

```
import csv
file_handle = open("items.csv","r")
reader = csv.reader(file_handle)
for row in reader:
    print(row)
file_handle.close()
```

Figure 3.19

Output:

```
['Item ', 'Quantity', 'amount']
['soap', '6', '42']
['shampoo', '2', '350']
['washing powder', '1', '150']
['conditioner', '1', '75']
['toilet cleaner', '1', '95']
['disinfectant', '1', '100']
```

Figure 3.20

Reading a specific row from a csv file

If you want to read only the second column (i.e. **quantity**) of the csv file then you can use the index of the row. The index of first column is 0 and the index of second column is 1.

```
import csv
file_handle = open("items.csv","r")
reader = csv.reader(file_handle)
for row in reader:
    print(row[1])
file_handle.close()
```

Figure 3.21

Output:

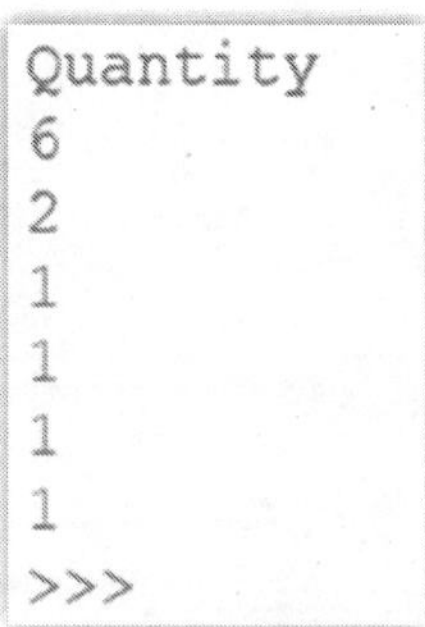

```
Quantity
6
2
1
1
1
1
>>>
```

Figure 3.22

If you do not want to display the heading **Quantity** in the output then insert next(reader) before iterating through the file using the "for" loop.

```
import csv
file_handle = open("items.csv","r")
reader = csv.reader(file_handle)
next(reader)
for row in reader:
    print(row[1])
file_handle.close()
```

Figure 3.23

```
6
2
1
1
1
1
>>>
```

Figure 3.24

Let's insert values from the csv into the dictionary.

```
import csv
file_handle = open("items.csv","r")
reader = csv.reader(file_handle)
next(reader)
items_dict = dict()
for row in reader:
    items_dict[row[0]]=row[1]
file_handle.close()
print(items_dict)
```

Figure 3.25

Here a new dictionary object items_dict is created and while iterating. For every item in the row the dictionary object store the data as "key" from colum 1 and value from column 2.

Output:

```
{'soap': '6', 'shampoo': '2', 'washing powder': '1', 'conditioner': '1', 'toilet
 cleaner': '1', 'disinfectant': '1'}
>>> |
```

Figure 3.26

Writing to csv files

Writing to csv files is similar to reading a csv file and we are going to work on that in this section. For reading a csv file we used the reader function of the csv module. Similarly, for writing a csv function we will use the **writer** function of the same module. This function returns a writer object which can be used to write rows into a csv file.

Suppose we want to insert another row in **`items.csv`** file. This is how we go about it.

```
import csv

# open object in append mode
file_handle = open("items.csv","a")

writer = csv.writer(file_handle)

#define a list or a tuple to insert data
row_data = ["Hair oil", 3, 215]

#use writerow() to insert the row at the end of csv file
writer.writerow(row_data)

#close the file
file_handle.close()
```

Figure 3.27

Output:

Item	Quantity	amount
soap	6	42
shampoo	2	350
washing powder	1	150
conditioner	1	75
toilet cleaner	1	95
disinfectant	1	100
Hair oil	3	215

Figure 3.28

Let's write a code that inserts a heading "Table of five" in the first column of a csv and then under it the table of five is displayed.

```
import csv

# open object in write mode
file_handle = open("table_of_five.csv","w")

writer = csv.writer(file_handle)
writer.writerow(['table of five'])

#writerow() takes only iterable parameter
for row in range (1,11):
    row_data = 5 * row
    writer.writerow([row_data])

#close the file
file_handle.close()
```

Figure 3.29

Output:

	A	B
1	table of five	
2		
3	5	
4		
5	10	
6		
7	15	
8		
9	20	
10		
11	25	
12		
13	30	
14		
15	35	
16		
17	40	
18		
19	45	
20		
21	50	
22		

Figure 3.30

Suppose for the same example you want to insert 2 columns in the manner: 5 X 1 5 and so on. For this we will modify the code slightly.

```
import csv

# open object in write mode
file_handle = open("table_of_five.csv","w")

writer = csv.writer(file_handle)
writer.writerow(['table of five', 'Values'])

#writerow() takes only iterable parameter
for row in range (1,11):
    row_data1 = " 5 X " +str(row)
    row_data2 = 5 * row
    writer.writerow([row_data1, row_data2])

#close the file
file_handle.close()
```

Figure 3.31

Output:

table of fi	Values
5 X 1	5
5 X 2	10
5 X 3	15
5 X 4	20
5 X 5	25
5 X 6	30
5 X 7	35
5 X 8	40
5 X 9	45
5 X 10	50

Figure 3.32

Conclusion

With this you come to the end of this chapter. Files are used to store data. Data can also be stored in a tabular form in a database. In the next chapter you will learn about MySQL database and how Python can be used to access a database and execute all types of SQL queries.

? EXERCISE

Multiple choice questions

1. Which of the following allows you to perform read and write operations on an existing binary file.

   a. rb+ b. wb+ c. ab d. ab+

   Answer: rb+

2. __________ allows you to perform read and write operation on a binary file. If the file does not exist then a new file will be created with the same name.

   a. rb+ b. wb+ c. ab d. ab+

   Answer: wb+

3. ________ appends content to the end of the file.

   a. rb+ b. wb+ c. ab d. ab+

   Answer: ab

4. ________ read and append a file. New content are added at the end of the file. If the file does not exist then a new file will be created with the same name.

   a. rb+ b. wb+ c. Ab d. ab+

   Answer: ab+

5. What does the following statement do?

   ```
   file_handle = open("my_bin_file.bin","rb")
   ```

   a. Opens file for writing only.
   b. Opens file for both reading and writing.
   c. Opens a file for both reading and writing in binary format.
   d. Opens a file for only reading in binary format.

   Answer: Opens a file for only reading in binary format.

Short questions and answers

1. Name the function that is used to delete files.

   Answer: `remove()`

   ```
   >>> import os
   >>>os.remove("fileName.txt")
   ```

2. Name the method that is used to create directory in the current directory.

   Answer:
   ```
   >>> import os
   >>>os.mkdir("directory_name")
   ```

3. What is the use of chdir() method?

   Answer: The `chdir()` method is used to change the current directory. It takes one argument which is the name of the directory that we want to make the current directory.

   ```
   >>> import os
   >>>os.chdir('directory_name')
   ```

4. Which method is used to check the current working directory?

   Answer: `getcwd() method`

   ```
   >>> import os
   >>>os.getcwd()
   ```

5. What is the purpose of rmdir()?

   Answer: The `rmdir()` method is used to remove or delete a directory. The name of the directory that has to be removed is passed as an argument.

6. Fill in the Blanks

   a. __________ are used to store huge collection of data and files permanently.

   Answer: Files

   b. A file can be stored in two ways: ________ and ________.

Answer: Text, Binary

c. The type of operations to be performed on open file are specified by the ______.

Answer: Access Modes

d. A ________ file stores information in ASCII or Unicode characters.

Answer: Text

e. In text file each line of text is terminated by a special character known as ________.

Answer: End of line(EOL)

f. _________ files are files that have information stored in the same format in which it is stored in the memory.

Answer: Binary

g. In binary files there are no _________ for a line.

Answer: delimiter

h. fileObject.__________(sequence_of_strings), writes the strings to the file.

Answer: 'writelines

i. ___________ function reads the whole file and returns the text as a string.

Answer: 'read()

j. The_________ method used to find current position of the file .

Answer: 'tell()

k. The __________ method of a file object flushes any unwritten information and closes the file object .

Answer: 'close()

l. The tell() method returns an ______ value that provides the current position of file pointer in the file.

Answer: Iinteger

Coding Questions and Answers

1. Look at the code given below and answer the following questions.

```
fileHandle = open('x','a')
/_______________
fileHandle ()
```

a. What type of file is x?

b. Fill in the blank with a statement that would write 'Hello World' in file x.

Answer: a. x is a text file

b. `fileHandle.write('Hello World')`

2. There is a folder by the name 'mar2020' which must be changed to 'jun2020'. How would you do that?

Answer: `>>> import os`

`>>>os.rename("mar2020","jun2020")`

3. Write a statement in Python to perform the following operations:
   1. Open a file "MYPET.TXT" in write mode
   2. Open a file "MYPET.TXT" in read mode

   Answer:
   1. file_handle = open("MYPET.TXT ","w")
   2. file_handle = open("MYPET.TXT ","r")

Descriptive Questions and Answers

1. What is the difference between file modes r+ and w+ with respect to Python?

   Answer:
   1. w+ - is Read and write operation.

   This opens the file in both read and write mode and if the file does not exist then a new file will be created with the same name for reading and writing.
2. r+ - is Read and write on existing file.

   This access mode opens the file for both read and write. The file pointer is placed at the beginning of the file.
2. Differentiate between the file modes r+ and rb+ with respect to Python.

   Answer:
   1. r+- Read and write on existing file.

      This access mode opens the file for both read and write. The file pointer is placed at the beginning of the file.
   2. rb+ - Read and Write on existing file

   Allows you to perform read and write operations on an existing binary file.rb+ - Read and Write on existing file. Allows you to perform read and write operations on an existing binary file.
3. How do you use with statement?

   Answer:

   The 'with' statement can be used to write two statements that are related to each other as pairs:

   'with open(filename,mode) as fileHandle:

   -----code to be execute-----

   This statement automatically closes the file after the nested block of code even if an exception occurs before the code ends.

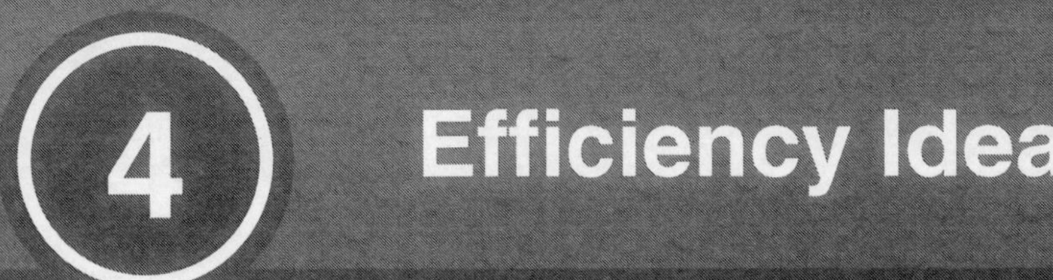

4 Efficiency Idea

In this chapter, you will cover:

Idea of efficiency: Number of comparisons in Best, Worst and Average case for linear search

An algorithm is a procedure or set of instructions that are carried out in order to solve a problem. Coding demands procedural knowledge which is expressed in the form of algorithms. An algorithm provides a recipe or a roadmap or a simple sequence of instructions that are required to accomplish a particular programming task. So, for things as simple as adding two numbers or as complex as designing a banking program, everything requires a systematic approach. It is important to create a meaningful roadmap before going ahead with the coding part. For simple programs it is easy to create algorithm by logical thinking. There are also some famous algorithms that can be used for complex problem solving and hence frequently used for coding.

4.1 Steps involved in writing an algorithm

There are three main steps involved in writing an algorithm:

1. **Data Input**
    - Formulate the problem and decide what data types will be the input.
2. **Data Processing**
    - Decide what computation will be carried of to get the desired result.
    - Also identify the decision points, conditions under which various functions will operate.
3. **Results Output**
    - One should know the expected results so that it can be verified by the actual results.

4.2 Characteristics of Algorithm

An algorithm has following five characteristics:

1. **Precision:** It clearly defines one singe starting point and one or more well defined ending points.
2. **Effectiveness:** It is composed of effective primitives that are understood by the person or machine using it.

3. **Input/Output Specified:** The algorithm must receive an input and it must also produce an output.
4. **Finiteness:** An algorithm must stop after executing of finite number of steps.
5. **Uniqueness:** In an algorithm the result of every step is uniquely defined and its value depends only on the input provided and the output generated by the previous steps.

4.3 Sorting Algorithm

An algorithm that puts elements of a list in certain order is called **sorting algorithm**. It uncovers a structure by sorting the input. Sorting is often required for optimizing the efficiency of other algorithms. The output of a sorting algorithm is in non-decreasing order where no element is smaller than the original element of the input and the output reorders but retains all the elements of the input which is generally in array form.

Some very commonly known sorting algorothms are as follows:

1. Simple sorts:
   a. Insertion sort
   b. Selection sort
2. Efficient Sorts:
   a. Merge sort
   b. Heap sort
   c. Quick sort
   d. Shell sort
3. Bubble sort
4. Distribution sort
   a. Counting sort
   b. Bucket sort
   c. Radix sort

4.4 Some important definitions

Recursive Algorithm: A recursive algorithm calls itself with smaller input values. It is used if a problem can be solved by using its own smaller versions.

Divide and Conquer Algorithm: As the name suggests the divide and conquer algorithm divides the problem into smaller parts. These smaller parts are solved and the solutions obtained are used to solve the original problem. It is used in Binary search, Merge sort, quick sort to name a few.

Dynamic programming: In a dynamic problem, an optimization problem is broken down into much simpler sub-problems, each sub problem is solved only once and the result is stored. For example, Fibonacci Sequence (Explained in Chapter on Recursion).

4.5 Big-O Notation

Big-O notation helps you analyse how an algorithm would perform if the data involved in the process increases or in simple words Big-O notation simplified analysis of how efficient an algorithm can be.

Since, algorithms are an essential part of software programming it is important for us to have some idea about how long an algorithm would take to run, only then can we compare two algorithms and a good developer would always consider time complexity while planning the coding process.

It helps in identifying how long an algorithm takes to run.

Big – O

- Gives us the algorithm complexity in terms of input size n.
- It considers only the steps involved in the algorithm.
- Big-O analysis can be used to analyse both time and space.

An algorithm's efficiency can be measured in terms of best- average or worst case but Big-O notation goes with the worst case scenario.

It is possible to perform a task in different ways which means that there can be different algorithms for the same task having different complexity and scalability.

4.5.1 Constant Complexity [O(1)]

A task that is constant will never experience variation during runtime, irrespective of the input value. For Example:

```
>>> x = 5 + 7
>>> x
12
>>>
```

The statement x = 5+7 does not depend on the input size of data in any way. This is known as O(1) (big oh of 1).

Example 4.1 Suppose, there are sequence of steps all of constant time as shown in the following code:

```
>>> a=(4-6)+ 9
>>> b = (5 * 8) +8
>>>print(a * b)
336
>>>
```

Now let's compute the Big-O for these steps:

Total time = O(1)+O(1)+O(1) = 3O(1)

While computing Big – O we ignore constants because once the data size increases, the value of constant does not matter.

Hence the Big-O would be O(1).

4.5.2 Linear complexity: [O(n)]

In case of linear complexity the time taken depends on the value of the input provided.

Suppose you want to print table of 5. Have a look at the following code:

```
>>> for i in range(0,n):
print("\n 5 x ",i,"=",5*i)
```

The number of lines to be printed, depends on 'n'. For n =10, only ten lines will be printed but for n= 1000, the for loop will take more time to execute.

The print statement is O(1).

So, the block of code is n*O(1) which is O(n).

Consider following lines of code:

```
>>>j = 0                                  ------(1)
>>> for i in range(0,n):                  ------(2)
        print("\n 5 x ",i,"=",5*i)
```

(1) is O(1)

(2) block is O(n)

Total time = O(1)+O(n)

We can drop O(1) because it is a lower order term and as the value of n becomes large (1) will not matter and the runtime actually depends on the for loop.

Hence the Big-O for the code mentioned above is O(n).

4.5.3 Quadratic Complexity:[O(n^2)]

As the name indicates quadratic complexity, the time taken depends on the square of the input value. This can be the case with nested loops. Look at the following code:

```
>>> for i in range (0,n):
    for j in range(0,n):
        print("I am in ", j," loop of i = ", i,".")
```

In this piece of code the print statement is executed n^2times.

4.5.4 Logarithmic Complexity

Logarithmic complexity indicates that in worst case the algorithm will have to perform log(n) steps. To understand this, let's first understand the concept of logarithm.

Logarithms are nothing but inverse of exponentiation.

Now let's take a term 2^3. Here 2 is the base and 3 is the exponent. We therefore say that base 2 log of 2 log of 8 ($\log_2 8$)= 3. Same way if 10^5=100000 then base 10 log of 100000 ($\log_{10} 100000$) = 5.

Since the computer works with binary numbers, therefore in programming and Big O we generally work with base 2 logs.

Have a look at the following observation:

$2^0 = 1, \log_2 1=0$

$2^1 = 2, \log_2 2=1$

$2^2 = 4, \log_2 4=2$

$2^3 = 8, \log_2 8=3$

$2^4 = 16, \log_2 10=4$

This means that if n =1, number of steps = 1.

If n = 4, number of steps will be 2.

If n = 8, then number of steps will be 3.

So, as data doubles the number of steps increase by one.

The number of steps grow slowly in comparison to the growth in data size.

4.6 Big-O analysis is also known as Asymptotic analysis

It is very important to know how fast a program would run and as mentioned earlier we do not want to consider the exact run time because different computers have different hardware capabilities and we may not get the correct information in this manner.

In order to resolve this issue, the concept of asymptotic notation was developed. It provides a universal approach for measuring speed and efficiency of an algorithm. For applications dealing with large inputs we are more interested in behaviour of an algorithm as the input size increases. Big O notation is one of the most important asymptotic notations.

4.7 Sequential Search

In class XI, we learned how we can make use of membership operator **'in'** to check if a value exists in a list or not.

```
>>> list1 = [1,2,3,4,5,6,7]
>>> 3 in list1
    True
>>> 8 in list1
     False
>>>
```

This is nothing but searching for an element in a list. We are going to look at how elements can be searched and how process efficiency can be improved. We start by learning about **sequential search**.

The simplest way of searching for an element in a sequence is to check every element one by one. If the element is found then the search ends and the element is returned or else the search continues till the end of the sequence. This method of searching is known as **linear search** or **sequential search**. It follows a simple approach but it is quite an inefficient way of searching for an element because we move from one element to the other right from beginning to end and if the element is not present in the sequence we would not know about it till we reach the last element.

Time analysis for sequential search:

- Best scenario is that the element that we are looking for is the very first element in the list. In this case the time complexity will be O(1).
- The worst scenario would be if we traverse throughout the entire sequence and realize that the element that we are looking for, does not exist. In this case the time complexity will be O(n).
- The average(i.e. average of comparisons) case scenario would be O(n/2)

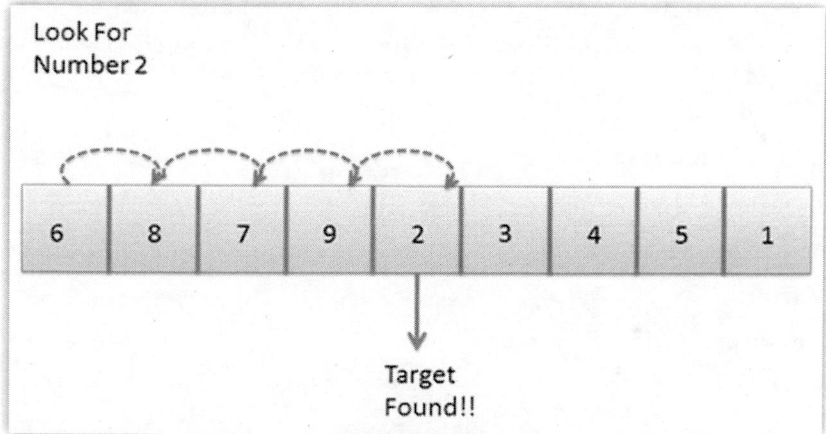

Figure 4.1

? EXERCISE

Short questions and answers

1. **What is worst-case time complexity of an algorithm?**

   Answer: The worst-case time complexity in computer science means worst- case in terms of time consumed while execution of a program.It is the longest running time that an algorithm can take. The efficiency of algorithms can be compared by looking at the order of growth of the worst-case complexity.

2. **What is the importance of Big-O notation?**

   Answer: Big-O notation describes how fast the runtime of an algorithm will increase with respect to the size of the input. It would give you a fair idea about how your algorithm would scale and also give you an idea about the worst-case complexity of the algorithms that you might be considering for your project. You would be able to compare two algorithms and decide which would be a better option for you.

3. **What is the need for run time analysis for an algorithm when you can find the exact runtime for a piece of code?**

   Answer: Exact runtime is not considered because the results can vary depending on the hardware of the machine, speed of the processor and the other processors that are running in the background. What is more important to understand is that how the performance of the algorithm gets affected with increase in input data.

4. **Why is Big O notation expressed as O(n)?**

Answer: Big-O notation compares the runtime for various types of input sizes.The focus is only on the impact of input size on the runtime which is why we use the n notation. As the value of n increases, our only concern is to see how it affects the runtime. If we had been measuring the runtime directly then the unit of measurement would have been time units like second, micro-second, and so on. However, in this case 'n' represents the size of the input and 'O' stands for 'Order'. Hence,O(1) stands for order of 1, O(n) stands for order of n and O(n^2) stands for order of the square of the size of input.

Big-O notations and names:

1. Constant – O(1)
2. Logarithmic – O(log(n))
3. Linear – O(n)
4. Log Linear – O(nlog(n))
5. Quadratic – $O(n^2)$
6. Cubic – $O(n^3)$
7. Exponential – $O(2^n)$

5. **Write a code in python that takes a list of alphabets such as ['a', 'b', 'c', 'd','e','f','g'] and returns a list of combination such as ['bcdefg', 'acdefg', 'abdefg', 'abcefg', 'abcdfg', 'abcdeg', 'abcdef']. Find the time complexity for the code.**

Answer:

Code:

```
input_value = input("enter the list of alphabets separate by comma : ")
alphabets = input_value.split(',')
final = []
str = ''
for element in range(0,len(alphabets)):
    for index, item in alphabets:
        if(item != alphabets[element]):
            str = str+item
    final.append(str)
    str=''
```

Execution:

```
print(final)
```

Output:

```
enter the list of alphabets seperate by comma :a,b,c,d,e,f,g
['bcdefg', 'acdefg', 'abdefg', 'abcefg', 'abcdfg', 'abcdeg', 'abcdef']
>>>
```

Conclusion:

The code has a runtime of $O(n^2)$.

6. **The following code finds the sum of all elements in a list. What is its time complexity?**

```
def sum(input_list):

    total = 0

    for i in input_list:

        total = total + i

    print(total)
```

Answer:

```
def sum(input_list):
  total = 0                                   ------(1)
  for i in input_list:                        -------(2)
    total = total + i
  print(total)                                -------(3)
```

time for block (1) = O(1)

time for block (2) = O(n)

time for block (3) = O(1)

Total time = O(1) + O(n) + O(1)

Dropping constants

Total time = O(n)

7. **What are the pros and cons of time complexity?**

Answer:

Pros:

It is a good way of getting an idea about the efficiency of the algorithm.

Cons:

It can be difficult to assess complexity for complicated functions.

8. **What is the difference between time and space complexity?**

Answer: Time complexity gives an idea about the number of steps that would be involved in order to solve a problem. The general order of complexity in ascending order is as follows:

$$O(1) < O(\log n) < O(n) < O(n \log n) < O(n^2)$$

Unlike time, memory can be reused and people are more interested in how fast the calculations can be done. This is one main reason why time complexity is often discussed more than space complexity. However, space complexity is never ignored. Space complexity decides how much memory will be required to run a program completely. Memory is required for:

1. Instruction space
2. Knowledge space for constants, variables, structured variables, dynamically altered areas etc
3. Execution

9. What is the difference between auxillary space and space complexity?

Answer: Auxillary space is the extra space that is required while executing an algorithm and it is temporary space.

Space complexity on the other hand is the sum of auxillary space and input space:

Space complexity = Auxiliary space + Input space

10. What is memory usage while execution of algorithm?

Answer: Memory is used for:

1. Saving the compiled version of instructions.
2. In case of nested functions or one algorithm, calling another algorithm, the variables are pushed to a system stack and made to wait till the internal algorithm hasfinished executing.
3. To store data and variables.

Space Complexity

You have learnt about time complexity. Now, let's move on to space complexity. As the name suggests space complexity describes how much memory space would be required if size of input n increases. Here too we consider the worst case scenario.

Now have a look at the following code:

```
>>> x = 23          ...(1)
>>> y = 34          ...(2)
>>> sum = x + y     ...(3)
>>> sum


57
>>>
```

In this example we need space to store three variables: x in (1), y in (2), and sum in (3). However, this scenario will not change, and the requirement for 3 variables is constant and hence the space complexity is O(1).

Now, have a look at the following code:

```
word = input("enter a word : ")
word_list = []
```

```
for element in word:
    print(element)
word_list.append(element)
print(word_list)
```

The size of the **word_list** object increase with n. Hence, in this case the space complexity is O(n).

Suppose there is a function by the name **function1** which has three variables and this **function1** calls another function named **function2** that has 6 variables then the overall requirement for temporary workspace is of 9 units. Even if function1 calls function2 ten times the workspace requirement will remain the same.

11. What would be the space complexity for the following piece of code? Explain.

```
n = int(input("provide a number : "))
statement = "Happy birthday"
for i in range(0,n):
        print(i+1,". ",statement)
```

Answer: The space complexity for the above code will be O(1) because the space requirement is only for storing value of integer variable n and string statement. Even if the size of n increases the space requirement remains constant. Hence,O(1).

12. What is the time and space complexity for the following:

```
a = b = 0
for i in range(n):
    a = a + i
for j in range(m):
    b = b + j
```

Answer: Time Complexity

Time for first loop = O(n)

Time for second loop = O(m)

Total time = O(n) + O(m) = O(n + m)

Space complexity

O(1)

13. Find the time complexity for the following code:

```
a = 0
for i in range(n):
    a = a + i
    for j in range(m):
        a = a + i + j
```

Answer: Time complexity: $O(n^2)$

14. What will be the time complexity for the following code?

```
i = j = k =0
for i in range(n/2,n):
    for j in range(2,n):
        k = k+n/2
       j = j*2
```

Answer: Time complexity for the first for loop O(n/2).

Time complexity for second for loop: O(logn) because j is doubling itself till it is less than n.

Total time = O(n/2)*O(logn)

= O(nlogn)

15. What is the time complexity for the following code:

```
i = a = 0
while i>0:
    a = a+i
i = i/2
```

Answer: Time complexity will be O(logn).

Big O for Python Data Structures

Python language comprises of mutable and immutable objects. Numbers, strings, and tuple come in the latter category whereas lists, sets, and dictionary data type are mutable objects. The reason why lists and dictionaries are called mutable is because they can be easily altered anytime. They are like array because the data elements can be inserted or deleted easily by providing an index value and since the values can be easily added or removed from any point, the lists are considered to be dynamic. Hence, lists are known to be dynamic arrays. You can also say that lists are called dynamic array because:

1. Its size can be dynamically modified at run time.
2. You need not define the size of the list when you create it.
3. They allow you to store more than one variable.
4. Dynamic arrays, once filled allocate bigger chunk of memory and elements of the original array are copied to this section of memory as a result it can continue to fill available slots.

The most important operations that are performed on a list are as follows:

1. Indexing
2. Assigning value to an index value

Both the methods mentioned above are designed to run at constant time O(1). The Big-O for common list operations are given as follows:

1. `index[] : O(1)`
2. `index assignment : O(1)`
3. `append: O(1)`

```
4. pop() : O(1)
5. pop(i): O(n)
6. insert(i, item): O(n)
7. delete operator: O(n)
8. contains(in): O(n)
9. get slice[x:y]: O(k)
10. del slice: O(n)
11. set slice : O(n+k)
12. reverse: O(n)
13. concatenate:  O(k)
14. sort: O(nlog n)
15. multiply O(nk)
```

Dictionaries

Dictionaries are implementation of hashtables and can be operated with keys and values. Big-O efficiencies for common dictionary objects are given as follows:

```
1. copy : O(n)
2. get item : O(1)
3. set item : O(1)
4. delete item : O(1)
5. contains(in) : O(1)
6. iteration: O(n)
```

16. Sequential search is also known as _______

Answer: Linear Search

17. How are the elements reviewed in sequential search?

Answer: The elements are reviewed one at a time in sequential term.

18. When does the sequential search end?

Answer: The sequential search ends when an element is found or when the end of the sequence is reached.

19. Write code to implement sequential search.

Answer: The sequential search can be implemented as follows:

- The function takes two values: seq_list which is the list and target_num which is the number to search in the list.
- We set search_flag = 0 if the target number is found in the list we will set the search_flag to 1 else we let it be 0.
- We iterate through the list comparing each element in the list with the target_num.

- If a match is found we print a message and update the search_flag to1.
- After the "for" loop if the search_flag is still 0 then it means that the number was not found.

Code:

```
def sequential_search(seq_list, target_num):
    search_flag = 0
    for i in range(len(seq_list)):
        if seq_list[i] == target_num:
            print("Found the target number ", target_num, " at index", i,".")
            search_flag = 1;
        if search_flag == 0:
            print("Target Number Does Not Exist. Search Unsuccessful.")
```

Execution:

```
seq_list = [1,2,3,4,5,6,7,8,2,9,10,11,12,13,14,15,16]
target_num = input("Please enter the target number : ")
sequential_search(seq_list, int(target_num))
```

Output1:

```
Please enter the target number : 5
Found the target number  5  at index 4 .
```

Output2:

```
Please enter the target number : 2
Found the target number  2  at index 1 .
Found the target number  2  at index 8 .
```

Output3:

```
Please enter the target number : 87
Target Number Does Not Exist. Search Unsuccessful.
```

20. How would you implement sequential search for an ordered list?

Answer: When elements in a list are sorted, then many times there may not be the need to scan the entire list. The moment we reach an element that has a value greater than the target number, we know that we need not go any further.

Step 1: We define a function **`sequential_search()`** that takes two areguments – a list (**`seq_list`**) and the number that we are looking for (**`target_num`**).

```
def sequential_search(seq_list, target_num):
```

Step 2: The first thing we do is set define a flag (search_flag) and set it to "False" or "0" value. The flag is set to "True" or "1" if the element is found. So, after traversing though the list if the search_flag value is still "False" or "0" , we would know that the number that we are looking for does not exist in the list.

```
def sequential_search(seq_list, target_num):
    search_flag = 0
```

Step 3: Now, it's time to check the elements one by one so, we define the for loop:

```
def sequential_search(seq_list, target_num):
    search_flag = 0
    for i in range(len(seq_list)):
```

Step 4: We now define how the elements are compared. Since it is an ordered list for every "i" in **seq_list** we have to check if i>target_num. If yes, then it means that there is no point moving further as it is an ordered list and we have reached an element that is greater than the number that we are looking for. However if **seq_list[i] == target_num** then, the search is successful and we can set the **search_flag** to 1.

```
def sequential_search(seq_list, target_num):
    search_flag = 0
    for i in range(len(seq_list)):
        if seq_list[i] > target_num:
            print("search no further.")
            break;
        elif seq_list[i] == target_num:
            print("Found the target number ", target_num, " at index", i,".")
            search_flag = 1;
```

Step 5: After the for loop has been executed if the value of **search_flag** is still 0 then a message stating that the target number was not found must be displayed.

Code:

```
def sequential_search(seq_list, target_num):
    search_flag = 0
    for i in range(len(seq_list)):
        if seq_list[i] > target_num:
            print("search no further.")
            break;
        elif seq_list[i] == target_num:
           print("Found the target number ", target_num, " at index", i,".")
            search_flag = 1;
    if search_flag == 0:
        print("Target Number Does Not Exist. Search Unsuccessful.")
```

Execution:

```
seq_list = [1,2,3,4,5,6,7,8,2,9,10,11,12,13,14,15,16]
target_num = input("Please enter the target number : ")
sequential_search(seq_list, int(target_num))
```

Output1:

```
Please enter the target number : 2
Found the target number  2  at index 1 .
Found the target number  2  at index 2 .
search no further.
>>>
```

Output2:

```
Please enter the target number : 8
Found the target number  8  at index 8 .
search no further.
>>>
```

Output3:

```
Please enter the target number : 89
Target Number Does Not Exist. Search Unsuccessful.
>>>
```

5 Stack and Queue

In this chapter, you will cover:

Data Structure: Stack, operations on stack (push & pop), implementation of stack using list.

5.1 Stack

Stack is an ordered collection of items where the addition and removal of items take place at the same end which is also known as the **TOP**. The other end of the stack is known as the **BASE**. The base of the stack is significant because the items that are closer to the base represent those that have been in the stack, for the longest time.

The most recently added item is the one that is in the top position so that it can be removed first. The items are added on to the stack using **push** operation and removed using **pop** operation.

To understand **push** and **pop,** let's take a look at a familiar situation. Suppose, you start working on a word document; you type in a title and then you change its Font size followed by change of color.

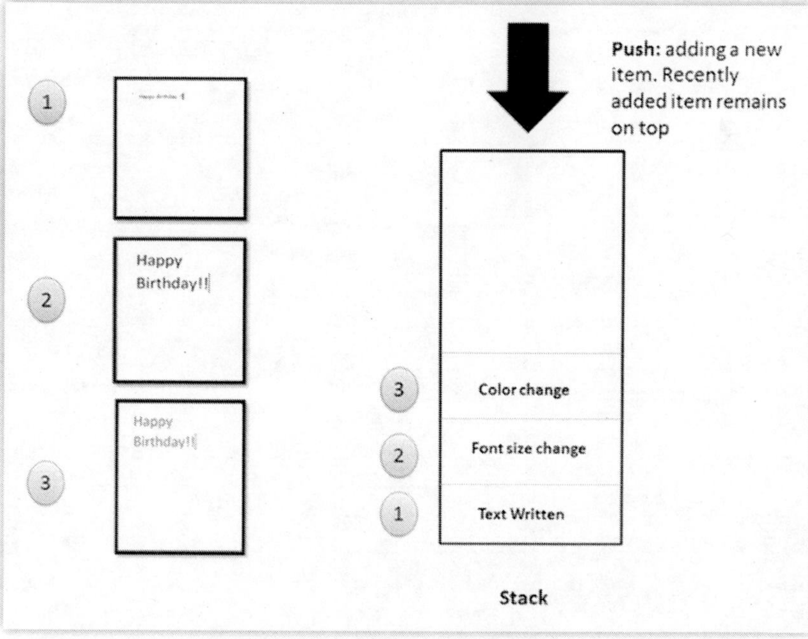

Figure 5.1 (a): *Push operation*

So, you can do whatever you want to do on the word file but when you hit the undo button, only the last task done is undone.

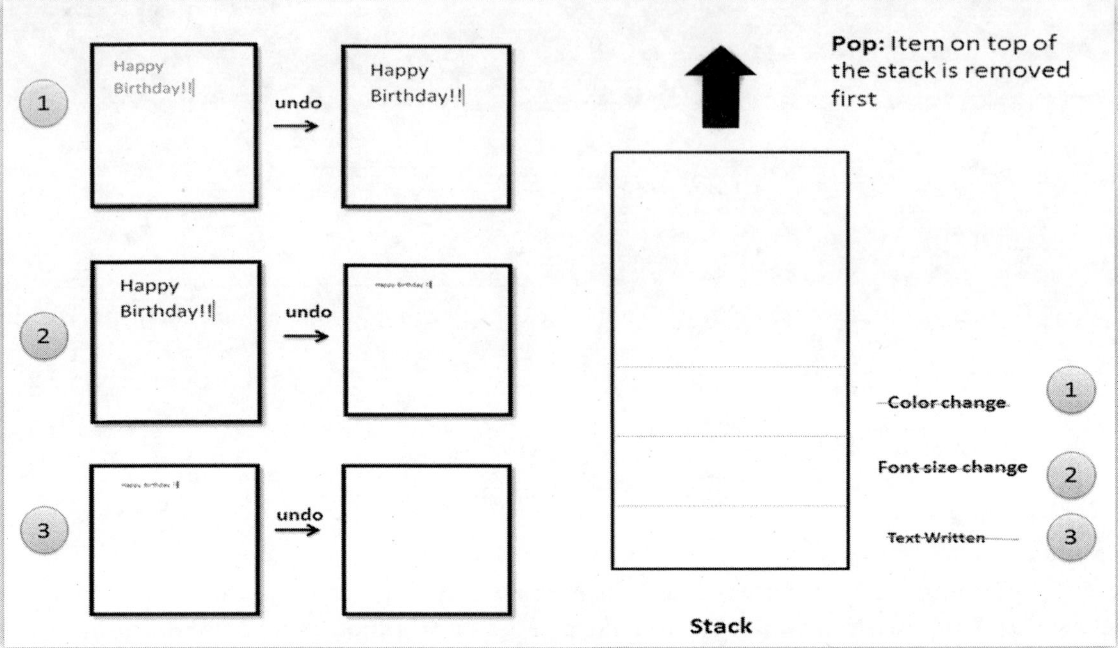

Figure 5.1(b): *PopOperation*

Similarly, in case of stack you can add as many items you want using **push** but you can **pop** or remove only the object which is on the top which means last in is first to be removed. This principle of ordering is known as LIFO-that stands for **Last –in-first-out**, where the newer items are near the top, while older items are near the base.

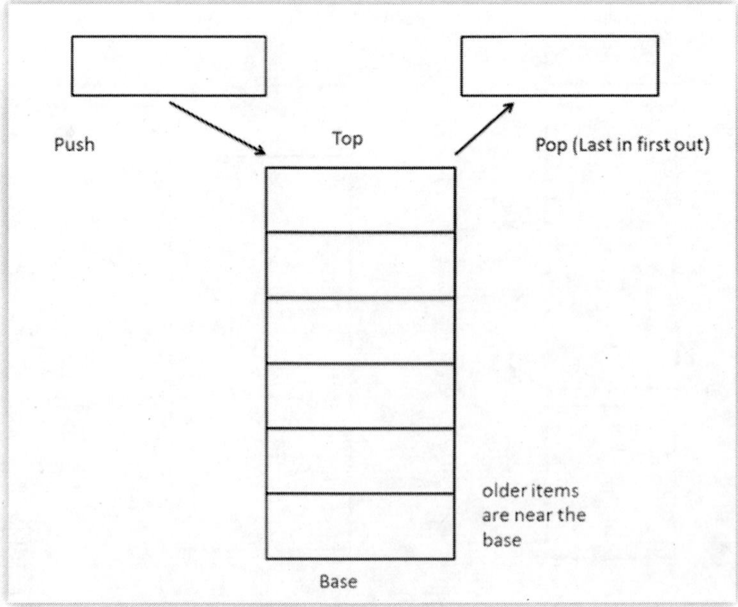

Figure 5.2: *LIFO*

Stacks are important because they are required whenever there is a need to reverse the order of items as the order of removal is reverse of the order of insertion.

Example:

- Pushing back button on browser while surfing on internet.
- Ctrl+Z (undo) in Microsoft applications.
- Remove recently used object from cache.

Stacks are commonly used by software programmers; it may not be quite noticeable while using a program as these operations generally take place at the background. However, many times you may come across **Stack overflow** error. This happens when a stack actually runs out of memory.

Stacks are simple yet one of the most important data structures as you will see very soon. Stacks serve as a very important element of several data structures and algorithms.

5.1.1 Implementation of a stack in Python

Here we will implement Stack using lists.

Step 1: Define a list by the name stack

```
#Define Stack
stack = []
```

Step 2: Define Push Function

A push function will take only one argument and that will be the element that we want to push in the list. In this function we call the append method to push the element to the stack.

```
#push method
def push(element):
    stack.append(element)
```

Step 3: Define POP Function

This function checks the stack. If the stack is empty, it prints: *Stack is empty. Nothing to POP!!*. If it is not empty pop the last item from the stack.

```
#pop method
def pop(stack):
        if(stack == []):
            print("Stack is empty. Nothing to POP!!")
        else:
            stack.pop()
```

The complete code will be as follows:

Code:

```
stack = []

#push method
def push(element):
    stack.append(element)

#pop method
def pop(stack):
        if(stack == []):
            print("Stack is empty. Nothing to POP!!")
        else:
            stack.pop()
```

Execution:

```
push(6)
push(3)
print(stack)
pop(stack)
print(stack)
pop(stack)
print(stack)
pop(stack)
```

Output:

```
[6, 3]
[6]
[]
Stack is empty. Nothing to POP!!
>>>
```

5.2 Queue

A **queue** is a sequence of objects where elements are added from one end and removed from the other. The queues follow the principle of first in first out. The removal of items is done from one end called the ***Front*** and the items are removed from another end that's referred to as ***rear***. So, just as in case of any queue in real life, the items enter the queue from the rear and start moving towards the front as the items are removed one by one.

So, in a queue the item at the front is the one that has been in the sequence for the longest and the most recently added item must wait at the end. The insert and delete operations are also called **enqueue** and **dequeue**.

5.2.1 Basic Queue Functions

Basic Queue functions are as follows:

- **`enqueue(i)`:** Add element "i" to the queue.
- **`dequeue()`:** Removes the first element from the queue and returns its value.
- **`isEmpty()`:** Boolean function that returns "**true**" if the queue is empty else it will return false.
- **`size()`:** Returns length of the queue.

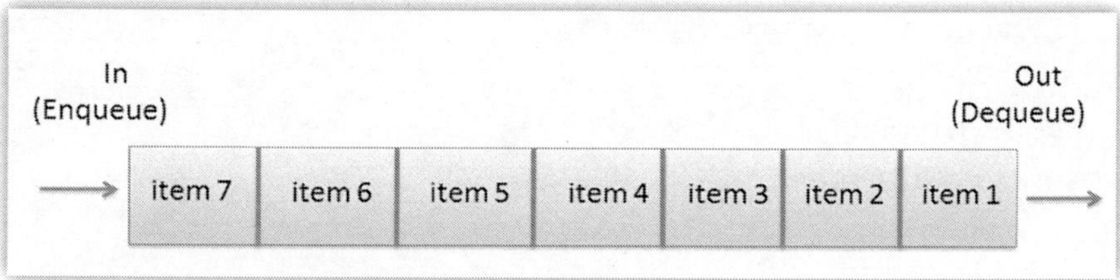

Figure 5.3: *Basic Queue functions*

5.2.2 Implementation of Queue

Let's write a program for implementation of queue.

Step 1: Define isEmpty() function

As the name suggests, this method is called to check if the queue is empty or not. The **`isEmpty()`** function checks if the queue is empty. If yes, it prints a message - ***Queue is Empty*** or else it will print a message - ***Queue is not Empty***

```
def isEmpty(queue):
    if queue ==[]:
        print("Queue is Empty")
    else:
        print("Queue is not empty")
```

Step 2: Define enqueue() function

This function takes an element as parameter and inserts it at index "0". All elements in the queue shift by one position.

```
def enqueue(queue,element):
    queue.insert(0,element)
```

Step 3: Define equeue() function

This function pops the oldest element from the queue.

```
def dequeue(queue):
    queue.pop()
```

Step 4: Define size() function

This function returns the length of the queue.

```
def size(queue):
    print("size of queue is",len(queue))
```

Code:

```
def isEmpty(queue):
    if queue ==[]:
        print("Queue is Empty")

    else:
        print("Queue is not empty")

def enqueue(queue,element):
    queue.insert(0,element)

def dequeue(queue):
    queue.pop()

def size(queue):
    print("size of queue is",len(queue))
```

Execution:

```
queue = []
# Check if queue is empty
isEmpty(queue)

#enqueue
print("inserting element no.1")
enqueue(queue,"apple")
print("inserting element no.2")
enqueue(queue,"banana")
print("inserting element no.3")
enqueue(queue,"orange")
print("The queue elements are as follows:")
print(queue)

#check if queue is empty?
print("check if queue is empty?")
isEmpty(queue)
```

```
#dequeue
print("remove first element")
dequeue(queue)
print("what is the size of the queue?")

size(queue)
print("print contents of the queue")
print(queue)
```

Output:

```
Queue is Empty
inserting element no.1
inserting element no.2
inserting element no.3
The queue elements are as follows:
['orange', 'banana', 'apple']
check if queue is empty?
Queue is not empty
remove first element
what is the size of the queue?
size of queue is 2
print contents of the queue
['orange', 'banana']
>>>
```

UNIT II

Computer Networks

- Evolution of Networking
- Data Communication Terminologies
- Network Devices
- Network Topologies and Types
- Network Protocol
- Mobile Telecommunication Technology
- Introduction to Web Services

1 Evolution of Networking

In this chapter, you will cover:

- Evolution of networking: Introduction to computer networks, evolution of networking (ARPANET, NSFNET, INTERNET)
- Data communication terminologies: IP address, switching techniques (Circuit switching, Packet switching)

In this chapter you will learn how the first network evolved to today's internet.

1.1 Evolution of Networking

Apranet

In the year 1969 a project name APRANET (Advanced Research Project Agency Network) was sponsored by the US Department of Defense. This marked the beginning of evolution of the networking. As **APRANET** was the first network, it eventually led to the development of the internet. The US Defense and various universities were connected together using packet switching. The goal was to design an effective communication method for the military. It was desired to have a network that continues to work even if there is a catastrophic event such as a nuclear attack. This was achieved by linking different computers together, so that the overall computer power increases and information storage can be decentralized. So, the maximum damage in case of attack is that a link would be destroyed but the network and its other components would continue to work. APRANET allowed users to login from a remote location. A **Terminal Interface Protocol (TIP)** was used so that users on individual computer terminal could dial into the network. This allowed users to access information in the other computer systems and also allowed them to exchange files, copy and save data. The electronic mail system for the **APRANET** was created in the year 1972 by a Programmer by the name **Ray Tomlison**. He is the one who used '@' symbol to connect the username of the recipient to his or her host computer. We still use this convention.

In 1980s, came a more superior and high – capacity network known as the **NSFNET .NSFET** was created by a federal agency known as National Science Foundation and it was strictly meant for academic and engineering research. This initially started as off with handful of computers but with time the team working on it expanded. The team members that comprised of scientists, engineers, researchers and students soon began to exchange data and messages. With time, more private companies started building their own network. These networks along with **NSFNET** and **APRANET** were linked to create the Internet. The work on the internet began in the year 1986 but it came fruition in the 1990s. The original APRANET was closed in the year 1990 and in 1995 the NSFNET too was discontinued. The commercial interservices however continued to remain a part of the internet.So, you see that eventhough for many people the experience with internet began in the 1990s, internet in itself is way older than that.

1.2 Internet

The internet is a worldwide network of interlinked computers. A super world-wide network is created by interconnecting larger and smaller networks belonging to different organizations across the world so that the computers across the world can communicate and exchange information with each other. A device known as a gateway is used to connect the dissimilar networks and thus forms the backbone of the internet. It is called a backbone because it works as a central interconnecting structure that can connect one or more networks. In order to achieve communication via the internet all computers have to follow certain protocols. A protocol is a common set of rules for communication and in case of the internet the set of protocol used is called TCP/IP(Transmission Control Protocol/Internet Protocol.). The internet standards are required to allow users from different networks to connect with each other.

How the Internet Functions?

The Internet functions as follows: the information that needs to be passed on to the other machine is first divided into small sections known as Packets and then these sections are sequentially numbered. These packets are then forwarded over the internet. They reach the destination computer in random order and are then rearranged in the right order to provide the right information. All machines connected to the internet are able to use it because they all follow the protocol defined for communication. As mentioned earlier the Internet uses the TCP/IP protocol. The TCP(Transmission Control Protocol) is responsible for breaking information into packets on the source computer and also for rearranging the packets on the destination computer. The IP(Internet Protocol) ensures that the packets reach the right destination as it keeps track of the address of the destination computer.

Interspace

Interspace is what we see as the future of internet. The internet transmits data by interconnecting networks whereas interspace would provide an environment that would interconnect spaces to manipulate data.

1.3 Switching Techniques

Data is transmitted across the network using switching techniques. This includes:

1. Circuit Switching
2. Packet Switching

1.3.1 Circuit Switching

Circuit switching makes use of a dedicated channel for the period of communication. This method was used in old traditional telephone communication where calls were carried over by what we know as **Public Switched Telephone Network (PSTN)** or **Plain Old Telephone Services (POTS)**. *Figure 1.1* shows how a typical traditional telephone network functions. The PSTNs work as telephone exchanges and each PSTN serves a particular region. These networks are connected through central offices.

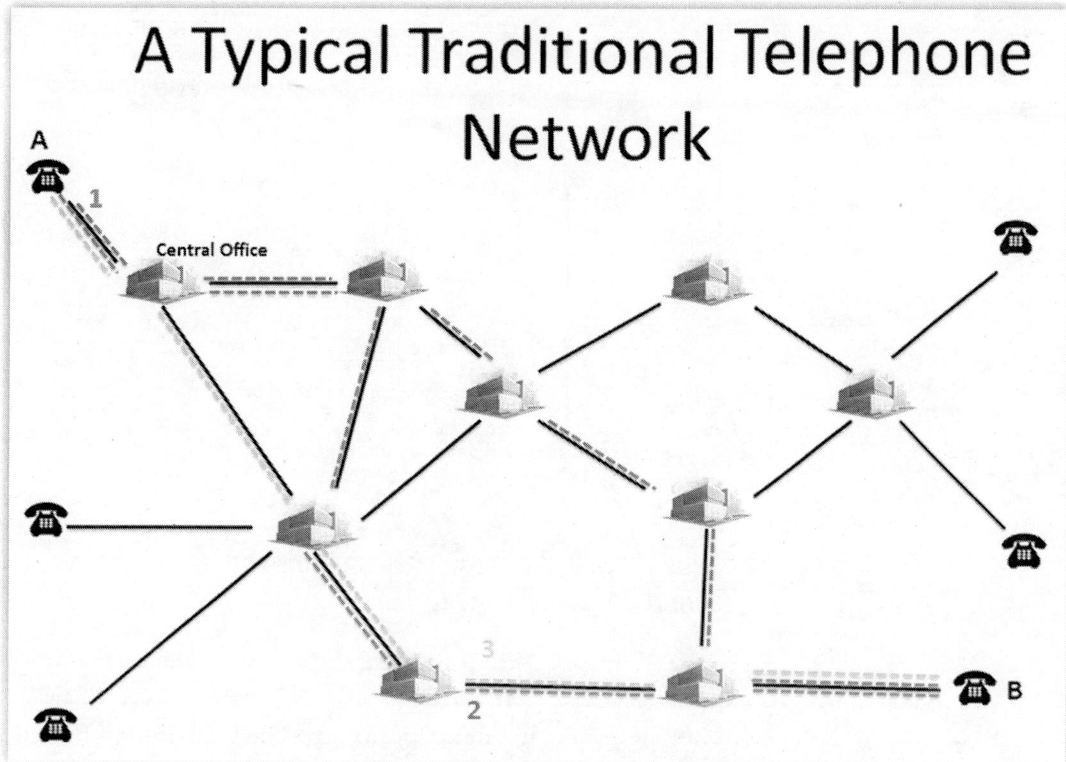

Figure 1.1: *A typical traditional telephone network*

Let's say that a person at **location A** wants to connect to the person at **location B**. In order to start the conversation the phone must establish a channel. As you can see in the figure there are many different paths that can be taken. Once the channel is finalized, the full bandwidth will be provided to the communication session till it terminates. This is why international calls were so expensive because one was actually renting the while line while making a PSTN call.

1.3.2 Packet Switching

In the last section you read about how circuit switching technique works. In this section we will look at how the Packet switching network works. Packet switching is made possible with the help of different routers. As you can see in figure 1.2, the information has to move from desktop at **position A** to laptop at **position B**. The information is broken into data packets before transferring. All packets are free to take any path. Every packet has the information related to the IP address and sequencing order so they can independently move on different paths. Each packet identifies the fastest channel and takes that route. Once all the packets reach the destination they are arranged in order so that the user can access it. As mentioned earlier the set of rules defined for communicating on the internet is defined by TCP/IP which is a packet switching protocol.

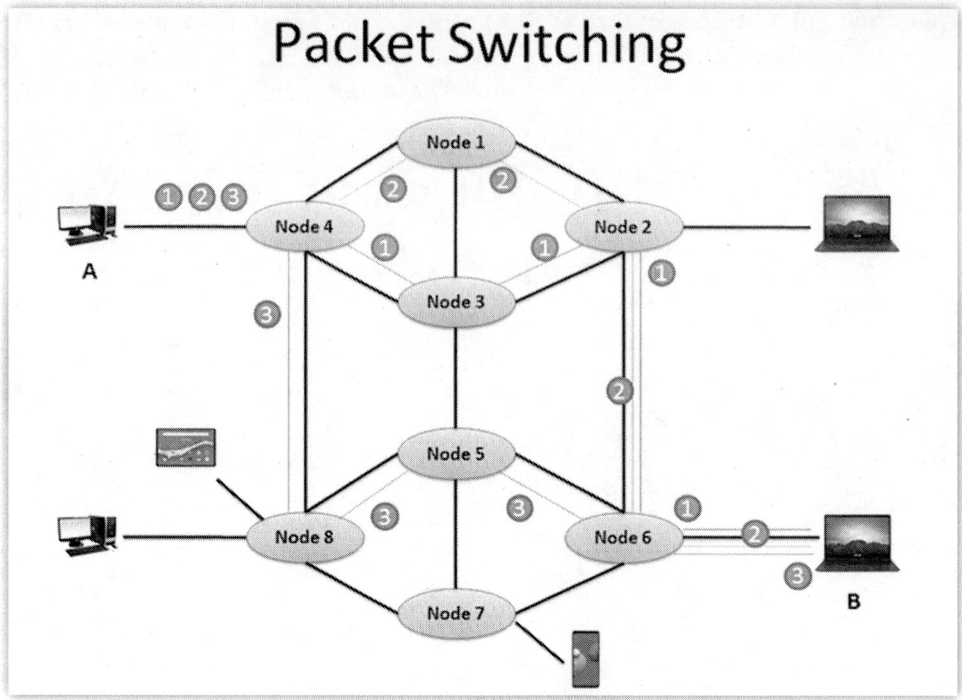

Figure 1.2: *Packet switching*

1.3.3 Circuit Switching vs Packet Switching

Circuit switched networks are used where information is required to be transmitted in real time and delay is not acceptable and are used for traditional phone calls. The packet switched networks on the other hand deal with digital data. These networks are very flexible and efficient. Nowadays phone service is available on the internet and is known as **Voice over IP** or **VoIP**.

Circuit Switching	Packet Switching
• It is important to find a channel before the communication is established between the source and the destination computer. • The entire data is passed through a fixed path. • This method guarantees delivery of message. • Mostly used for Voice calls.	• Uses TCP to break a huge piece of information into smaller packets (size varying from 128 to 4096 bytes). • Every packet can take an independent path. It has information related to the address and sequencing order. • The Internet protocol (IP) is responsible for tracking various paths that are available between the source and the destination. If there is a issue in one route then it looks for alternate route to the destination. • Packets are reassembled in the right order at the destination by the TCP. • If any packet is lost or damaged a request is sent to send the same message again.

2 Data Communication Terminologies

In this chapter, you will cover:

- **Data communication terminologies:** Concept of communication, components of data communication (sender, receiver, message, communication media, protocols), measuring capacity of communication media (bandwidth, data transfer rate.
- Transmission media: Wired communication media (Twisted pair cable, Co-axial cable, Fiber-optic cable), Wireless media (Radio waves, Micro waves, Infrared waves).

2.1 Concept of Channel

The path followed by the data from source to destination is called a channel, you can also say that it is the connection or a pathway between the transmitter and the receiver through which the information travels. A channel is formed with the help of many things such as wires, free space and other networks, Information is transmitted between networks of different characteristics such as from Wi-Fi to an Ethernet LAN or to the one with the fibre optic backbone. The data rate and the reliability of a network is dependent on its physical characteristics. Channels can be either wired or wireless. This is shown in *Figure 2.1*.

Computer Networks Based on Communication

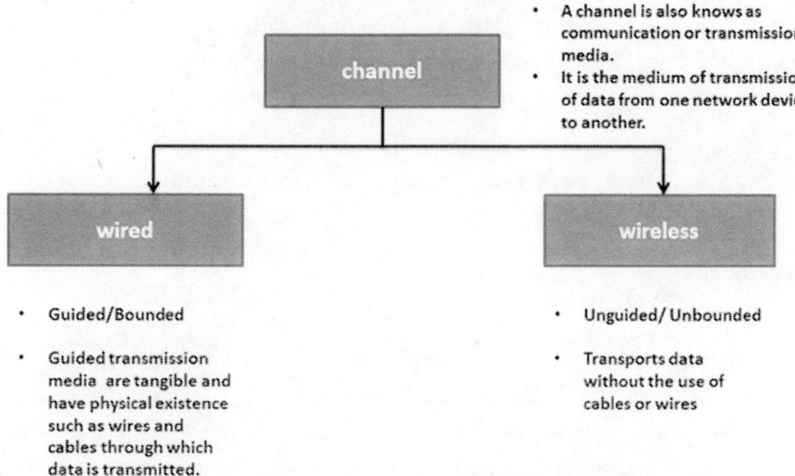

Figure 2.1: *Computer networks based on communication*

The information is converted to binary digits which are then encoded into a signal that can be sent from the transmitter to the receiver with the help of an appropriate medium. In case of bounded transmission the source and the destination are connected through wires and the signals have to travel through this physical media channel. Figure 2.2 shows further classification of wired and wireless networks.

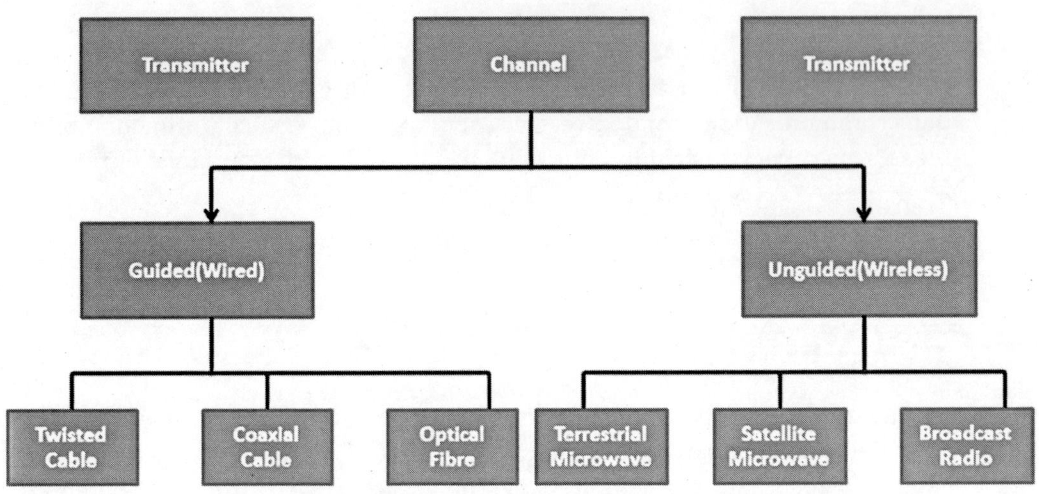

Figure 2.2: *Classification of wired and wireless networks*

You know that the channel or the transmission media carries information from one place (Sender) to the other (Receiver). This transmission medium can be of two types:

1. **Guided:** In case of guided medium the signals are transmitted through solid medium such as copper twisted pair cable or coaxial cable that comes under the category of Metallic cable. Another example of guided medium is Fibre optic Cable. The limitations of transmission are determined by the type of medium used. Any signal travelling along the guided medium is directed by its physical limits and data is transported in the form of electric signal. In a short while you will learn about how the twisted pair and the coaxial cables work. The fibre optic cables transport signals in the form of light.

2. **Unguided :** The unguided transmission medium uses the free space. In this case the bandwidth of the signal produced by the antenna is more important. The commonly used wireless or unguided media comprises of Radio waves,Micro wave and Infra Red Waves.

2.2 Twisted Pair Cable

Figure 2.3 displays the diagram of a twisted pair cable that was discovered by Alexander Graham Bell. Twisted pair cable is a wiring that comprises of two metallic conductors (copper) twisted together in its own insulation(plastic covering) in order to improve the electromagnetic compatibility of the wire. Copper wires are known for low cost and good performance hence copper is the best choice for twisted pair cable. It is the cheapest medium available.

Twisted Cable

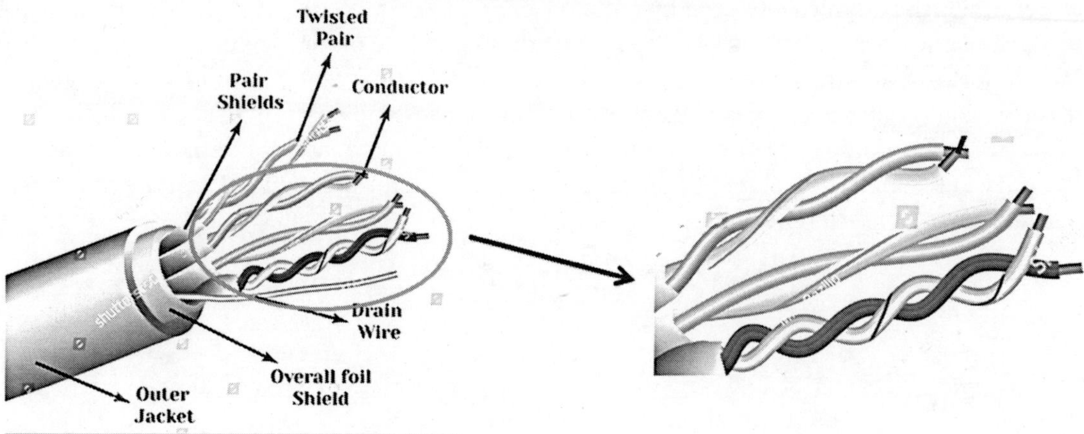

Figure 2.3: *Twisted Cable (Source: shutterstock.com)*

You may be aware of the fact that a current carrying wire has a magnetic field around itself, and when this current carrying wire comes in close proximity with another wire the magnetic field is prone to encounter interference. A single conductor or an untwisted pair of parallel wires are prone to electromagnetic radiation and often face the issues related to cross talk with neighbouring pairs but that is not the case with twisted pair. The electromagnetic radiations and cross talk is greatly reduced in case of twisted pair cable because when two wires are parallel one wire is closer to the noise and the other is a bit away and so the distribution of interference is not the same as a result the quality of signal suffers. Balance is maintained by twisting cables together. so in one twist one wire is close to the noise and the other is little far away where as in the second twist the second wire comes closer to the noise and the first wire moves away so both wires are equally affected by the noise and cross talk, the unwanted signals are cancelled out and the receiver receives a clear signal. The performance of twisted pair cables increases as the number of twists increases. The wires of a twisted pair cable are generally 1 to 2 mm thick. In computer networks , the Ethernet cable used generally comprises of 4 pairs. These pairs are bundled together and covered with protective shield. Every cable is color coated so that it is easy to identify. A twisted pair cable can be further classified as:

1. **Shielded twisted pair cable (STP)**
   a. Each pair of conductor is encased in a metal foil covering.
   b. Metal case shielding eliminates cross talk and prevents noise penetration.
   c. Has a mesh shielding which allows higher transmission rate and protects from electromagnetic interference.
   d. More expensive than UTP.
2. **Unshielded twisted pair cable (UTP)**
   a. UTP is less costly easily available therefore more commonly used.
   b. Extensively used for LAN and telephone connections.

2.3 Coaxial cable

Coaxial cable consists of an inner conductor. This inner conductor is held in place by a solid Di-electric material which is in turn enclosed by an outer conductor. The outer metallic wrapping works as a shield against noise and also works as a second conductor. The outer conductor is also enclosed in an insulating shield and the whole cable is protected by a plastic jacket. As compared to twisted pair cable, the coaxial cable can carry signals of higher frequencies and has a higher bandwidth. They are less susceptible to interference or cross talk as compared to the twisted cables mainly because of its shielding. The crosstalk is regulated because the outer conductor is grounded and the inner conductor is shielded from interference.

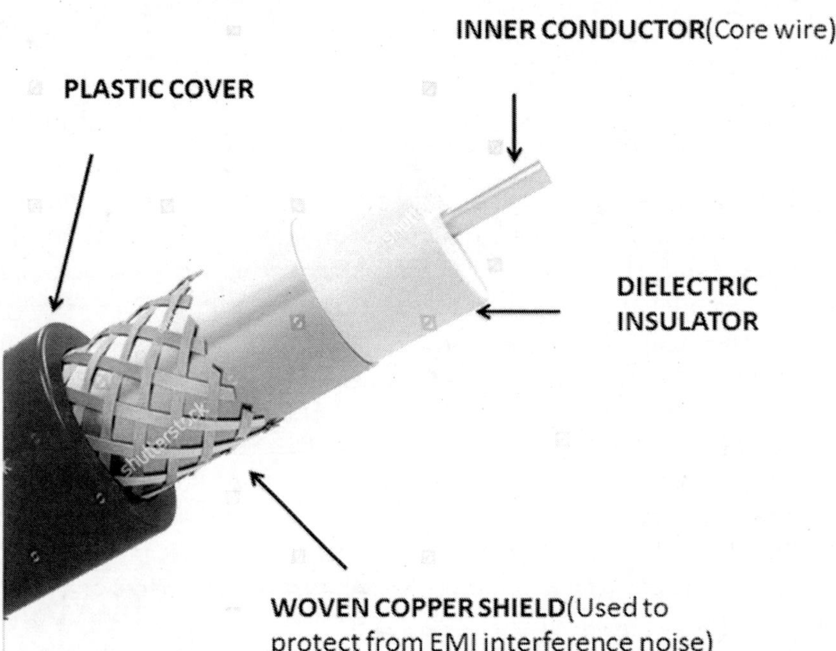

Figure 2.4: *Coaxial cable (Source: Shutterstock.com)*

When it comes to performance, the coaxial cables have a much higher bandwidth and the signal weakens rapidly hence there is a frequent requirement of repeaters. The coaxial cable performance is dependent on the diameter of the inner and outer conductors, the bigger the better. Coaxial cables are used for both digital and analog signals. When transmitting digital signals repeaters are required every 1 Km and for analog signals amplifier is required every few Kilometers.

Coaxial cables offers good data rate and less signal attenuation and are effectively used for higher data rate and higher bandwidth. As you can see in the diagram a coaxial consists of a central conductor which is surrounded by a foil shield. The foil shield is further covered by a braided shield to protect fromm EMI interference (noise). The conductor and the foil shield is separated by a dielectric insulator

Coaxial cables offer better shielding as compared to twisted pair cables. These cables are able to transmit signals that can cover long distances at greater speed. The shielding in these cables greatly reduces the electrical and radio frequency interference. It is for this reason that coaxial cable is often the **primary type of cabling** for **Cable TV** and **computer networks**.

2.4 Optical Fibre

The optical fibre transmits data at a very high rate and hence it is the most expensive wired medium available for transmission. Optical fibre are extensively used for long distance communication, the transmission does not get affected by any electromagnetic interference because it involves light hence the noise and distortion is very less. The optical fibre is a flexible, thin and transparent medium that works on the principle of total internal reflection. It is made of high quality very fine glass or plastic fibres slightly thicker than human hair and is able to transmit digital data signals in the form of light over huge distances of thousands of miles.

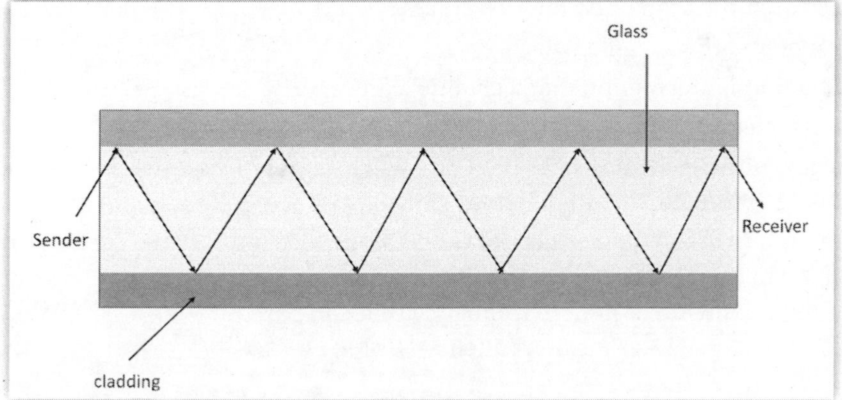

The centre of each fibre or strand is known as the core through which the light travels. The core is surrounded by a layer of glass (cladding) that reflects light inwards so that the signal is not lost and it also allows the light to pass through the bends in the cable. Because of this reflective cladding the light does not escape the glass core.

An optical fibre has an outer jacket made of PVC or Teflon.

Advantages of optical fiber

1. useful in backbone networks
2. High bandwidth(refer to section 2.5), therefore higher data rate.
3. Not affected by electromagnetic noise.
4. Signal can travel longer distances.

Disadvantages of fiber optics

1. Expensive
2. Unidirectional
3. Two cables are required for full duplex communication.

2.5 Bandwidth

Bandwidth is the frequency range (portion of electromagnetic spectrum) that a signal occupies. It is the maximum amount of information that a signal can carry. You can also say that bandwidth is the difference between the upper and the lower frequency limits of a signal.

When discussing about signal bandwidth refers to:

1. Difference between the upper and lower frequency limit.
2. Range of frequencies occupied by a signal.
3. The section of the electromagnetic spectrum occupied by the signal.
4. The range over which a signal is transmitted.

When discussing about channel bandwidth refers to:

1. Difference between the upper and lower frequency limit
2. Range of frequencies that a cable will carry.
3. Maximum amount of information that a channel can carry
4. The range of frequency required to transmit the desired information

The **data rate** is dependent on bandwidth. Data rate will be higher for a greater bandwidth. Generally, channel must provide more bandwidth whereas signal must occupy less bandwidth.

Signals can be either be **analog type** or **digital type**. Bandwidth for both the cases is calculated in different ways. Coming to calculating the bandwidth of an analog signal, we know that bandwidth is the difference of the upper and lower limit of frequency that can pass through a channel. The bandwidth of an analog signal is defined in terms of frequency (Hz)

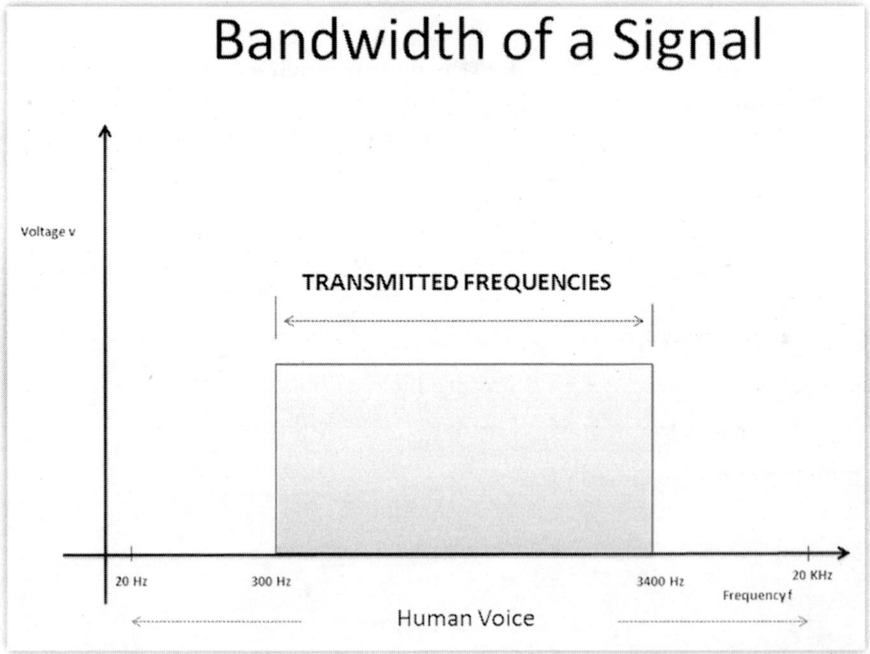

***Figure 2.5:** Bandwidth of a signal*

In *figure 2.5* you can see that the range for human voice is between 20 Hz to 20 KHz but in the communication only voice frequencies within the range of 300 Hz to 3400 Hz are transmitted as it is ideal for efficient and cost effective transmission. So, we can say that the effective speech bandwidth is 3400Hz – 300 Hz which is equal to 3100 Hz.

Now, if we talk about a channel, it is a medium through which the input signal passes so the bandwidth of a channel would be the range of frequencies that it can carry in terms of analog signal or number of bits per second in case of digital signal that a channel can carry. It is important for a channel to have a bandwidth greater than the bandwidth of a signal to avoid loss of information. The following table lists down the Frequency range for various channels:

Table 2.1: *Channels and their Frequency Range*

Channel	Frequency range
Twisted Pair	1MHz – 100MHz
Coaxial Cable	0 – 750 MHz
Satellite	1 GHz – 40 GHz
Fibre Optics	180 THz – 330 THz

As you can see that Frequency range for channels is expressed in Hertz(HZ) which is a unit of Frequency defined by International System of Units(ISI). This unit is named after Heinrich Rudolf Hertz and is defined as one cycle per second.

1 Kilo Hertz = 10^3Hz

1 Mega Hertz = 10^6Hz

1 Giga Hertz = 10^9Hz

2.6 Data Transfer Rate

The **Data Transfer Rate (DTR)** is defined as the amount of digital data transferred from one point to the other in a given time. In simple words, it is the speed at which data travels from one place to another. The data travels at a faster rate when the path has greater bandwidth. In Telecommunications DTR is expressed in terms of bits per second in Telecommunications. A low-speed internet connection will transfer data in terms of Kbps(stands for Kilobits per second) whereas a LAN network connected by Ethernet will transfer data in Mbps(Megabits per second). There are network switches designed to transfer data at a high speed of Terabits per second. When you talk of data transfer time between the microprocessor and various devices it is measured in milliseconds. DTR is expressed as bytes per second in computer networks.

2.7 Wireless Network

The one and only medium for transmitting and receiving data through a wireless network is by usage of radio waves. As you can understand by the name itself wireless means "without wires". The Wi-Fi router in your house is an example of wireless network. *Figure 2.6* displays few examples of wirelesss networks

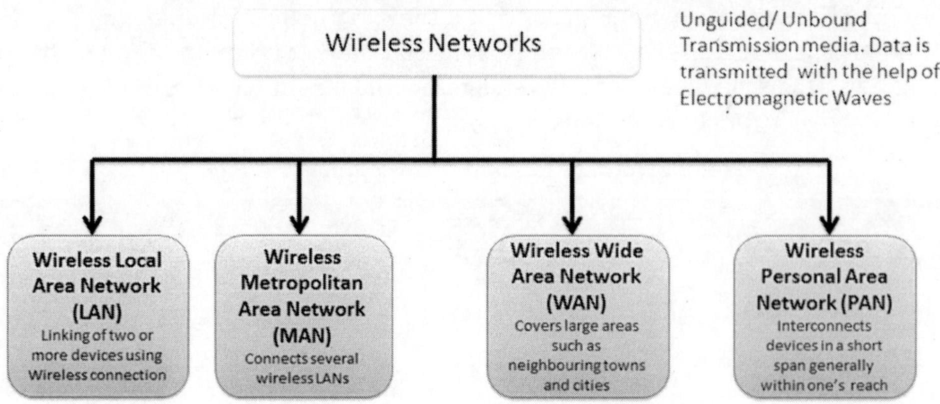

Figure 2.6: *Wireless network*

These networks are not connected by any cables. The purpose of wireless network is to eliminate the process of installing cables in buildings so as to get a connection between different locations of the equipment. The wireless networks are based on radio waves and its implementation takes place at the physical level of the network structure. If you look at the electromagnetic spectrum given in *figure 2.6* you will see that the radio waves are electromagnetic waves that are transverse in nature and they have the longest wavelength on the electromagnetic spectrum. The Frequency range for Radio waves is between 3 KHz to 3GHz and these wave travel with the speed of light. Radio waves can be easily absorbed by most materials. Radio waves can get affected by the near electromagnetic fields which can also cause loss of data rate.

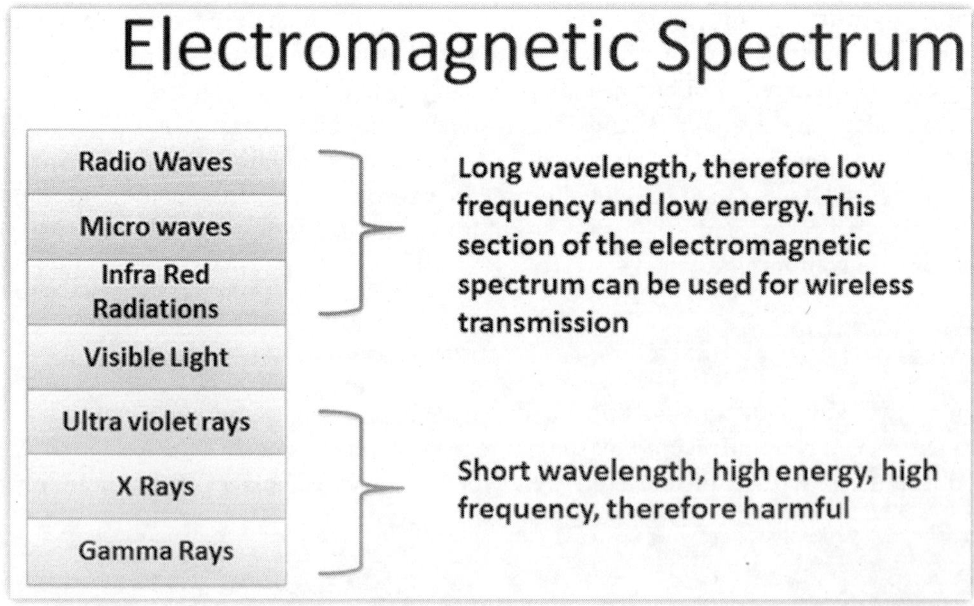

Figure 2.7: *Electromagnetic spectrum*

You must be familiar with waves such as sound waves or water waves. These waves are nothing but disturbance that travels through a medium to reach from one point to the other. Electromagnetic waves on the other hand do not require any medium (solid , liquid or air) to travel. They can travel over vacuum space. We are able to see lights of other stars because light too is electromagnetic in nature. Electromagnetic waves are created when an electric field comes in contact with a magnetic field. Radio waves, Microwaves, gamma rays and x-rays are all different forms of electromagnetic (EM) radiations. The sunlight is also a form of electromagnetic radiation. The light from the sun reaches the earth in the form of radiation. *Figure 2.7* describes different types of electromagnetic waves in the electromagnetic spectrum.

2.7.1 Radio Waves

Radio waves are electromagnetic waves having the wavelength between 300 GHz to 3 KHz. These wave are easy to generate. They have large wavelength so they can travel over long distances. They are transmitted with the help of radio transmitters and received by radio receivers that are installed in the devices. Antennas are required both to transmit and receive radio signals. Radio waves can be used for communication indoors as well as outdoors as they are easily penetrated through the walls. They are omni directional in nature and can travel in any directions from the source. So, you can say that the antenna transmitting radio waves propagates it in all directions and can be received by any receiving antenna. The disadvantage of this omni directional property is that radio waves being transmitted from one antenna can face interference from waves of same frequency or band being transmitted from another antenna.

Figure 2.8: *Radio waves are omni directional*

2.7.2 Microwaves

Microwaves are subclass of Radiowaves or you can also say that they are radio waves with higher frequencies (300 MHz – 300GHz). Microwaves are unidirectional so in order to transmit and receive data, the antennas must be aligned. These waves are ideal for point to point communication, it is important that each antenna is in line of sight of the next antenna. These signals are of small wavelength and must be focussed into a narrow beam. Electromagnetic waves having frequencies above 100 MHz are not omni directional, they travel in straight line this makes alignment of the transmitting and receiving antennas to be strictly within the line of sight.

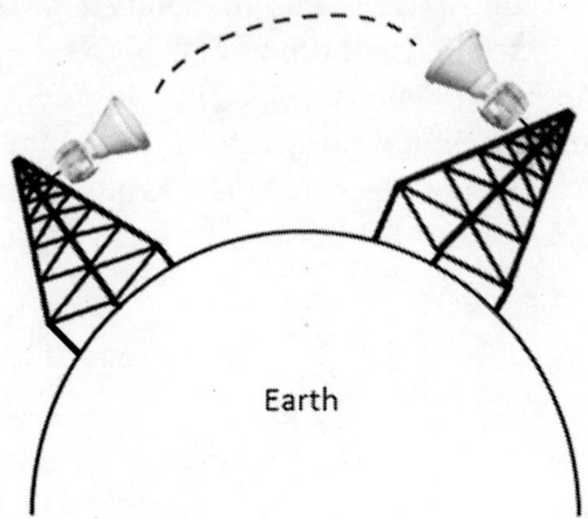

Figure 2.9: *Microwaves*

Microwave do not penetrate into obstacles such as walls. These wave have high frequencies and are therefore used for short distance communication systems such as navigation, remote sensing, radar etc.

3 Network Devices

In this chapter, you will cover:

- Network devices (Modem, Ethernet card, RJ45, Repeater, Hub, Switch, Router, Gateway, WIFI card).

3.1 Introduction

The human race thrives on communication and networking skills and as the technology is advancing it is upgrading the way we communicate with each other. Can you imagine a world without printers, emails, Google, WhatsApp, Amazon, Netflix etc.? Have you ever wondered how we get access to all these facilities by just one click on our phone or computer. In this chapter we are going to look at Computer Networking and how it is implemented in our day to day life.

We use computer networks for:

- Sharing files and data.
- Sharing devices such as scanners, printers etc.
- Sharing applications such as a management software in a school or office which is based on Client/server applications.
- Communication via emails, chat etc.
- Voice over network protocol.

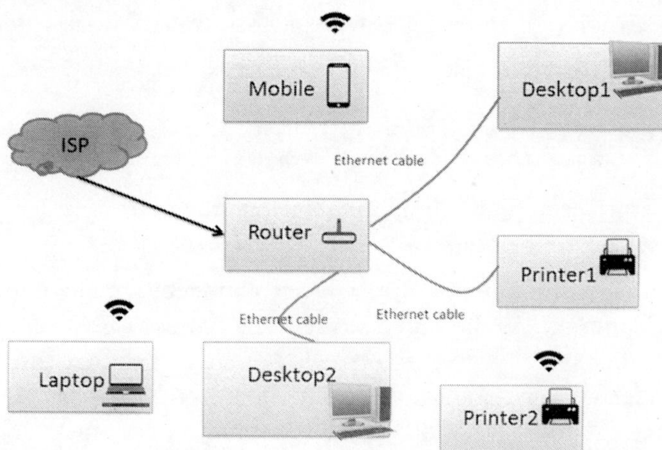

Figure 3.1: *Computer network*

On this note, let's begin our journey to explore the world of Computer Networks.

Computer Network: As the name suggests a computer network is a group of computers that are connected together. These connected computers can be used to share network resources such as printers, access to internet, file servers etc. A computer network is like a multiuse connection that allows a computer to accomplish much more than what it could have achieved if it was a standalone machine.

3.2 Advantages of Computer Networks

- Sharing resources such as printers is much cheaper than purchasing a separate equipment for each machine.
- ***Site licenses*** turns out to be much cheaper than purchasing software license for each and every machine.
- Computer Network allows users to share files easily.

> ***Site license*** refers to use of rights-protected software which is used for single site having multiple users. These users are given the permission to right to use copy protected work, but only at that particular location.

- Computer networks offer good security and users cannot access files on each other's system.
- Computer Networks allows simple and instant communication with the help of emails and chat messengers.
- It is easy to take backup of data as all the data is stored on the server.

3.3 Disadvantages of Computer Networks

- Purchase of expensive network cables and file server would add to costs. Also, if the company requires a large sophisticated and complicated network then it would require a separate network management team to ensure that the computer network functions properly.
- If the server fails then all the files and software that are available centrally will become inaccessible which can bring work to halt.
- If a virus finds its way into the network it can spread to other computers on the network.
- It is important to ensure that the network is well protected as they are vulnerable to hackers.
- Fault in the network can lead to loss of data and resources.

3.4 Components of a Network

A computer network comprises of many components which together in order to make it possible to transfer data from one system to the other.

- **Hosts and Nodes**: Host is computer or other device connected in a computer network and has at least one network address. As the name suggest the network host offers resources, services and applications to other systems on the network. A node is a connection point in the network. If a computer is connected to a network it is a **network node**. So, basically anything connected to a network is a node. All hosts are node but all nodes may not be hosts. A host is an endpoint of communication like a computer, storage or printer. A node on the other hand is any device that is active on a network. Any data communication system such as modem, hub, switch etc or data terminal equipment such as phone, printer, host computer is a node. It is a point where information may start, stay or change directions.

- **Server:** Server is one of the most interesting component of the network. A server is dedicated to network resource management and it is not used for any other task except for accepting and responding to requests made over a network. It allows other machines on the network to communicate with each other and share data and resources. A network can have more than one server and every server has a unique name by which it is identified by other users on the network.
- **Client:** A client computer on the system is the one that avails the services provided by the server. It is preferred to keep the server on a separate machine but that is not always necessary. In order to access the services the client has to send request to the server and wait for its response. Once the access is granted the client can carry out the necessary tasks
- **Network Hardware:** In order to facilitate operations of a computer network such as controlling the network traffic, establishing connections, transmitting data etc, the network requires specialized hardware. Some basic hardware components of a computer network are as follows:
    - **Network Interface Card (NIC):** is a hardware component which is required to connect a computer and a network, it can also be thought of as a point of interconnection between a system and a network (private or public). A NIC can be a built-in card within the computer which means that it is part of the motherboard or it can be fitted into an expansion slot like an add-in card. Irrespective of whether the network is wired and wireless, the network card works as the interface between the computer and the network. Network adapters that connect over USB drives are not cards but are regular USEB devices enabling connection over the USB port.

      What does NIC do?

      The NIC is required so that the computer or a device on a network can communicate with other computers on the same network. NIC is required whether the devices are on a network or communicating directly. It is the most essential hardware device required to establish communication between two computers. Every participating computer in a network has a NIC but there are ways to connect computers without a NIC such as by using modem over phone lines which would obviously be a very inconvenient option. You must also note that NIC is important but it is not the only requirement for establishing a connection. You would require a router to connect your computer to a larger network such as the internet. NIC helps the device to connect to the router which is connected to the internet and this is how a computer is able to connect to the internet.
    - **Hub:** Connects all of the network devices together on an internal network. It has no intelligence on where to send data hence all the information is broadcasted on each connection. A hub only knows when a device is connected to it. So, when a data packet is received at a port it is copied to all other ports. A hub has ports to accept Ethernet connections from various network devices.
    - **Switch:** A switch is a small network hardware device very similar to a hub that can be used to join multiple computers together with one LAN or Local Area as it accepts Ethernet connections from network devices. However, unlike a hub a switch is intelligent. It has knowledge of physical devices connected to it. So, when it receives a data packet it forwards it only to the

intended destination which is not the case with the hub, Switches reduce unnecessary traffic over network and are hence preferred over a hub.

- **Router:** A router routes data from one network to another based on the IP address. So, when a router receives a data packet it first analyses whether the information received is for its own network or the outside network. This analysis is done based on the IP address. If the data packet is meant for the internal network then the router receives it else it is sent to another network. Hence a router is known to be a gateway of network

Both hubs and switches are used to exchange data within an internal network but a hub only knows about the device that is connected to it whereas a switch can detect specific devices connected to it. Both can exchange data within the internal network but they cannot exchange data outside their network because they cannot read the IP addresses. When two networks have to communicate with each other the data packets will have to leave the respective networks and go on to the internet. This is achieved with the help of a router. So, basically Routers are used to connect networks whereas hubs and switches create networks.

- **Communication channel:** The communication channel is the physical path through which the information travels from one computer to the other. The communication channel can be wired or wireless.

Access Point

An access point is nothing but a device used to create a wireless local area network(WLAN). It works as a portal for connecting devices to a LAN of an office or a large building. The advantage of access point is that it can extend wireless coverage of an existing network and can also increase the number of users connected to it.

A high-speed Ethernet cable running from a router, switch or hub to an access point transforms the wired signal into a wireless or Wi-Fi signal and projects in the given area.

Compare Server and Host

Server	Host
Can be a physical device or a software program	It is always a physical device
A server is always installed on a host computer.	It can have a server or client installed
It provides services only to client	It provides services to many users and devices on the network
It is dedicated to server specific services	Provides specific services

Check Your Progress

From you understanding list 3 differences between a node and a host?

Node	Host

3.5 RJ45 Connector

Cables help in transferring information along their length. To actually get the information the cable must end into a connector that requires a jack to plug into.

RJ45 is a standard physical connector for network cables. It looks similar to a telephone jack but it is a bit wider and very commonly used for Ethernet networking. **"RJ45 cables"** is another name for Ethernet cables. It has RJ45 connectors on each end of the cable. The Ethernet cable has a plastic plug at the end of each cable device. This plug is inserted into RJ45 Jacks of Ethernet. In the name RJ45, RJ stands for **"Registered Jack"** and the number "45" is the number of **interface standard**. The RJ45 connector has 8 pins which means that the Ethernet cable has 8 wires. You can actually see that at the Ethernet cables, all of the 8 wires are in different colors.4 are solid colors and 4 are striped.

RJ45 Cables have two wiring standards:

(1) T-568A and (2) T-568B

T-568A is widely used but T-568B seems to be more common. As a matter of fact there are some applications that require cross over Ethernet cables which means that one end of the cable has T-568A connector and the other has T-568B connectors. Such cables are required for direct computer to computer connection.

Cables that terminate with RJ45 connectors at both ends are called RJ45 Ethernet cables. The most common Ethernet cables in use are cat5, cat6 and cat7.

3.6 Wi-Fi Card

Wi-Fi stands for **"Wireless Fidelity"**. It was invented in 1991 in Netherlands by NCR Corporation/ AT&T. It was initially invented for mobile computing devices such as laptops but now we see that it is widely used to interact with television, smart watches, mobile phones, digital cameras etc, Wi-Fi is a wireless technology also known as wireless LAN. With Wi-Fi connection a LAN can operate without any cables or wire connections. Let us see how wireless technology works.

A wireless connection comprises of three very important elements:

1. Radio Signals
2. Antenna
3. Router

The router transmits the radio signal. This signal is picked up by Wi-Fi cards in the device. A device within the range of 100- 150 ft for router can easily connect to the router. The signal is received by the Wi-Fi cards which in turn creates a connection between the user and the network.

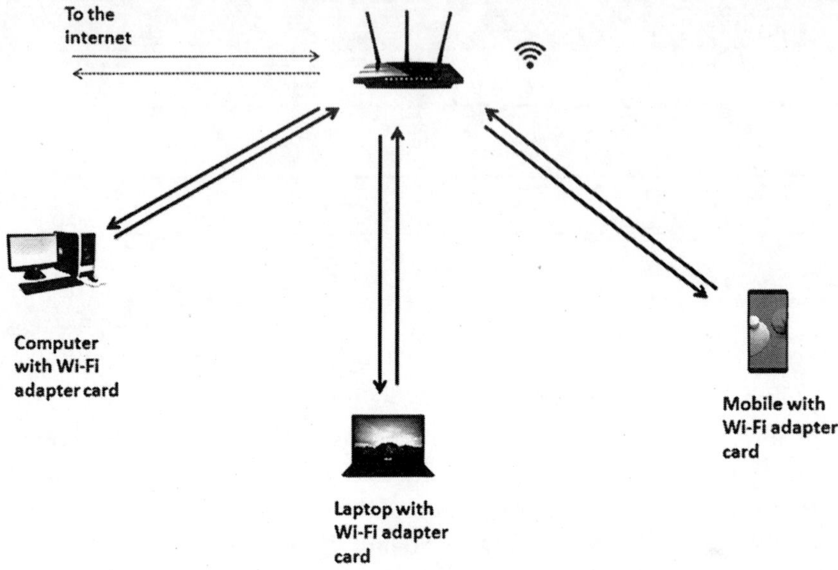

Figure 3.2: *Router*

Wireless cards are also known as LAN cards. They come in different form for different devices. Some devices come with pre installed Wi-Fi cards. Instead of transmitting data through **digital subscriber line (DSL)** or a high speed cable, a Wi-Fi network transmits data through radio waves.

The Wi-Fi hotspot or the router or the access point receives information through wires. This information is then converted from binary format to radio waves. The router then broadcasts this information (radio waves) in the surrounding area (within 75-150 ft). However, if there are no obstacles in between, these waves can be transmitted up to 1000 ft.

Wireless cards have a tiny antenna that picks up these signals, converts it back to binary code so that it can be read by the device. When you want to transmit some information, the Wi-Fi card converts the binary information back to radio waves and transmits it so that the router can receive it and convert info back to binary format and send the information into the internet.

The wireless networks are designed to work at higher radio frequencies compared to radio and cell phones. The cards and routers can communicate on one of three channels. When in crowded area the cards and routers can switch between channels to reduce interference.

4 Network Topologies and Types

In this chapter, you will cover:

- Network topologies and Network types: Types of networks (PAN, LAN, MAN, WAN), networking topologies (Bus, Star, Tree)

4.1 Introduction

A computer network can be classified on the size into following three categories (*figure 4.1*):

1. Local Area Network
2. Metropolitan Area Network
3. Wide Area Network

Wireless Network Classification Based on Size

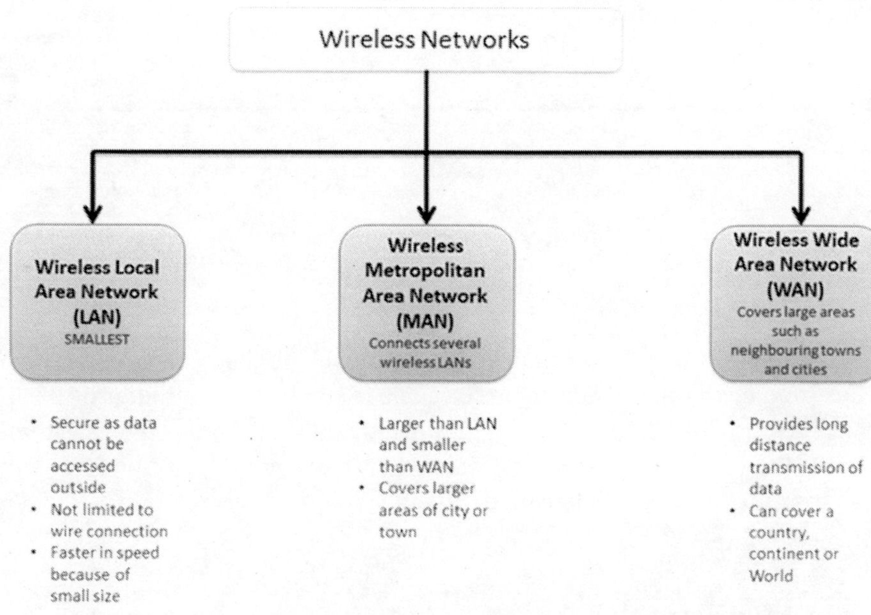

Figure 4.1: *Classification of wireless network on the basis of size*

4.2 LAN

A LAN consists of limited devices connected together (physically or virtually) in a limited space. The best example for this would be a home router. In many homes devices such as laptops, phone, Television are connected to each other via Wi-Fi, cables, Bluetooth, hotspot etc.

In case of LAN devices are connected to each other in a limited area. Wired connections are used to connect computers to each other and to the other peripheral devices such as printers. All the systems on the network can access each other's data and can also communicate with each other using chat or email.

A network topology is the structure of a network or a network architecture that describes how computers are connected in a network. It is the logical layout pattern in which a network is created. All devices that exists on a networks are referred to as Nodes and how all these nodes are connected to each other is defined by the network topology.

4.3 Point to Point topology

Point to Point topology is the direct link between two nodes. It is a low cost, fast and reliable method.

Point to Point Topology

Figure 4.2: *Point to Point Topology*

4.3.1 Bus Topology

A **Bus** has all nodes connected directly to one cable. This cable is the back bone of the network. It is easy to set up Bus topology as the requirement for cable is small. Any computer or peripheral device can be easily connected to this network. The biggest disadvantage of this network is that if there is an issue with the cable then the entire network goes down. This topology cannot be implemented for a large network as trouble shooting will become difficult.

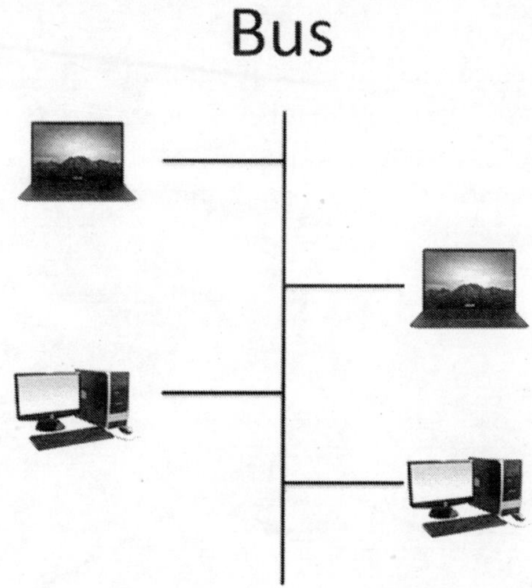

Figure 4.3: Bus topology

4.3.2 Star Topology

The star topology is a very popular topology. It consists of a central hub and each node is connected to this hub using Point to point connection. The hub can be a simple device that makes a connection possible. It can also be a computer acting as a server. It is a low cost topology and it is very easy to add new nodes to the network. The star topology is considered o be quite robust. The whole connection will fail if the hub goes down but if the there is a problem in connection between one node and the hub it will not affect the functioning of the other nodes.

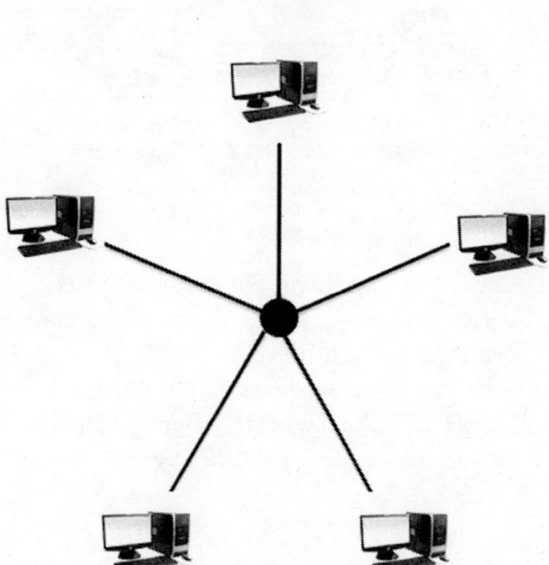

Figure 4.4: Star topology

4.3.3 Ring Topology

A Ring topology has all the nodes connected to each other in a circular manner allowing the data to flow in one direction. It has a single pathway so it is very easy to detect defects. Ring topology is easy to install and very easy to manage but adding nodes to this network is a tedious task. For this network to work properly it is very important for all nodes tofunction properly. Defect in one node can bring the network down.

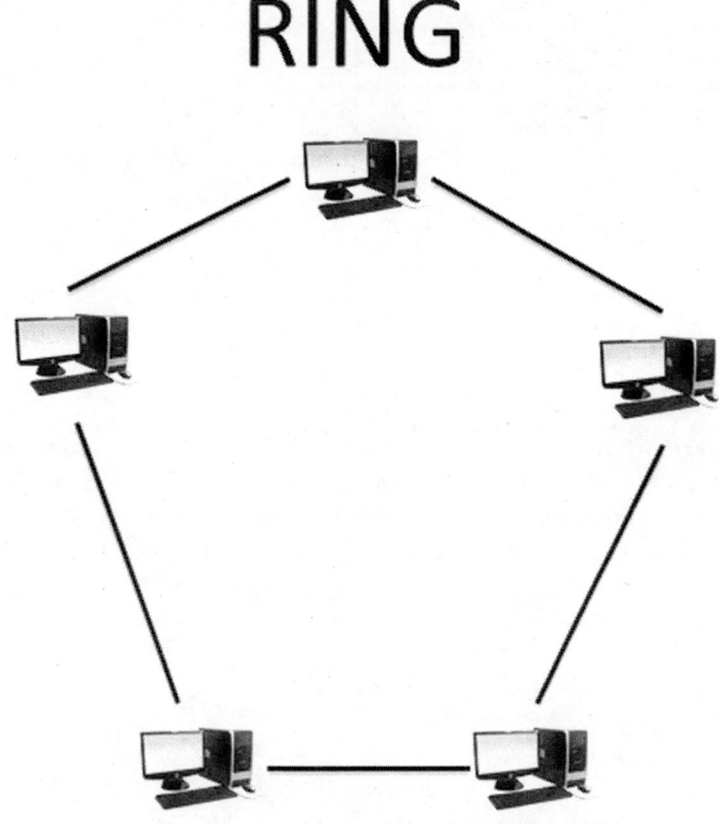

Figure 4.5: *Ring topology*

4.3.4 Tree topology

Large networks often incorporate Tree topology. This topology has few nodes at the bottom and branches out at the top as you can see in *figure 4.6*. A device can communicate with other device on the network without interfering with any other node. You can see in *figure 4.6* the central nodes of two star networks are connected to form a tree structure. Both the star networks are connected through the main cable. If this main cable stops working then information cannot be shared between the devices of different stars but the devices will be able to communicate with other devices on the same network.

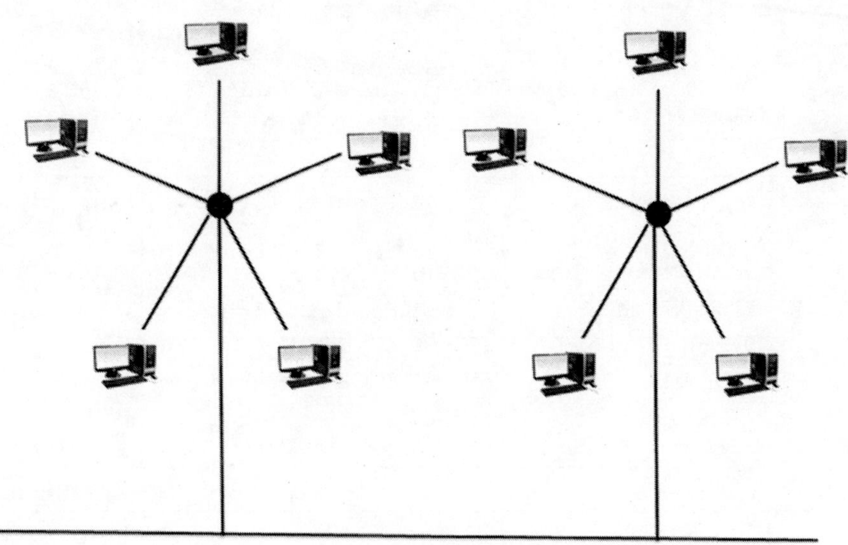

Figure 4.6: *Tree topology*

4.4 MAN

You have learnt about Local Area Network which is the smallest type of network in terms of size. The **Metropolitan Area Network (MAN)** is bigger than LAN in size but smaller the Wide Area Network (WAN). MAN can be used to connect the networks of a city into one large network and interconnect several LANs by bridging them with backbone lines.

4.5 WAN

As the name suggests **Wide Area Network (WAN)** can cover network over huge geographical areas. WAN is provided by satellite companies or service providers. A wide area network can span over several cities and no one other than the customer can access the network. WAN provides increased bandwidth. Users can store data online saving the system from getting loaded. WAN is safe because it offers strong privacy and also allows data encryption. WAN can cover very large areas allowing you to connect to people in different countries. The installation charges for WAN are high. Resolving of issue in WAN is not an easy task and can take time. Systems on WAN must have antivirus installed to protect themselves from threats.

4.6 LAN vs MAN vs WAN

So far you have studied that a computer network allows various systems on the network to communicate with each other and based on area a computer network can be classified as LAN, MAN and WAN. Now let's compare the three networks. This is shown in Table 4.1.

Table 4.1: *LAN vs MAN vs WAN*

	LAN	MAN	WAN
Meaning	Local Area Network	Metropolitan Area Network	Wide Area Network
Size	Covers smaller area	Bigger than LAN but smaller than WAN	Covers area that is much larger than MAN
Nature	Connects all systems in an office. All computers on the network can share data and tools	Connects cities. Connects two or more computers that are apart by a great distance. They can be placed anywhere within a city or at times two different cities.	Can consist of one LAN connecting to another LAN via telephone lines, radio waves. It may be limited to an enterprise or be accessible to public.
Ownership	Private	Public	Organization
Transmission speed	High	Average	Low
Congestion	Less	More than LAN	More than MAN
Fault tolerance	More	Less	Less
Cost	Inexpensive	Expensive	Expensive
Communication Medium	Coaxial Cables	Optical fibres, Cables etc.	PSTN or Satellite Link
Examples	Smallest LAN would be two computers connected to each other Students playing a game from their systems without internet	Used for communication in military Communication between banks in a city	The internet

4.7 Personal Area Networks (PANs)

PAN or Personal Area network is set up for one or a small group of people. It can have a machine such as laptop or computer, a phone or some wearable smart devices. These networks are generally wireless. Bluetooth is a popular wireless technology used for creating PAN. PAN can also be created by infra-red or NFC. The radius of a PAN network is generally about 10 m.

5 Network Protocol

In this chapter, you will cover:

- HTTP, FTP, PPP, SMTP, TCP/IP, POP3, HTTPS, TELNET, VoIP, wireless/mobile communication protocol such as GSM, GPRS and WLL

5.1 Network Protocol

While communicating over a network it is important to follow certain standards or set of rules so that the data can be transferred securely and systematically over the network. These standards are followed by all the nodes on the network. The nodes cannot communicate with each other in absence of these standards. These standards are called **network protocol** and to do anything on the internet such as emails, chats or website surfing one must follow these protocols. These protocols exist in layers and in this chapter we will look at some important Network Protocols that are important for communication.

5.2 Transmission control protocol (TCP/IP)

The **Transmission Control Protocol (TCP)** is the backbone of all the communication that takes place over the internet. The systems are able to communicate with each other by establishing connection defined by these protocol.

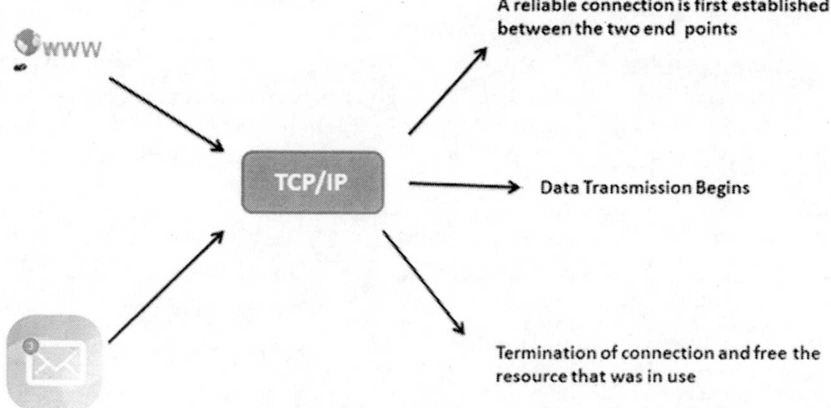

Figure 5.1: *Transmission control protocol (TCP/IP)*

The **Internet Protocol (IP)** defines how the packets of data will be sent and received by the computers on a network. TCP keeps track of the packets and if any packet is lost or gets dropped the TCP will ask to resend it.

TCP/ IP works in Layers as shown below:

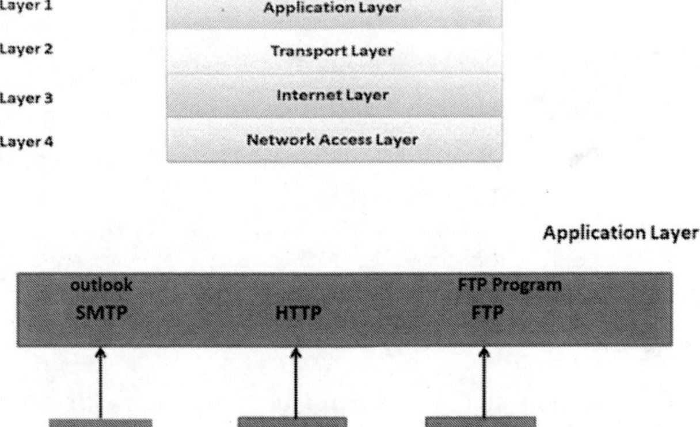

Figure 5.2: *TCP/IP model*

The topmost layer of the TCP/IP model i.e. **Layer 1** is known as the **application Layer**. The web browser directly interacts with the application layer. The application layer has the protocols for visiting web site(HTTP), Checking mails(SMTP) and File Tansfer(FTP). The transport or the TCP layer is useful in applications that have interactive modules such as online games. The application layer receives data from the program that is being used by the user. It then uses the port to talk to the transport layer. Through this port it informs the TCP layer where the data is coming from. The TCP then splits the data into smalls chunks so that these chunks can be sent over the internet through the shortest route. *Table 5.1* explains various Network Protocols .

Table 5.1: *Network protocol*

	HTTP	FTP	TCP/IP	PPP
Stands for	Hypertext Transfer Protocol	File Transfer Protocol	Transmission Control Protocol/ Internet protocol	Point- to – point protocol
Designed For	Viewing Webpages	Transfer of files from one system to another	• IP tells how the data packets will be sent over the network. • The TCP is responsible for transmission of data over the internet networks.	Used with dial-up internet connections including ISDN.

Proper-ties	Generic, stateless and object oriented protocol. Comprises of: (a) set requests from a browser on a local system to the web server and (b) set of response from the server back to the browser.	• Allows people in different geographical locations to work on a common project. • It is designed to promote sharing of files. • Encourages indirect use of remote computers. • Any type of file can be transferred using FTP.	• The IP has the packet addressing method. • It allows any computer to send packet of data to another computer. • The TCP makes sure that data packets are delivered to the destination. • It checks data packets for errors. • If an error is found , a request is submitted for re-transmission.	• PPP is layered protocol. • It is used for transmission of data over normal telephone lines. • It can provide connection, authentication, transmission, encryption and compression.

A network protocol is a set of rules and regulations that are applied on a network. It provides the standard format for transmitting data packets over the network. It also has techniques defined for identifying and correcting errors over a network. We will now look at each of these protocols in detail.

5.2.1 Transmission Control Protocol/Internet Protocol (TCP/IP)

TCP/IP is a communication protocol that interconnects various devices on the Internet. As mentioned in Table 5.1, TCP is responsible for ensuring that the packets are transmitted correctly over the Internet. This protocol breaks the data in packets that can be easily handle by the network. The TCP assigns a header to each packet. This header contains information about the order in which the data packet must be reassembled. It also provides error checking information so that the computer that receives the data packet can ensure that it has note encountered any mishaps. The packets then move on to the Internet layer where the Internet protocol(IP) attaches the information of the origin as well as the destination IP address so that the packets have the information of their starting point and the final stop. **The IP is responsible for the address part of every packet**. It provides a distinct IP address to each data packet. Each node has IP address, so you can say that an IP address is a unique identifier for a node on a network. It is a 32 bit binary number which is represented by 4 decimal numbers. Each decimal value represents 8 bits in 0-255 range and is separated from the next value by a dot or a decimal point, For E.g. 192.62.56.02. This is known as **dotted IP notation**. The IP address is checked by every gateway on the network to know where the packets have to go. All packets of the same message may not follow the same route but they will be reassembled at the destination.

The data packets are now ready to be sent over the network. TCP/IP is responsible for assembling of data packets on the internet into original message or file. All packets are verified when they arrive at the destination and are assembled back in the correct order. In order to ensure that the data is not lost midway. TCP provides support for error detection and requests re-transmission if an error is found or if the data received is incomplete.

So, you see that TCP/IP has two components TCP and IP, together these protocols form the **backbone of the Internet**. These two protocols can also be used for private networks such as intranet and extranet. TCP/IP follows the client-server mode of communication. The user on the internet making a request(such as opening a website on the bowser) is the **client**. The computer responding to the request and providing the service desired by the user is the **server**. At the base level the TCP/IP works more like a point to point communication that means that the communication occurs between one computer to the other and then from that computer to the next one and so on. Every request made by the user is considered as a new request and is not related to previous ones hence TCP/IP is considered to be **stateless**. The connection between two computers remains intact till all the packets are delivered after that the transmission path is made available and the network path is available for anyone who wants to use it. This is much more convenient than having a dedicated phone connection for the entire call duration.

5.3 File Transfer Protocol (FTP)

As the name suggests **File Transfer Protocol (FTP)** is used to transfer files from one computer to another. We all often use FTP unknowingly, the best example is while uploading or downloading files on the internet. Uploading is a process by which a user transfers the file from his machine on to the server. Downloading is the reverse of it. Downloading is transferring files from the server on to the local system.

Files can be transferred over any two computers as long has they have a stable internet connectivity. You can also share folders that have data. We often share folders having images, books and music files using FTP. FTP uses TCP/IP to transfer files.

One must be cautious about security while downloading files using FTP. Downloading files from unreliable sources can be an open invitation for viruses. You can avoid malware and viruses by using FTP client. FTP clients just makes downloading and uploading easy it is not a mandatory option though.

5.4 Point to point protocol (PPP)

Point to point protocol (PPP) is used for communication between two computers by making use of a serial interface such as a computer connected to a server using a phone line. There is no host or any other networking in between. It is a direct connection. So, an **Internet service provider (ISP)** can provide a PPP connection to the user. The user forwards the request to the ISP which in turn forwards it to the internet and similarly gets the response from the internet and forwards it back to the user. PPP was designed so that two computers could communicate with each other over the telephone lines.

Point to Point Protocol is also known as **RFC1661**. It is a duplex protocol because both the computers connected together can communicate with each other. PPP was created by **Internet Engineering Task Force (IETF).** The idea was to create a data link protocol for point to point links. It is a widely used protocol. It is used to connect the computer to the ISP via modem. For many years people used point to point protocol for establishing a dial connection with the ISP. However, they have now been greatly replaced by broadband devices.

5.5 Hyper Text Transfer Protocol (HTTP)

Hypertext transfer Protocol or HTTP is an underlying request response protocol used by the World Wide Web. So, this protocol is used for transferring of hypertext such as images, audio, video etc. between two computers. It is part of internet protocol suite and is a TCP/IP based communication protocol. **Hyper Text Markup Language (HTML)** is used to code hypertext.

HTTP defines how messages can be formatted and transmitted and how a webserver and browsers can respond to a request. HTTP defines the standards for commands and services used by the clients (browsers) and the servers to communicate with each other.

So, when you type in the URL of the webpage that you wish to visit an HTTP request is forwarded to the web server asking it to fetch and display the requested web page. The browser that you used to surf the web is called the clients to the HTTP and the web applications that respond to the request such as Facebook, Google, YouTube etc are the server for HTTP. It is thus said that HTTP follows a client- server or request/response model.

All transactions made using HTTP are independent of each other therefore, it is a stateless protocol. There is no information about the commands that were sent before. It is therefore difficult to have a website that responds intelligently to a user input. This can be considered as a shortcoming of this protocol and is being addressed in new technologies such as Javascript, ActiveX etc.

HTTP is an application layer protocol that generally used TCP as transport level protocol. Therefore it is a TCP- IP based communication protocol. However, its concern is only about the getting some data back. It is not concerned about how data is handled and assembled (that is done by TCP). It is only interested in getting a response for the request made.

Client Action

When the client forwards a request it is actually asking the server to perform an action such as:

1. **GET**: This action refers to 'Read Only' such as get a page or read a page.
2. **POST**: This action asks the server to receive the data posted by the client.
3. **DEL**: This action refers to Deletion of web resources.
4. **PUT**: This action is similar to POST the difference being that PUT can update the data posted before.
5. **CONNECT**: This action asks the server to establish a connection with the client.
6. **OPTIONS**: This action asks the server to provide a list of options for requests.
7. **HEAD**: this request is similar to **GET**. It asks for a response similar to GET but without a response body.

A lot of numbers are defined as server status code. Such as **200 means OK, 404 means Not Found** etc. It is frustrating when you encounter an error while surfing on the net. Knowing the meaning of the status code can help you understand what actually when wrong. E.g. if you get a 404 error you can check the URL spelling probably a there is a typing error and the website was not found.

Headers are tiny bits of information that you can forwarded with requests and response. HTTP supports headers. A header is nothing but a text record. It is used to inform the server regarding certain details such as the type and version of the browser. Knowing the capabilities of the browser, the server would respond back with information that is compatible with the browser. On receiving a request header the server responds by forwarding a HTTP response header as an attachment to the information that is being sent.

HTTP is connectionless. As mentioned earlier, HTTP is stateless. The HTTP client which is generally the web browser forwards a request and waits for a response. Once the client gets a response it disconnects. If the browser has to make a new request, it will be done on a new connection as a fresh request.

HTTP can be used to transfer any type of file. It is up to the client and server system to handle the data. HTTP is therefore known to be **media independent**. It is important for the client and the server to use appropriate MIME- type to specify the type of content used.

HTTP Basic architecture

As mentioned before, HTTP is based on client server architecture where the client and server communicate with each other using request/response protocol. To establish a connection the client first forwards a request, HTTP identifies the resource requested by the client and informs the server about the action that it must take in response to the request. When a user clicks the hyperlink, the client on the computer contacts the server with the help of HTTP. In this section you learnt about HTTP. How it is used for transferring files on the internet and also about its three important features:

1. HTTP is connectionless.
2. HTTP is stateless and
3. HTTP is media independent

5.6 Email Protocol

In this section you will learn about two types of email protocols:

1. Simple Mail Transfer Protocol(SMTP)
2. Post Office Protocol 3(POP3)

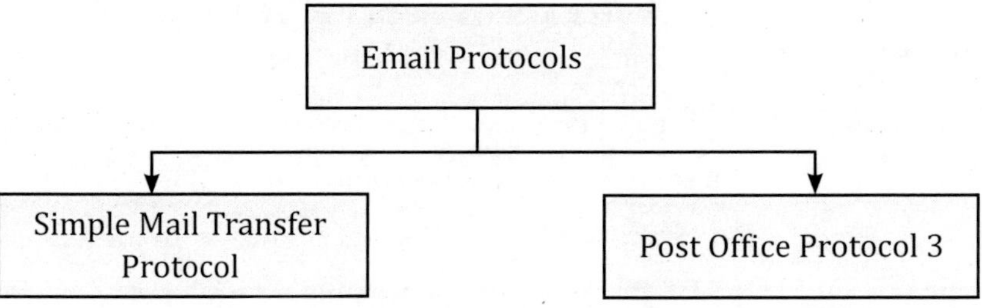

Figure 5.3: *Email protocol*

5.6.1 Simple Mail Transfer System (SMTP)

As the name suggests **Simple Mail Transfer System** is an application level program that handles message services or transfer of emails over the TCP/IP networks. It is a set of instructions or commands used to direct the transfer of emails. However, SMTP only works for outgoing email messages (So, you may want to remember its purpose as **S**ending **M**ail **T**o **P**eople). All email systems are designed to incorporate SMTP for forwarding emails. While forwarding an email the ISP's address must be provided. The client's system must have a client **Message Transfer agent (MTA)** and the server's system must have a **server MTA**. The mail is transferred through MTA. SMPT is easy to implement and is a very simple and reliable way of forwarding messages over the server. If the messages are not delivered to the recipient then an error message is displayed. This message explains what went wrong and why the message could not be delivered.

While forwarding emails you must have noticed that an email has various sections: to, cc, bcc, message body etc. All this information gets converted to text string when the message is sent out on the internet. Texts related to different sections are assigned a code word or a number to make identification of each section easy. The software on the server interprets the code to access the message.

The SMTP is also responsible for setting up rules of communication between the servers. So, basically, whenever there is a transaction, the SMTP server provides its identification and informs about the operation that it is going to carry out and the message will be sent only if the recipient server authorizes the operation. In case there is an error in sending the message, the receiving server will reply with an error message.

A big issue with SMTP is that it is very easy to use hence people are able to create fake ids. Virus infected emails can be forwarded via SMTP using fake ids. This problem still exists but people are getting aware of this issue. One must ensure that the email comes from a reliable source.

The advanced version of SMPT – **Extended Simple Mail Transmission** is widely implemented in many servers. **ESMTP** is used for forwarding multimedia files. ESMTP helps in forwarding audio files, images etc. via emails. Another supplementary protocol **Multi-purpose Internet Mail Extension(MIME)** is used to forward Non ASCII data via SMTP but it cannot replace SMTP.

Figure 5.4 shows how SMTP works. Path1 shows how the mail travels from the user's computer using SMTP protocol and reaches the email or the SMTP server when the user clicks on the send button. The SMTP server is configured in the email client. So, if you are using your gmail account to send an email then the SMTP server will have an address of smtp.gmail.com. Path 2 shows that the SMPT server forwards the emails to the reciepient's email server where the mail remains till the time the recipient logs into the account to check mail. Path 3 shows how the email is downloaded from the recipient server to the recipient's computer when he/she logs into the account. This is done using **POP3**. You will read about it in the next section.

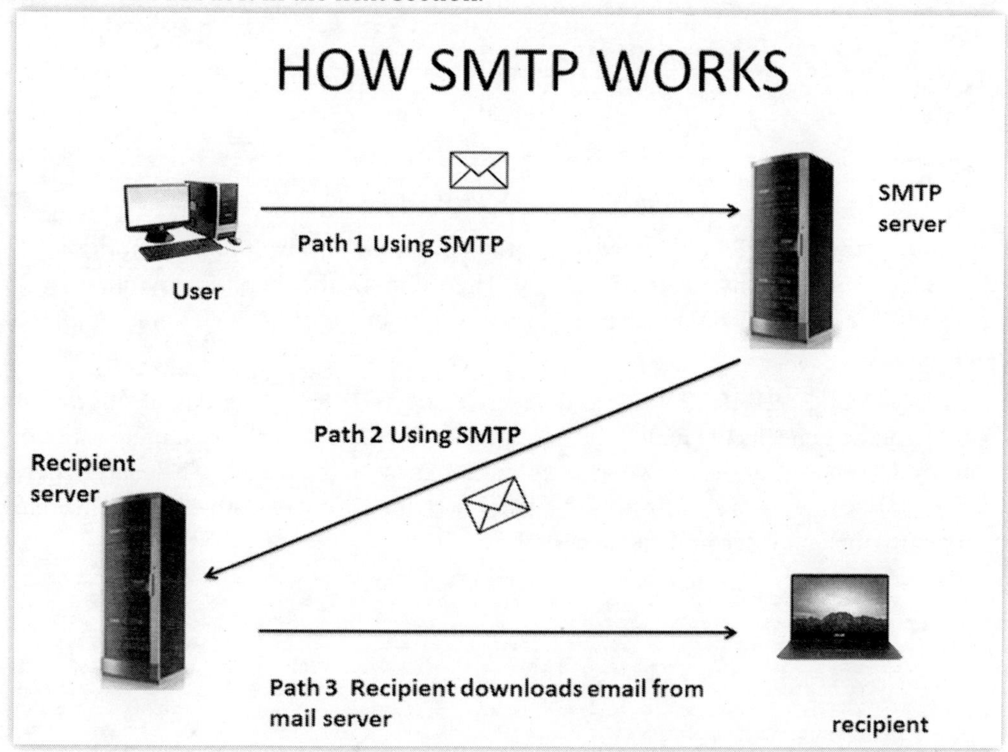

Figure 5.4: *How SMTP works*

5.6.2 Post Office Protocol (POP3)

PoP3 is used for receiving emails and is the third version of this protocol. Incase of SMTP, the email can be sent only if the destination computer is online but that is not the case with POP3. POP3 receives the email and holds it till it is picked up by the recipient. The SMTP server is used to receive the mails for all the hosts and then each hosts retrieves its messages from the SMTP server using POP3 (Client server protocol).

POP3 simplifies the concept of emailing. It is very commonly used with most mail servers. It can work with any email program as long as the email program is configured to host POP3.

If you check Microsoft Outlook on your system you will realize that it is designed to work with POP3. POP3 can work with any email program that is configured to host the protocol. It assures high success rate with minimum errors. To connect a email program it is important to know the address of the POP3 server which is provided by the web hosting company. Each POP3 server has a different address. Those users who wish receive their POP3 emails must provide the email id and the password in order to receive email. *Figure 5.5* shows how POP3 works.

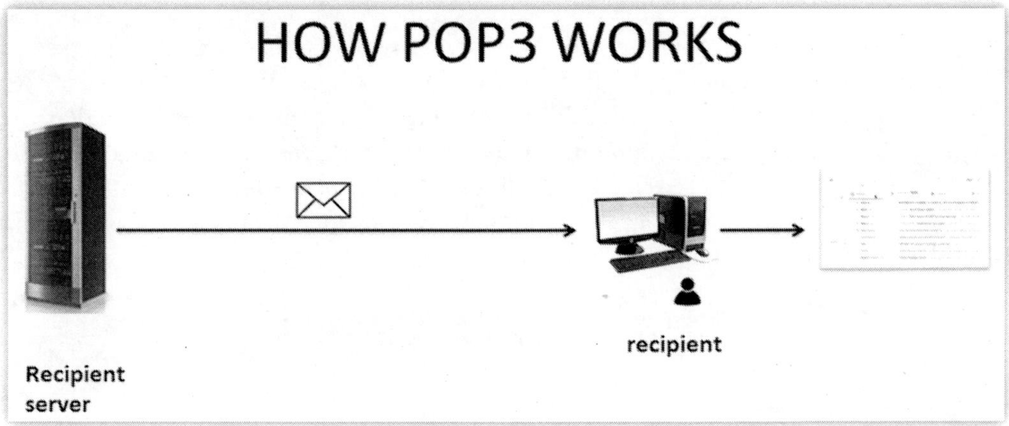

Figure 5.5: *How POP3 Works*

It is important to note that POP3 only downloads the content of inbox. It has got nothing to do with other folders such as sent items, drafts, Trash etc. The moment the email is downloaded on to the recipient's device it is deleted from the server. So, what happens if two devices are configured to the same email account.

Suppose reciepient1 and recipient2 are two devices connected to same email account as shown in Figure 5.6. If recipient 1 checks the mail first then the email will be downloaded on to that device and it will be removed from the server. So, when recipient2 logs on to the account little later, there will be no copy available. But there is a setting option available to let a copy remain on the server so that all devices connect to one email account can access the mail.

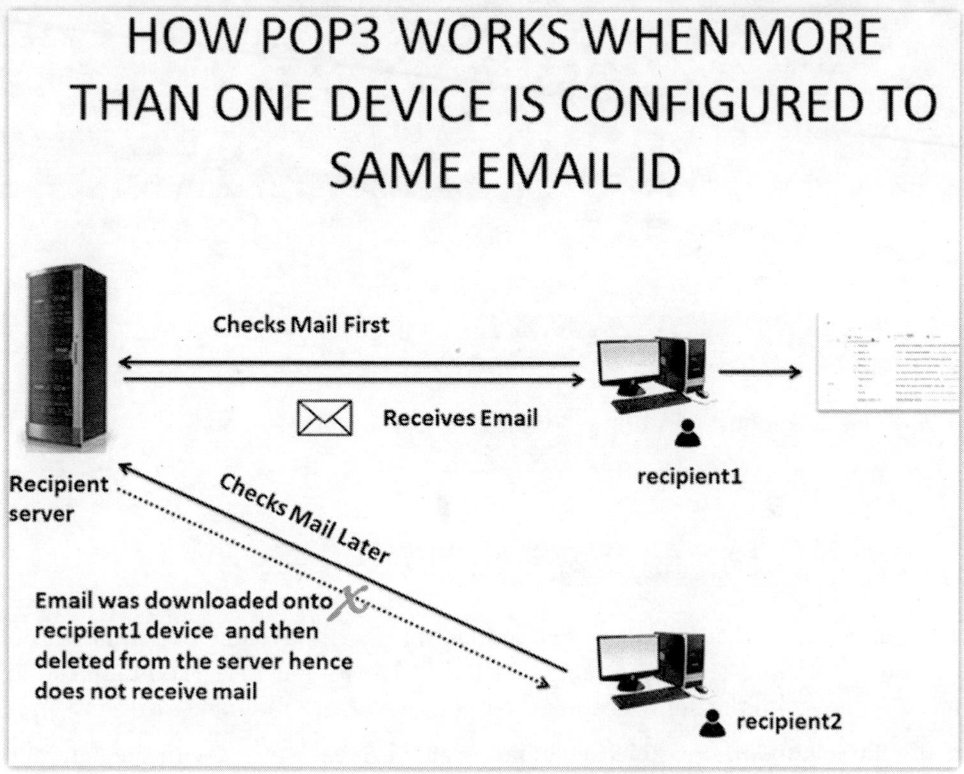

Figure 5.6: Working of POP3

5.7 Remote Login (Telnet) and Internet

Internet's remote login service by the name **TELNET** (Teletype Network Protocol) allows users to interact with other computers through their computers. So, in other words TELNET allows you to virtually access a computer and it creates a two-way, joint text-based communication channel between two computers. TELNET uses Transmission Control Protocol/Internet Protocol (TCP/IP) networking protocol for enabling remote sessions.

To use remote login via TELNET the user will have to:

1. Start a local application program where the details of the remote machine can be provided.
2. This local application then becomes the client that can request for a connection to the server on the remote machine.
3. The client can use the keyboard and mouse to work on the remote machine the output of which is displayed on user's screen.

Advantages of TELNET

1. Remote login shows how the Internet can provide interactive services.
2. It allows users to interact with applications running on a remote computer.
3. The remote program responds to input from the user.

6 Mobile Telecommunication Technology

In this chapter, you will cover:

- Mobile telecommunication technologies: 1G, 2G, 3G, 4G and 5G

6.1 Generations of wireless technologies

Mobile is a portable device that has greatly simplified our lives. Have you ever thought of how two people are able to communicate with each other using mobile phones? Well communication over the mobile phone happens with the help of cellular network which is a radio network.

Subscribers of mobile network are able to communicate with each other with the help of mobile or radio communication. The location of these subscribers may change but that does not interrupt the call. Cellular communication is a type of mobile communication. When we talk about cellular communication the picture that comes instantly in our mind is of people communicating with each other from different geographical location without having any sort of physical connection such s wires or cables attached to their device. Your mobile phone is the best example for this scenario.

A mobile phone network comprises of several overlapping geographic areas known as **cells**. So, if you look at a cellular design it would look like hexagonal mesh with base station at the centre. So that the user doesn't drop a call while travelling from one base station to the other. The cells are designed in such a way that they overlap at the edges. The phone transmits RF signals which is received by the base station. The base station forwards the signal to the destination mobile phone. It transmits and receives signals at two slightly different frequencies. Central switching centres connect the base stations and track calls so that when the user moves from one cell to another the calls can be transferred without any problem.

Radio coverage over a huge geographical area can be provided when the cells are combined together and this is how the mobile are able to communicate with each other. In last two decades we have witnessed a huge growth in the mobile telecommunication industry. In this chapter you will learn how the mobile technology has evolved over the years. This first mobile service started in the 1940s in USA and it was introduced in the Europe in 1950s. There were lot of issues regarding mobility, speech quality, capacity and service availability. The device was bulky and susceptible to interference. Over a period of time advanced technologies introduced microprocessors which helped in developing small, compact, efficient and smart devices which slowly got popular with the masses. In today's word it is difficult to do without mobile phones and you must keep in mind that during the COVID times mobile phones have helped several offices, schools and institutions to continue providing their services.

Figure 6.1: *Wireless network*

6.1.1 1G – First Generation of Wireless Technology

The first generation of wireless technology was introduced in late 1970s and early 1980s. 1G refers to analog telecommunication standards. **Nippon Telegraph and Telephone (NTT)** in Japan launched the first commercially automated cellular network in the year 1979 by. Within a span of 5 years the whole of Japan was covered by NTT network and Japan thus became the first nationwide 1G network. This network provided only voice facility. Compared to today's standards, 1G network offered poor battery life and poor quality. Phones came in big size, were inconvenient to use and offered no security. 1G mobile systems used radio towers for transmission and voice was modulated to frequency of 150 Hz or higher.

Figure 6.2: *1g – first generation of wireless technology*
(Source: http://www.cntr.salford.ac.uk/comms/etacs_mobiles.php)

6.1.2 2G – Second Generation of Wireless Technology

2G or second generation mobile or cellular networks emerged in the 1990s. These networks used digital signals and were based on **Global Systems for Mobile (GSM)** for wireless transmission. In 1991, 2G cellular networks were commercially launched in Finland on GSM standard by **Radiolinja**. GSM offered reliable wireless transmission and secure communication. 2G networks provided better call quality. It provided data speed up to 64 Kbps. In addition to making and receiving calls, the user could send text messages (SMS) and MMS. It also provided better quality voice call. Users could put calls on hold, conduct conference calls and had the facility for internal roaming. It also allowed sending emails. The advantage of 2G networks over 1G network was that the phone conversations were digitally encrypted,

Figure 6.3: *2G – second generation of wireless technology (Source: https://www.electronics-notes.com/articles/connectivity/2g-gsm/basics-introduction.php)*

it efficiently used radio frequency and users could also forward text messages.

GSM as designed specifically for second generation mobile phone technology with the aim to achieve a greater capacity than the first generation analog systems. GSM **used Time Division Multiple Access (TDMA)** to achieve this. TDMA is a digital cellular telephone communication technology that allows multiple users to use the same frequency channel without any kind of disturbance. A signal is divided into different time slot and users are allowed to transmit within certain time intervals. Multiple users can transmit one after the other each using its own time slot. TDMA's capacity is triple of **FDMA (Frequency division Multiple Acess)** which was the cellular standard for 1G cell phone systems. In case of FDMA all users share the frequency channel simultaneously and each user is transmitting at one frequency hence it is important to have good quality filters in the radio hardware which is not the case in TDMA.

6.1.3 3G – Third Generation of Wireless Technology

The third generation wireless mobile telecommunication technology emerged in the 2000s. The mobile phones were available in the market at affordable prices and almost everyone owned a phone. Users could download videos, conduct internet search, interact on social media and also make video calls. They even had access to playing games and watching mobile TV. 3G technology was based on **IMT-2000(International Mobile Telecommunications)**. It is a standard defined for mobile and telecommunication technology. 3G allowed masses to experience improved data capacity service and transmission at a very low cost. It allowed users to access various types of applications with the help of their phones.

Figure 6.4: *3G – third generation of wireless technology*

6.1.4 4G – Fourth Generation of Wireless Technology

The Fourth Generation Wireless Technologies were introduced in the 2010s. It focussed on long term development and evolution and is being used by us on the present day. This technology is more evolved and allows higher data transfer rate. You can expect higher speed of transmission which is 100 Mbps while moving and 1Gbps while stationary, better quality, better security, lower cost, IP telephony, gaming services, HD mobile TV , video conferencing etc. 4G networks are based on packet switching only.

Figure 6.5: *4G – fourth generation of wireless technology*

6.1.5 5G – Fifth Generation of Wireless Technology

5G would focus on development of new standards to meet the growing requirements of IoT. It is expected that mobile phones based on 5G technology will provide much higher speed, will improve capability and reliability resulting in great consistency and performance. It is expected to bring in lot of new features that would provide unified experience for all.

You just had a look at how the mobile technologies evolved over a period of time. Let's have a look at some of the general features of mobile communication:

1. The first feature is **High Capacity and Load Balancing** which refers to the ability to deal with overloading and actively shifting users from one access point to another.
2. The next point is **Scalability**. Wireless networks can expand their coverage and capacity without deploying new networks.

3. A network is able to control the role of the user by imposing policies with the help of **Network Access Control** and **Mobile Device Registration.** A user cannot access a network without registering himself.
4. Several people access the network at the same time and in today's date there may be several apps running on each device. Mobile device Manageement controls how each user accesses programs and apps. Even if a device is stolen the data can be erased remotely.
5. A caller will not face any disruption in service when moving from one access point to the other.
6. Networks can be very complex and may consist of several components but can be managed from a central location.

Advantages of mobile Technologies

1. People can communicate with each other irrespective of their geographical location.
2. Communicating with mobile devices is cost effective as there is cost of installing wires and cables.
3. Mobile technologies these days offer great speed and network connectivity.
4. Allows you to connect to family and friends in case of emergency.

Table 6.1 : Difference among generations of wireless technologies

1G	2G	3G	4G
Basic Voice service	Designed for Voice and Messaging	Designed for voice with text, multimedia, internet	Designed primarily for data
Analogue based circuit	First Digital Standard	First mobile broad band	True mobile broadband
Person to person voice call. Mono service	Voice, SMS, Monomedia person to person	Integrated high quality audio and video data	Dynamic information access
No mobility, no security	Security, mobility, mass adoption	Better internet experience	Faster broadband and great internet experience
Major security issues	Limited data rates, impossible to meet the demands of internet and email	Failure of WAP (Wireless Application Protocol) for internet	More battery usage. Requires complicated and extensive hardware.

6.2 Global System for Mobile Communication (GSM)

European Telecommunication Standards Institute (ETSI) had developed a standard – Global System For Mobile Communication for second generation(2G) digital cellular networks to replace the first generation(1G) cellular network.

GSM is an open, digital cellular radio network that uses the **Time Division Multiple Access(TDMA)** technology which allowed users to use there mobiles for data computing and forwarding and receiving text messages. A GSM enabled phone could be connected to laptops for receiving emails, faxes, browsing internet etc.

The original GSM system operated at 900MHz.

Advantages of GSM

- Extremely secure.
- Extensive coverage in over the world.
- Clear voice calls compared to 1G
- Compatible with wide range of devices
- Introduced interesting features such as: short messages, caller ID, Call hold, Call forwarding etc.
- Compatibility with Integrated Services Digital Network (ISDN) and other telephone services.

Disadvantage of GSM

- As GSM allows multiple users to share the same bandwidth there are great chances of interference and bandwidth limitation.
- GSM can cause electronic interference. This is the reason why places like airplanes and hospitals request people to switch off their mobile phones.

6.3 General Packet Radio Services(GPRS)

General Packet Radio Service (GPRS) is a packet-switching protocol or packet-based mobile data service designed for mobile communications of 3G and 2G cellular systems. It is an advanced and very useful packet-switching technology characterised by non-voice and high-speed and is envisioned for GSM networks.

GPRS allows sending and receiving of large data volumes across mobile phone networks. Before forwarding the data on the mobile network, it is broken down into individual packets and then transferred via core network and radio. As in the case of packet switching techniques, the data is reassembled once it reaches the recipient.

Advantages of GPRS

- Low communication cost
- Fast data transmission
- Allows users to operate multiple devices simultaneously.
- Can be directly connected to the Internet.

GSM Vs. GPRS

GSM	GPRS
Abbreviation of Global System for Mobile Communications	Abbreviation for General Packet Radio Service
Circuit switching system	Packet switching system
Can only transfer data by sms	Can use wireless network channel to transfer large amount of data
Designed for 2G cellular devices	Designed for 2G and 3G cellular devices

6.4 Wireless in Local Loop(WLL)

The **Wireless Local Loop** system comprises of a user handset and a base station. The base station is connected to central exchange and an antenna. It uses the terrestrial microwave links to send and receive calls. Base station can provide support to multiple handsets.

Wireless support is often provided in homes and offices it is more secure than wired networks but allows data transfer over a short range.

7 Introduction to Web Services

In this chapter, you will cover:

- Introduction to web services: WWW, Hyper Text Markup Language (HTML), Extensible Markup Language (XML), domain names, URL, website, web browser, web servers, web hosting

7.1 API

API stands for Application Programming Interface. Where Application refers to the software that can be used to do some task. Programming refers to the code that makes an application do something and the Interface is the place which allows user to execute the program. For Example: On your mobile phone you have several apps installed. When you open any app such as, your personal banking app you will provide a username and password to the server. The server will interpret the information provided by you and retrieve all the data related to your account and present it to you in a readable format. This is an API, that makes things happen.

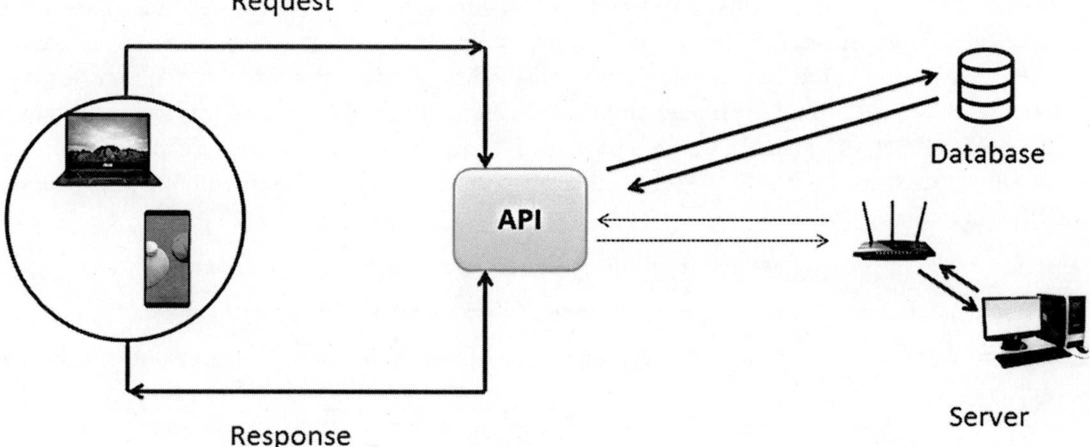

***Figure 7.1:** API*

It consists of set of programs that communicates with external software components or applications. Delivers the user's request to a system and gets a response from the system for the user.

7.2 What is a Web Service?

In the name "web service" web stands for the internet and the service refers to API. So, an API that uses the internet or API over the internet is known as a web service. So, you can say that all web services are API but all APIs are not web services.

7.3 World Wide Web (WWW)

WWW stands for **"World Wide Web"**. Many people believe that the World Wide Web or the "web" is the same as the Internet. This is not true. "www" is just a small part or subset of the Internet. The Internet is a network of networks where all the information resides. The web allows us to access this information with the help of a web browser. "www" is a small part of the internet just like FTP, IRC, Email protocols etc. It is also known as the universe of information available on the internet.

The web is a collection of websites which are residing on web servers. When the local computer is connected to the internet it can retrieve information from the webservers using the web browser. The websites reside on webserver. Each website is a collection of web pages that contain digital images, audios, videos etc. along with the text. All the content of a website residing on any web server can be accessed by any computer from any part of the world with the help of the Internet. The retrieved information including media is displayed on the browser of the device which is accessing it.

WWW was invented by Tim Berners –Lee. In the next section on HTML you will learn how HTML helps in creating the building blocks(web pages) of the web.

7.4 Hypertext Markup Language(HTML)

The web pages are formatted in HTML. HTML stands for Hypertext Markup Language, it is used for creating web pages. As a matter of fact HTML elements or tags define the complete structure of the web page. The reason why it is called a Hyper Text Markup Language is because (1) we can surf the web by clicking the hyperlinks,(2) it consists of markup symbols or codes also known as tags which which gives information about how an element must be displayed on the internet. The markup code is placed between '<' and '>' and (3) it uses code words like any other language. It is a standard markup language that allows you structure a web page and decide how and in which form you would like to present the content to the world. HTML is described by Standard Generalized Markup Language (SGML). Here are some facts:

1. HTML is a scripting language used to render web pages on the web.
2. The Hyper text allows user to jump from one page to another by clicking on a link.
3. The text between two pointed brackets(< and >) is called markup, rest is the content to be displayed.

7.5 HTTP

The API can be called over the Internet using **Hypertext Transfer Protocol(HTTP)**. HTTP is responsible for forwarding requests and getting a response over the internet. If you look at www.yahoo.com, It is a regular text that does nothing, but when you add HTTP in front of it , it becomes a hypertext which when clicked can take you to that site. If you type www.yahoo.com inside the address bar of your computer, it will automatically add http:// or http(s):// in front so that yo can visit the site.

The following figure shows how HTTP Request and Response works:

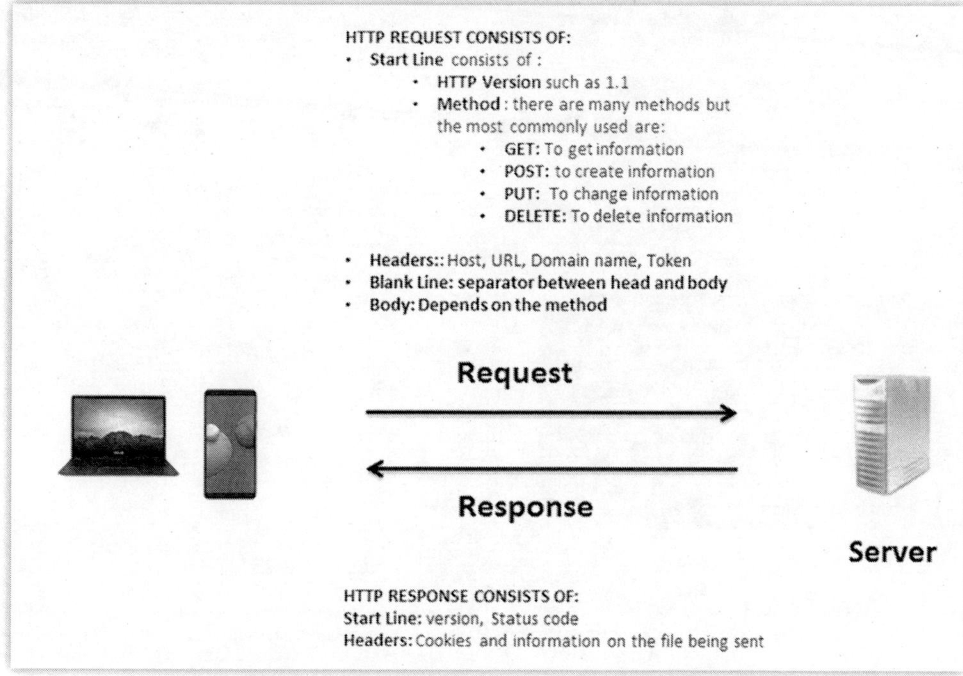

Figure 7.2; HTTP Request and Response

The first part of the HTTP Request as well as HTTP Response is the **start line**. In HTTP Request the start line is known as the **request line** whereas in HTTP Response it is known as the **response or status line**. In both cases the start line of the HTTP Request has the version such as HTTP 1.1 or 2. The request line will consists of methods such as GET, POST, DELETE, etc. The response line however does not have any method. The Request line has an API folder and parameters. These are not available in response line. On the other hand the response line has a status code which is not present in request line. You can view the request being sent by the computer and response you receive in chrome browser as shown below:

Step 1: Go to **More Tools > Developer Tools**

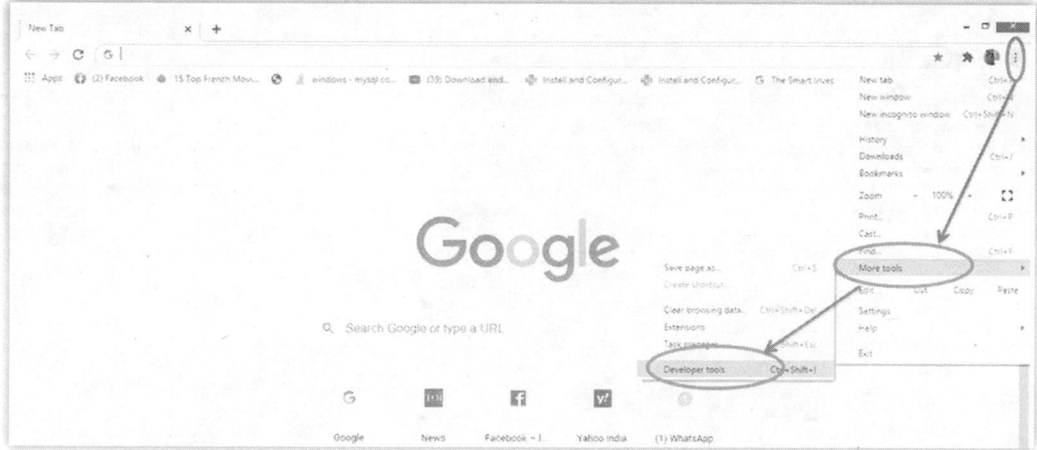

Step 2: Now go to any site. In this case it is www.yahoo.com Notice the activity under the Network Tab.

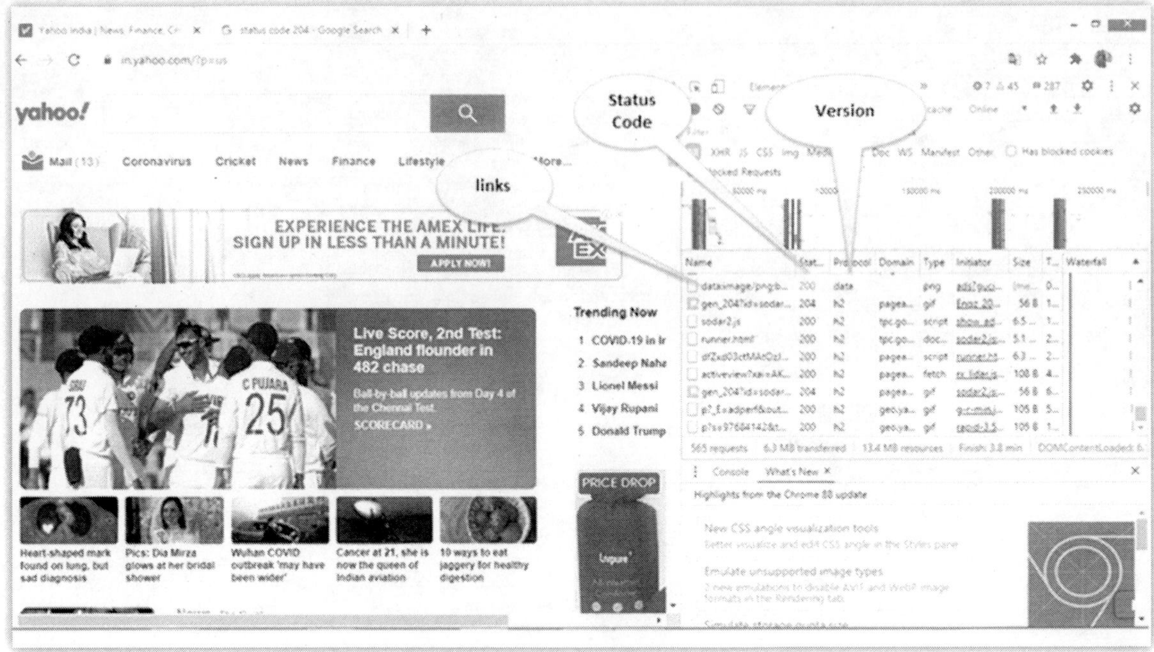

Step 3: Click on any link to view the headers

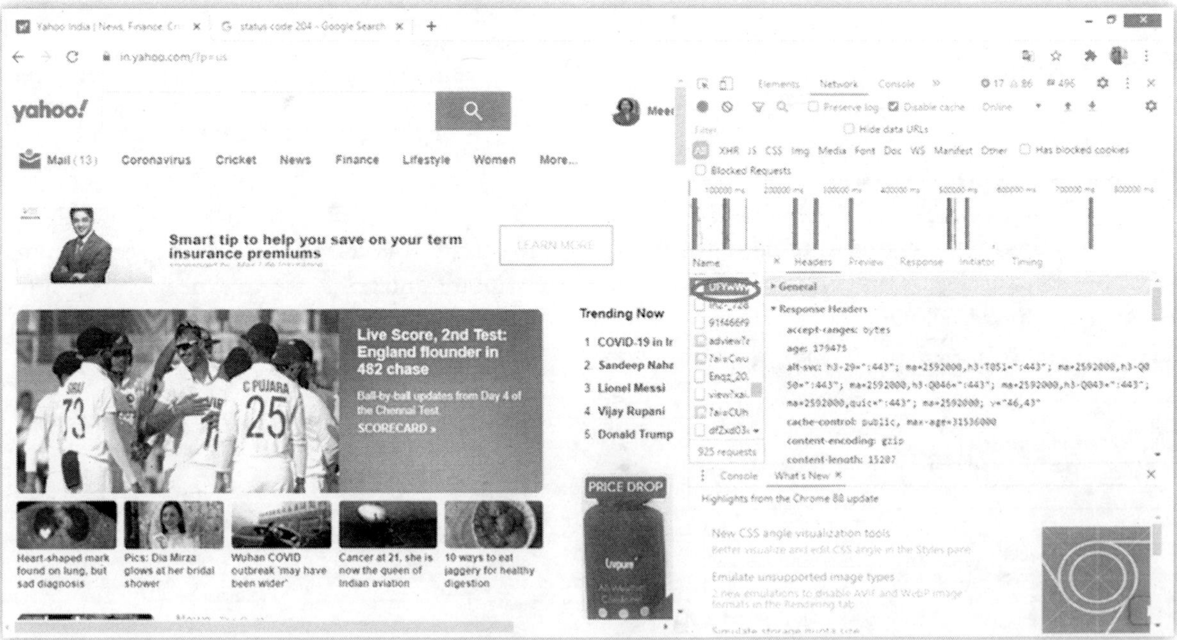

HTTP RESPONSE AND REQUEST LINE

VERSION	REQUEST http/1.1, http/2	RESPONSE http/1.1, http/2
METHOD	GET – to read POST – to create PUT – to update DELETE – to delete ETC.	-----
PARAMETERS	YES	NO
STATUS CODE	NO	YES Example : 1XX : Information 2XX: Success
FORMAT	<Method><API Folder location><Parameters><HTTP version>	<HTTP version><Status Code>

7.6 Extensible Markup language(XML)

XML stands for **Extensible Markup Language**. XML files are used to hold or contain data that is sent to an API or sent back from the API. The data in XML file is contained with the help of tags the same way as in case of HTML. However, there is a huge difference between the two. The tags “<>” in HTML are used to define some element such as body, header, table, button, font, list etc. whereas in XML it just means data.

So, <button>Click here to download</button> creates a button s shown below:

Click here to download

Where as in an XML file, this same line of code would mean that a tag by the name button contains data: “Click here to download”. So, this file is not defined to display any data, it can only define new tags.

XML is used to structure data so that it can be stored and transported. An XML of Tags that provides structure to data and text that can be stored within the tags. The purpose of using XML is that it helps in transferring information. HTML can only display but it cannot transfer data.XML also allows you to create your own mark up symbols.

7.7 URL

URL stands for **Uniform Resource Locator**. It is used to locate unique resource on the web. This unique resource can be a web page, an image, document etc. URL is the string that you type in the address bar of you browser.

Figure 7.3

In the figure shown above, the URL is https://bpbonline.com/. The first part of the URL is known as the **scheme**. The scheme refers to the protocol that is being used by the browser to forward the request. In this case it is **https**(s stands for **secure**), other examples are ftp, http, mailto: etc. The scheme is followed by **'://'** after which comes the authority which has the **domain name**. In this case the domain name is **bpbonline.com**. Other examples are www.google.com, www.facebook.com etc. The authority may also include a **port number** separated from the domain by a **colon(:)**. Next comes **path**. Now, suppose you click on a link on the site. It will take you the path where that resource is stored on the web server.

So, in https://bpbonline.com/collections/security-cyber-security-books-online-ebooks:

https is the scheme.

bpbonline.com is the domain and collections/security-cyber-security-books-online-ebooks is the path(It is located as **security-cyber-security-books-online-ebooks** file in collections folder in the root directory **bpbonline.com**) of the resource that the user is looking for.A resource is generally located in a host directory or folder. So, you can say that the format is **scheme(or protocol)://domain(or server name or host name):port(optional)/path**

So, now in simple word we can say **URL** is the address of a web page. It is a formatted text string that helps you find a resource on the internet. Every resource on the internet has a unique URL. Every domain name has an IP address. Server with one IP address can provide services for several hosts, so one or more websites can have the same IP address.

When you type in the address of a website in the address bar, you are able to locate the site with the help of **DNS server**. We know that each website has an IP address but it is near to impossible to remember the sites by ip address when we can't even remember the phone numbers of our near and dear ones. Websites should have meaningful name that can be easily remembered. Facebook, Instagram, twitter are social media, google and Bing are search engines, yahoo and gmail are for emails etc. We remember the websites by their hostname. **DNS server** is a server that maintains a record of which hostname is associated with which IP address and they translate the hostname to an IP address. DNS server is also known a Name server or domain name system server. Though, we are comfortable using hostname, the network devices can identify a website only by IP address. So, when we type the URL in the address bar, the DNS server retrieves the IP address that you want to visit and this is how your request is taken forward.

7.8 Webpage

A webpage is an HTML document that is viewed in a web browser. Every webpage on the internet has a URL. To access a web page its URL must be entered in the address bar of the browser. Since a web page is designed in HTML it can have any type of content such as audio, video, text, graphics etc. It can also contain links to other related web pages. Web pages can also be used to upload or download important documents.

A web page can be **static** or **dynamic**. A static webpage only provides information and has a **.html** or **.htm** extension. Dynamic pages on the other have actions associated with it. For example you log in to a site using username and password. The web pages forwards this information to check if you are a valid user and if yes then it takes you to the next page. Dynamic webpages generally have **.php, .asp or .jsp** as extension. They are created with the help of scripted languages made specifically for runtime environment to automate the code implementation. JavaScript, PHP, JSP, Ruby, Python etc. are common example of scripted languages.

Collection of related webpages that belong to the same domain name is known as a **website**. So, a website of a school will have webpages related to newletter, events, teachers, class information, list of holidays, awards and achievements etc. Similarly a social media site will have webpages for posting comments, uploading pictures, watching videos etc.

7.9 Web browser

A web browser is undoubtedly the most important window on your computer. It allows you to surf on the internet. A webpage is coded in HTML which can be interpreted only by a browser and displays the page as it is intended to be. The graphics of the page makes it easier for the user to surf on the internet. A web browser is a software application which is used to access the information on the internet. The information is retrieved from the resources residing on a web server on the internet and then displayed to the user.

Web browsers can be text based or graphic based. What we use in our day to day routine such as Chrome or Firefox are Graphic browser which display all the contents on the webpages, images, texts, ads etc. The text browser only provides the text of the web pages and completely ignores the graphic content.

7.10 Web servers

A remote computer that runs website is known as the web server. When you want to visit a website, you type in the URL of that site in the address bar. A request is passed from your local server to the webserver that is running the site and information is displayed on your computer in the form of web page as a response from the web page. Special programs such as **Apache** or **IIS run** on the web server and help in delivering the web page over the http protocol. Every server has a unique domain name and IP address.

- Database Concepts
- Working with Queries
- Joins
- MySQL for Python

1 Database Concepts

In this chapter, you will cover:

- Database concepts: Introduction to database concepts and its need.
- Relational data model: Relation, attribute, tuple, domain, degree, cardinality, keys (candidate key, primary key, alternate key, foreign key).

1.1 What is a Database?

Database is a data collection storing organized information. Database is required to store data permanently. It allows you to store information in files on the hard drive. Almost all software applications deal with huge volumes of data and so it is important to have a mechanism that not only allows us to store data in a structured manner but also allows retrieval, insertion and deletion of data. In this chapter you will learn how a database can be populated with data.

Software applications use **Structured query language (SQL)** so that the program that they are running can communicate with the database also known as the backend. It is a common language used to communicate with databases such as Oracle, MySQL, Microsoft SQL Server etc. When it comes to storing data in a structured manner and retrieving it when required we make use of **Relational Database Management Systems (RDBMS)**.

SQL is the common language for various databases such as Oracle, MySQL, Microsoft SQL Server, DB2, Informix etc. RDBMS has been the most in demand choice for storing data in databases be it financial institutions, manufacturing units, logistics or any other application. It provides a very structured way of storing data, this allows you to work with huge volumes of data within short duration of time. The data is stored in such a way that it can be easily located, retrieved, updated, created or deleted within no time. If the data is not stored in structured and organized manner then you would take a long time to retrieve the information that you require and honestly speaking that would be as inconvenient as the traditional way of storing records in books. With the help of database we are trying to automate the process of working in data and we are able to speed up the process. This can be done only with the help of **Relational database management system**.

Being a student of computer science you may be aware of the fact that there is a great demand for programmers specialized in object oriented programming. In object oriented programming the code is divided into entities or objects and then all the tasks are done by drawing a relationship between these objects and making them interact with each other. Relational database are ideal choice for object oriented programming.

So, for example If you want to make a campus management software, it will have objects like class, students, parents, teachers , events, clubs, exams, etc. and then by mapping them together we can easily work on complex data. So, if you need to find out information about one student you will instantly get records of his parents, teacher, clubs, events etc. This is done with the help of relational database management system.

Object oriented programming is all about how two or more objects are related to each other and the relational database is used to store this information in a tabular form. Example of relation between two objects is Employee and Employer, Customer and Address etc. The relational database provides a way to show that relationship exists between these objects as we will see shortly. The relationships that these objects have with one another can be defined as:

1. **One to One:** Like an email id can be associated with only one username and a username can be associated with only one email id. In this of relationship we can find out which username belongs to which user.
2. **One to Many:** A School can have many teachers but all teachers of that school belong to that school only. In this type of relationship we can find which teacher work in a particular school.
3. **Many to Many:** A teacher can teach many subjects and the subject can have more than one teacher. In this relationship we can find which subject is being taught by which all teachers and which all teachers are teaching which all subjects.

Couple of decades back all organizations stored records in thick long ruled books by drawing columns and manually filling in the details. Then came the computers with the popular MS Excel sheets and it became easier for anyone to fill in data in spreadsheets. Now, vendors come up with customised software which provide easy to fill form to the user once the user fills in the form all the data is collected and stored in the backend(the relational database) in a tabular form. So, now let's see how a database looks like. Databases are made of table in which data is stored in rows and columns.

BOOK_ID	BOOK_NAME	AUTHOR_NAME	PAGES	COST
1	The Secret	Rhonda Byrne	198	3
2	The Frequency	Linda West	180	4
3	The Power	Rhonda Byrne	272	6
4	The Magic	Rhonda Byrne	272	6
5	The Hero	Rhonda Byrne	240	6
9	One Truth, One Law	Erin Werley	87	6
10	Mind Magic	Merlin Starlight	265	19
11	Advanced Manifesting	Linda West	172	4

Figure 1.1: *Example of how data is stored in rows and columns*

1.2 Relationships in Database

You may ask why and how does a relationship exist in databases? Well, modern databases have been designed to have relationships between tables. Let's first understand what is a relationship, Suppose there are two tables: table A and table B . If table B has information pertaining to table A then a relationship exists between the two. This relationship between the tables is maintained by a pointer known as **Foreign Key**. Now, let's understand how the tables work. In the coming chapters we will be working with **my_first_database** that has tables related to customer. The first table **customer_detail** is described as follows:

```
+------------------+--------------+------+-----+---------+----------------+
| Field            | Type         | Null | Key | Default | Extra          |
+------------------+--------------+------+-----+---------+----------------+
| customer_ID      | smallint     | NO   | PRI | NULL    | auto_increment |
| customer_FN      | varchar(35)  | NO   |     | NULL    |                |
| customer_SN      | varchar(35)  | NO   |     | NULL    |                |
| customer_contact | bigint       | NO   |     | NULL    |                |
| email_id         | varchar(255) | NO   |     | NULL    |                |
+------------------+--------------+------+-----+---------+----------------+
```

Figure 1.2

Here **customer_ID** is the **primary key** of this table which means the value of this column is unique for every row and this key can help in identifying a row. A table can have more than one primary keys. If we look at the information of this table:

```
+-------------+-------------+-------------+------------------+---------------------------+
| customer_ID | customer_FN | customer_SN | customer_contact | email_id                  |
+-------------+-------------+-------------+------------------+---------------------------+
|       10000 | Eric        | Jackson     |       9898983434 | ericjackson@yahoo.com     |
|       10001 | George      |  Mathews    |       9089376511 | gm@yahoo.com              |
|       10002 | Riya        | Pathak      |       9089346521 | riya.patha2010@gmail.com  |
|       10003 | Aslam       | Khan        |       9602346833 | riya.patha2010@gmail.com  |
|       10004 | Rakesh      | Verma       |       7089676523 | rakesh.verma@gmail.com    |
|       10005 | Meenakshi   | Sinha       |       9989645523 | msinha@gmail.com          |
+-------------+-------------+-------------+------------------+---------------------------+
```

Figure 1.3

You can see that each customer is assigned a unique id.

Now, there is another table called **customer_login**

```
mysql> desc customer_login;
+-------------+-------------+------+-----+---------+----------------+
| Field       | Type        | Null | Key | Default | Extra          |
+-------------+-------------+------+-----+---------+----------------+
| login_ID    | smallint    | NO   | PRI | NULL    | auto_increment |
| username    | varchar(35) | NO   |     | NULL    |                |
| password    | varchar(35) | NO   |     | NULL    |                |
| customer_ID | smallint    | NO   | UNI | NULL    |                |
+-------------+-------------+------+-----+---------+----------------+
4 rows in set (0.00 sec)
```

Figure 1.4

You can see that table **customer_login** holds the primary key of **customer_details -customer_ID**. **customer_login** can be linked to **customer_details** with the help of customer_ID. Hence customer_ID becomes the foreign key in customer_login.

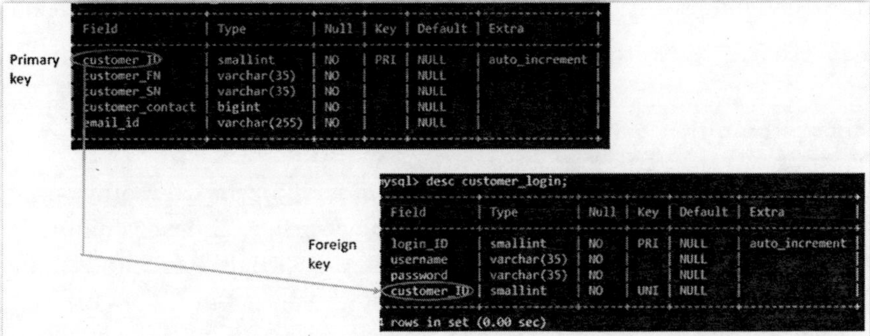

Figure 1.5

Now coming to Why have relationships in Database? Well, it is same as asking why break data into several tables? If you don't break data into multiple tables you will have one huge table with huge number of entries and it will be near to impossible to make sense out of that table. One big table will cause redundancy which means unnecessary repition of data which will lead to anamolies. As you work through the exercises given in this book you will understand the importance of relational database.

A relation between two tables is established using a foreign key which in turn is a primary key belonging to sôme other table. Multiple tables can use same primary key.

Domain: Domain is the set of possible values for an attribute

Relation: A table in database is known as a relation. The information in a table in database is organized into row and columns.

Tuple : A tuple is a row of a table

Attribute: An attribute is a column header of a table or relation in a database.

Degree: Total number of columns or attributes in a table is the degree of that table

Cardinality: Total number of rows in the table represents its cardinality.

Key: A column or a combination of columns that uniquely identifies a row in a table.

Primary key: One or more columns of a table that together uniquely identify a row is known as a primary key.

Alternate key: Contains one or more columns whose combined value uniquely identifies each row of a relation.

Foreign Key: One or more columns in whose values matches the values of the primary key of some other table of database.

1.3 Structured Query Language

SQL or structured query language is the language used to interact with database. You can SQL to interact with databases like SQL server, oracle, DB2, MS SQL server ,Postgre SQL and MySQL. The syntax of SQL can vary for different databases but broadly the concept is same. In this chapter you will learn how to use SQL for MySQL.

1.3.1 Why MySQL?

MySQL is gaining lot of popularity and is often preferred for development purposes for the following reasons:

1. MySQL is easy to learn and easy to use.
2. MySQL offers strong data security layers which allows data protection from hackers.
3. It is an opensource free software which can be used easily with any application.

1.3.2 How to work with SQL?

Working with SQL is easy. Its syntax and implementation is different from other programming languages. Most programming languages especially the object-oriented programming languages such as Python on JAVA are know for defining control flow whereas SQL is a declarative language with no control flow. It has only four main operations defined by the acronym **CRUD(Create Read Update Delete)**:

1. **Create:** used to create new data
2. **Read:** Used to retrieve data from the database
3. **Update** change existing data in the database
4. **Delete:** Remove data from database

These four statements are the heart and soul of SQL which are often used for creating and maintenance of data in the database.

1.4 Using SQL Command Line

In this section you will learn how to use SQL command line. Open your command prompt.

Step 1: Next to the Windows icon on the bottom left hand side type in command prompt and click on the circled option.

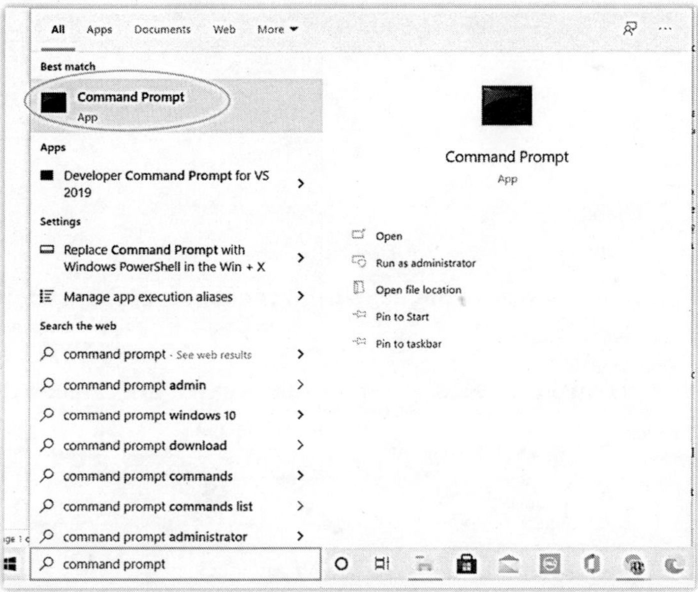

Figure 1.6

The following window will be displayed:

Figure 1.7

Step 2: In order to work with MySQL you have to locate where it is installed in your computer and navigate to the bin folder. For this example MySQL is installed at C:\Program Files\MySQL\MySQL Server 8.0.

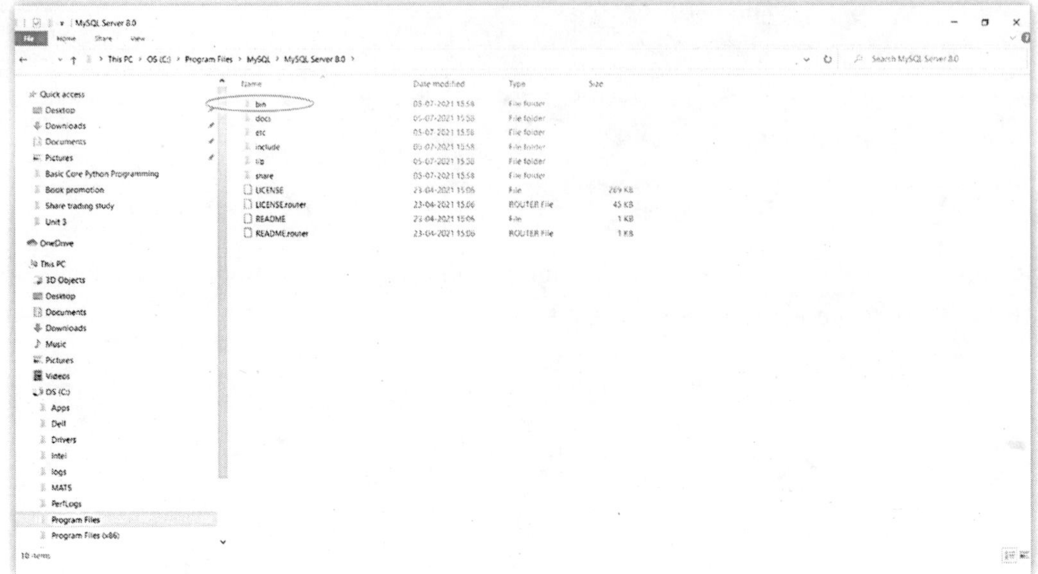

Figure 1.8

To go to this directory give the following command in your command prompt:

>cd C:\Program Files\MySQL\MySQL Server 8.0\bin

Your command prompt will now look as shown in the following figure (Figure 1.9).

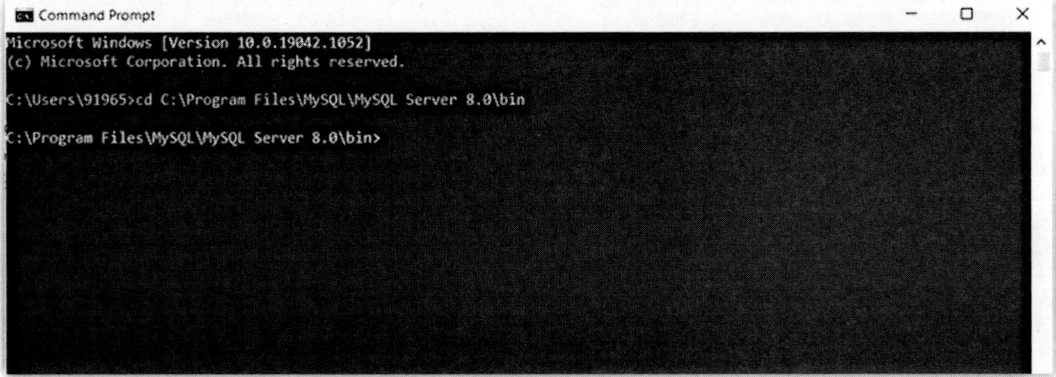

Figure 1.9

You are now ready to work with MySQL.

The first step to run MySQL is to provide login details that were provided at the time of installing MySQL. For this provide the following command :

```
>mysql -u [username] -p[password]
```

For this example, no username was provided at the time of installing the software so the username will be '**root**'. The password given was **'bpb21'**. So, the command provided will be as follows(please note the will be no space between -p and password i.e. bpb21):

```
>mysql -u root -pbpb21
```

Once you provide the password the command prompt will look as shown in the following figure (Figure 1.10):

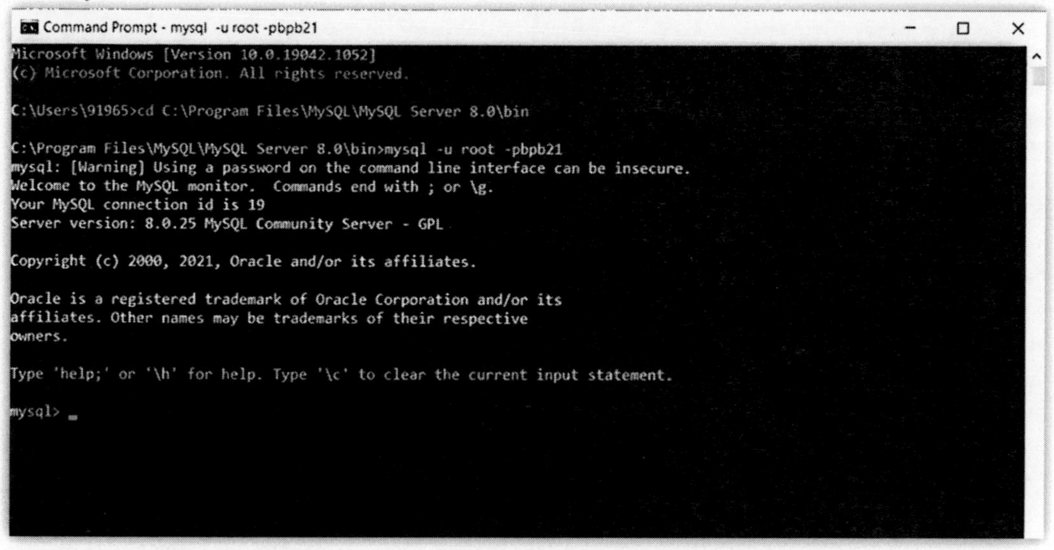

```
Command Prompt - mysql -u root -pbpb21
Microsoft Windows [Version 10.0.19042.1052]
(c) Microsoft Corporation. All rights reserved.

C:\Users\91965>cd C:\Program Files\MySQL\MySQL Server 8.0\bin

C:\Program Files\MySQL\MySQL Server 8.0\bin>mysql -u root -pbpb21
mysql: [Warning] Using a password on the command line interface can be insecure.
Welcome to the MySQL monitor.  Commands end with ; or \g.
Your MySQL connection id is 19
Server version: 8.0.25 MySQL Community Server - GPL

Copyright (c) 2000, 2021, Oracle and/or its affiliates.

Oracle is a registered trademark of Oracle Corporation and/or its
affiliates. Other names may be trademarks of their respective
owners.

Type 'help;' or '\h' for help. Type '\c' to clear the current input statement.

mysql> _
```

Figure 1.10

You are now ready to use MySQL.

1.5 Creating a Database using SQL

In this section you will start your SQL journey by creating a database and this is what this section is all about. Following steps will guide you on how to create a database.

Step 1: Log into MySQL database (follow the steps given in the section "using command line")

Step 2: Let's create a database by the name **my_first_database**. The command for this will be as follows:

```
> create my_first_database;
```

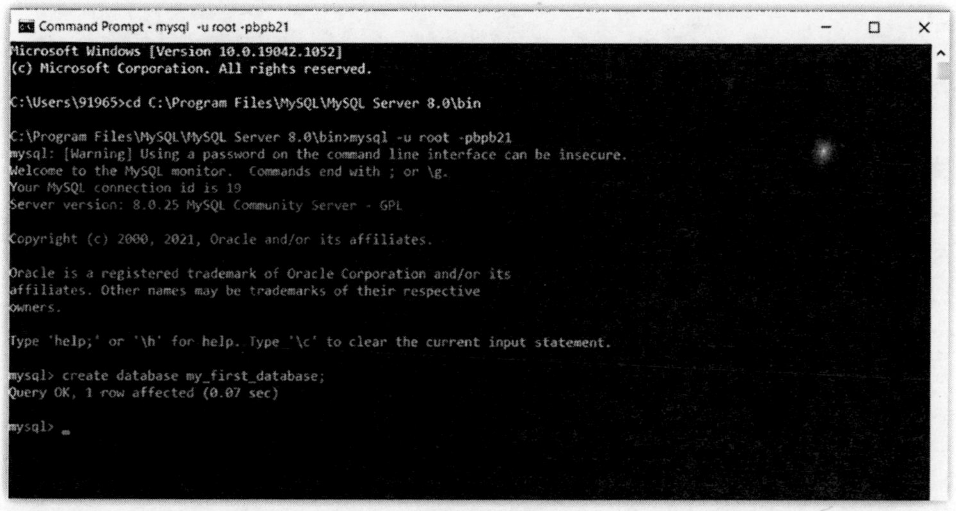

```
Command Prompt - mysql -u root -pbpb21
Microsoft Windows [Version 10.0.19042.1052]
(c) Microsoft Corporation. All rights reserved.

C:\Users\91965>cd C:\Program Files\MySQL\MySQL Server 8.0\bin

C:\Program Files\MySQL\MySQL Server 8.0\bin>mysql -u root -pbpb21
mysql: [Warning] Using a password on the command line interface can be insecure.
Welcome to the MySQL monitor.  Commands end with ; or \g.
Your MySQL connection id is 19
Server version: 8.0.25 MySQL Community Server - GPL

Copyright (c) 2000, 2021, Oracle and/or its affiliates.

Oracle is a registered trademark of Oracle Corporation and/or its
affiliates. Other names may be trademarks of their respective
owners.

Type 'help;' or '\h' for help. Type '\c' to clear the current input statement.

mysql> create database my_first_database;
Query OK, 1 row affected (0.07 sec)

mysql> _
```

Figure 1.11

Step 3: Check if the database has been created by giving the following command:

```
> show database;
```

On giving this command your database should reflect on the screen.

```
Command Prompt - mysql -u root -pbpb21
C:\Program Files\MySQL\MySQL Server 8.0\bin>mysql -u root -pbpb21
mysql: [Warning] Using a password on the command line interface can be insecure.
Welcome to the MySQL monitor.  Commands end with ; or \g.
Your MySQL connection id is 19
Server version: 8.0.25 MySQL Community Server - GPL

Copyright (c) 2000, 2021, Oracle and/or its affiliates.

Oracle is a registered trademark of Oracle Corporation and/or its
affiliates. Other names may be trademarks of their respective
owners.

Type 'help;' or '\h' for help. Type '\c' to clear the current input statement.

mysql> create database my_first_database;
Query OK, 1 row affected (0.07 sec)

mysql> show databases;
+--------------------+
| Database           |
+--------------------+
| information_schema |
| my_first_database  |
| mysql              |
| performance_schema |
| sys                |
+--------------------+
5 rows in set (0.05 sec)

mysql>
```

Figure 1.12

You should be able to see the name of your database in the list that has been created.

You can also provide privilege over this database. For this first create a user **'meenu'**.

Step 1: First create a user and password by giving the following command:

```
mysql>create user 'meenu'@'localhost' identified by 'bpb'
```

This command creates a username **'meenu'** and password **'bpb'**;

Step 2: Now grant all privileges to user 'meenu'. For this give the following command:

```
mysql>grant all privileges on my_first_database.* to 'meenu'@'localhost';
```

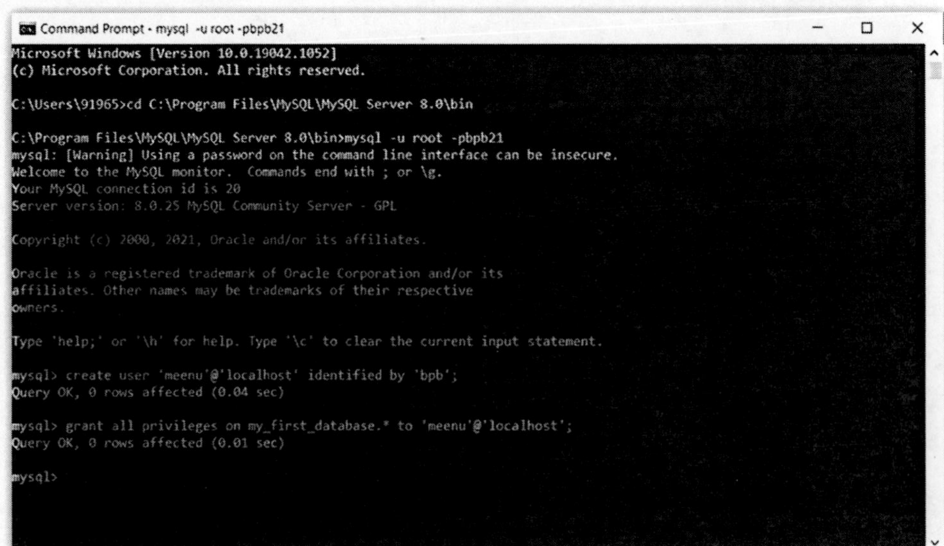

Figure 1.13

Step 3: Now exit the MySQL command using quit command as follows:

mysql> QUIT;

Step 4: Now try to log in back to MySQL with meenu. Give the following command:

>mysql -u meenu -p

Enter password: bpb (which is 'bpb')

Step 5: In this step you can attach to 'my_first_database' database with the following command:

mysql> use my_first_database;

Now, that we have created a database and a database user we can now start creating the tables in this database.

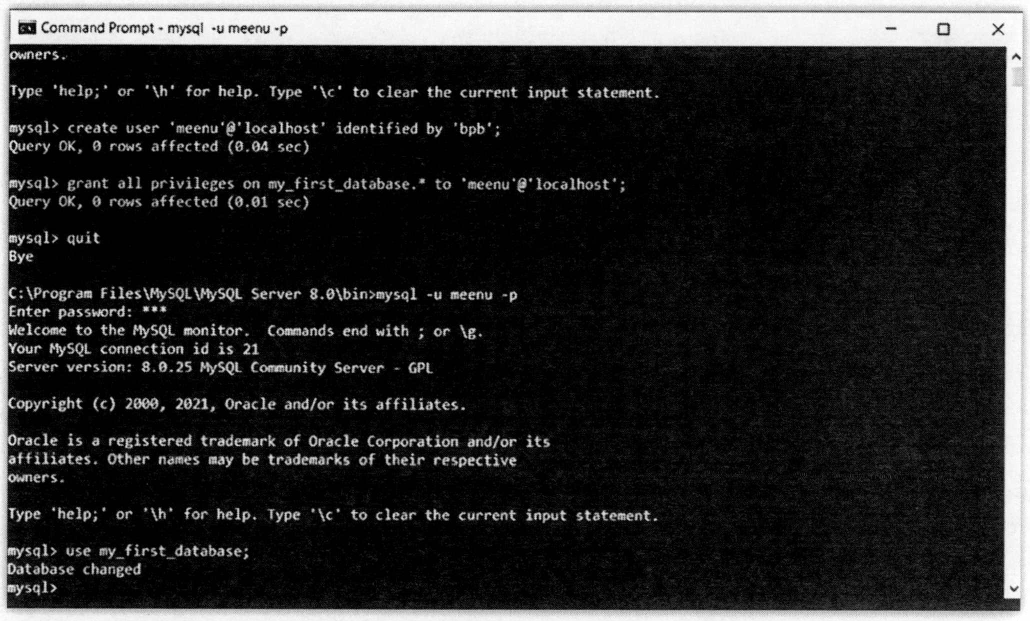

```
Command Prompt - mysql -u meenu -p
owners.

Type 'help;' or '\h' for help. Type '\c' to clear the current input statement.

mysql> create user 'meenu'@'localhost' identified by 'bpb';
Query OK, 0 rows affected (0.04 sec)

mysql> grant all privileges on my_first_database.* to 'meenu'@'localhost';
Query OK, 0 rows affected (0.01 sec)

mysql> quit
Bye

C:\Program Files\MySQL\MySQL Server 8.0\bin>mysql -u meenu -p
Enter password: ***
Welcome to the MySQL monitor.  Commands end with ; or \g.
Your MySQL connection id is 21
Server version: 8.0.25 MySQL Community Server - GPL

Copyright (c) 2000, 2021, Oracle and/or its affiliates.

Oracle is a registered trademark of Oracle Corporation and/or its
affiliates. Other names may be trademarks of their respective
owners.

Type 'help;' or '\h' for help. Type '\c' to clear the current input statement.

mysql> use my_first_database;
Database changed
mysql>
```

Figure 1.14

1.6 Data Types in MySQL

Data types are important part of all programming languages and SQL is no exception. So, before creating any table it is important to first understand what type of information you want to store in it. For example for creating a customer you would require home address, name, mobile number, address, pin code etc. For creating this table, you will have to provide details of data type for each field that will be stored in this table. For example, phone number can only be numeric. Addresses can be text and numeric and may also include special characters like '-', '/' or '#'. This is called defining the data type. You will also have to define the size of each data type. For example, phone numbers should not take more than 10 numeric values or address should not take more than 150 characters and so on. It is very important to define data type of every field of a table at the time it is created. For every field you have to define how many characters and what type of characters. You will understand the importance of datatypes as you start working on the database.

This is called defining the size of data field. In MySQL datatypes can be broadly classified into three types:

1. Numeric
2. Date and Type
3. Strings

1.6.1 Numeric Data Types

Different types of numeric Data Types are as follows, you would be referring to this again and again while programming:

1. **Integer (INT):** It is used for normal signed or unsigned integers and ranges from -2147483648 to 2147483647. It can take up to 11 digits. It is one of he most commonly used data types and stores a whole number. The common uses are: (1) for storing a count (2) often used for creating primary keys.
2. **Big Integer (BIGINT):** It is a larger integer with range of (-2^{63}) to$(2^{63}-1)$. An integer has the range of (-2^{31}) to$(2^{31}-1)$
3. **Very Small Integer (TINYINT):** It is a very small integer that can be signed or unsigned and within the range is from -128 to 127. It can take up to 4 digits.
4. **Small Integer (SMALLINT):** It is for small integer signed or unsigned within the range of -32768 to 32767. It can take upto 5 digits.
5. **Medium Sized Integer (MEDIUMINT):** Integers signed or unsigned within the range of -8388608 to 8388607 is in this category. I can take up to 9 digits.
6. **Large Integer (BIGINT):** Large Integers signed or unsigned within the range of -9223372036854775808 to 9223372036854775807. It can take up to 20 digits.
7. **Floating-point number (FLOAT(N,D)):** A floating point number is always signed and you will have to define the length of the number N and the number of the decimal. Unless specified otherwise the default value is 10, 2. Where 10 in the length of the number before decimal and 2 in the number of decimals digits it can take.
8. **Double (DOUBLE(M,D)):** Is signed floating point number (M = length of the number and D = number of decimals to include)with the default value of 16,4.

1.6.2 Date and Time Data Types

The date and time data type are of following types:

1. **DATE:** The format for DATE is **YYYY-MM-DD**. Where, DD is the date of the Month, MM is for month and YYYY is for the year.
2. **DATETIME:** This would display date and time in the format **YYYY-MM-DD HH:MM:SS**. Where YYYY is for 4 digits of the year, MM is for 2 digits of the month and DD is for two digits for the date of the month. HH is for hours, MM is for minutes and SS is for seconds.
3. **TIMESTAMP:** Time stamp displays date and time in DATETIME format but without the hyphens in between. So, the date and time is displayed as **YYYYMMDDHHMMSS**.
4. **TIME:** save the time in HH:MM:SS format.

1.6.3 String Data types

A string is a data type which is used to represent text. All characters in string data type are stored as text. It can also contain text and numbers. The string data types are as follows:

1. **CHAR(L):** This data type is used to define string characters with the fixed length of 1 to 255 characters. It is not necessary to define the length and the default value is 1.
2. **VARCHAR(L):** This data type is used to define string data of variable length between 1 to 255 characters. It is important to define the length of varchar data type.
3. **BLOB:** used to store large amount of binary data such as images or any other file. It can have maximum length of 65535 characters and is not case sensitive. There is no need to specify length.
4. **TEXT:** The only difference between BLOB and TEXT is that the latter is case sensitive.
5. **TINYBLOB:** is same as BLOB with maximum length of 255 characters.
6. **TINYTEXT:** is same as TEXT with maximum length of 255 characters.
7. **MEDIUMBLOB:** same as BLOB with maximum length of 16777215 characters.
8. **MEDIUMTEXT:** same as TEXT with maximum length of 16777215 characters.
9. **MEDIUMBLOB:** same as BLOB with maximum length of 16777215 characters.
10. **MEDIUMTEXT:** same as TEXT with maximum length of 16777215 characters.
11. **LONGBLOB:** same as BLOB with maximum length of 4294967295 characters.
12. **LONGTEXT:** same as TEXT with maximum length of 4294967295 characters.
13. **ENUM:** Enumeration is for list which is used to create a list of string objects.

While entering records in database there may be some fields which are not mandatory and there would be some mandatory fields. Like, all people may not have a middle name so in that case we can allow middle name to allow blank values whereas first name and surname or the last name should be mandatory. When, it is mandatory to have a field value. Define it as NOT NULL.

1.7 SQL Commands

There are different types of SQL commands and they are used for a variety of purposes for a smooth functioning of various transactions. Database commands can be categorized as follows:

1. **Data Definition Language:** These statements are used to add, modify or delete the structures that are containing the data. These commands are used to maintain the data in the database. The statements that come under this category are:
   a. CREATE
   b. ALTER
   c. DROP
2. **Data Manipulation Language:** Allows the user to update or delete existing data or add more data to the existing data. The statements that come under this category are:
   a. INSERT
   b. UPDATE

c. DELETE

3. **Data Query Language:** It is used to retrieve data, information related to metadata or help information. The statements that come under this category are:
   a. SELECT
   b. SHOW
   c. HELP
4. **Data Control Language (DCL):** these statements are used to control the access to data that exists in the database. You can grant or deny permissions given to the users. The commands that come under this category are:
   a. GRANT(We have used this statement while creating user for school database)
   b. REVOKE
5. **Transaction Control Language(TCL):** are used to manage database transactions. Following statements come under this category:
   a. START TRANSACTION
   b. SAVEPOINT
   c. COMMIT
   d. ROLLBACK

1.8 Creating a Table

In this section we will create our first table for our **my_first_database** database.

You should know the following things:

1. A table is made up of rows and columns.
2. To create a table you must use proper syntax.
3. You should define the primary key for the table.
4. You will create column for a table and assign appropriate datatypes.

Deciding the name of the table

In this example we will create a table that would have the details of a customer. The name of the table should be meaningful and must define its purpose of existence. This is important because a software program can have several tables in the database and it becomes easy to identify the table by its name. Since we want to create a table with details of the customer, let's call it **customer_details**. Separating the words of the table by underscore is the best practise.

Follow the step by step instruction given below.

We start with Designing of customer_details table. This table will be a small but important one.

Step1: Here we are considering following fields:

- **customer_ID:** This field should be unique identification number. It should be an integer and should auto increment.
- **customer_FN:** This field will be a varchar field to store customer's first name. Cannot be null.

- **customer_SN:** This field will be a varchar field to store customer's surname. Cannot be null.
- **customer_contact:** customer's contact number 10 digit.Cannot be null.
- **email_id:** home address is varchar field. Cannot be null.

Here, it is important to understand the concept of primary key and its importance in Relational database. In order to uniquely identify every row record it is important to have a field that can only accept unique values. So, this field will help you identify the record that you need. Primary key field must have unique value it is a mandatory field. When more than one fields are defined as primary key they are referred to as **composite key**. If a table has a primary key defined then you ***cannot*** have duplicate values for that field. You may wonder why this is important? Consider an example, a man called "Arun Mehra" has an account at Amazon. Is he the only Arun Mehra on Amazon? No, there would be several people by that name. So, we use the city name, let's say Delhi to identify which Arun Mehra he is. Do you think Delhi would have only one Arun Mehra who has an Account on Amazon? Let's filter it more and use the area let's say Dwarka. Is there only one Arun Mehra in Dwarka? So, we know that all Arun Mehras have different address and unique cell phone number. So, we can use that for identifying the right Arun Mehra. Though cell phone number would make a good primary key, it is subject to change. Therefore, for our example we are considering customer_id. Every customer is assigned a customer_id and that number auto increments for the next customer so that each customer is uniquely identified by his or her customer_id rather than names.

Step 2: Keeping the definition of all the fields given in step1 we will now create our table. This is how the CREATE statement should look:

The format for creating a table is as follows:

CREATE TABLE [table_name]

([column_name] [data_type]([size])

[table_constraint] ([column name]));

Constraints in MySQL

Constraints are required to restrict the values that are stored in a particular field. You can limit the type of data entered into a table with the help of constraint. Constraints can be applied at column level and at table level. Constraints are defined at the time the table is created. Following are the constraints that you would like to work with while working on MY SQL:

- **PRIMARY KEY:** You have already used the Primary Key constraint while creating family_data table. The primary key is required to accept unique data for one or more columns for faster access of values stored in the database.
- **NOT NULL:** This constraint specifies that a particular cannot accept blank entry.
- **UNIQUE:** this constraint does not allow duplicate entry in a column.
- **FOREIGN KEY:** In Relational database management system the link between tw tables is created with the help of FOREIGN KEY. Primary key of one table when used in another table for retrieving related records is called FOREIGN KEY.
- **CHECK:** As the name suggests, this constraint is used to check if valid value has been entered as per the logical statement.
- **DEFAULT:** Default is a value that must be fed into a column if no value is defined while inserting data.

CREATE TABLE Customer_details (

customer_IDsmallint NOT NULL AUTO_INCREMENT,

customer_FNvarchar(35) NOT NULL,

customer_SNvarchar(35) NOT NULL,

customer_contactbigint(10) NOT NULL,

email_idvarchar(255) NOT NULL,

PRIMARY KEY (customer_ID)

);

Step 3: We will now create the table.

- Open the command prompt
- Login to school database

  mysql -u meenu–p

  enter password: meenu
- Give the following command to connect to school database

  use my_first_database;

  The following message will be displayed:

  Database changed

  Write down the query to create the table.

```
Command Prompt - mysql -u meenu -p
mysql> quit
Bye

C:\Program Files\MySQL\MySQL Server 8.0\bin>mysql -u meenu -p
Enter password: ***
Welcome to the MySQL monitor.  Commands end with ; or \g.
Your MySQL connection id is 21
Server version: 8.0.25 MySQL Community Server - GPL

Copyright (c) 2000, 2021, Oracle and/or its affiliates.

Oracle is a registered trademark of Oracle Corporation and/or its
affiliates. Other names may be trademarks of their respective
owners.

Type 'help;' or '\h' for help. Type '\c' to clear the current input statement.

mysql> use my_first_database;
Database changed
mysql> CREATE TABLE Customer_details (
    ->     customer_ID smallint NOT NULL AUTO_INCREMENT,
    ->     customer_FN varchar(35) NOT NULL,
    ->     customer_SN varchar(35) NOT NULL,
    ->     customer_contact bigint(10) NOT NULL,
    ->     email_id varchar(255) NOT NULL,
    ->     PRIMARY KEY (customer_ID)
    -> );
Query OK, 0 rows affected, 1 warning (0.12 sec)

mysql>
```

Figure 1.15

Once your table has been created, the following message will be displayed:

Query OK, 0 rows affected

- To see the table in the database give the following command in the database:

  show tables;

  Following data will be displayed:

```
mysql> show tables;
+---------------------------+
| Tables_in_my_first_database |
+---------------------------+
| customer_details          |
+---------------------------+
1 row in set (0.04 sec)

mysql>
```

Figure 1.16

To have a look at the table definition use describe command as shown below:

desc customer_details;

The output will be as follows:

```
mysql> desc customer_details;
+------------------+--------------+------+-----+---------+----------------+
| Field            | Type         | Null | Key | Default | Extra          |
+------------------+--------------+------+-----+---------+----------------+
| customer_ID      | smallint     | NO   | PRI | NULL    | auto_increment |
| customer_FN      | varchar(35)  | NO   |     | NULL    |                |
| customer_SN      | varchar(35)  | NO   |     | NULL    |                |
| customer_contact | bigint       | NO   |     | NULL    |                |
| email_id         | varchar(255) | NO   |     | NULL    |                |
+------------------+--------------+------+-----+---------+----------------+
5 rows in set (0.03 sec)
```

Figure 1.17

We will now create another table for maintaining customer login data to give you clarity on few more concepts. We will be following the same steps:

Step1: Defining the fields:

- **login_ID:** This field should be unique identification number. It should be n integer and should auto increment.
- **username:** This field will be a varchar field to store student's first name. Cannot be null.
- **password:**This field will be a varchar field to store student's first name. Cannot be null.
- **customer_ID:** Foreign key to map parents with the child. customer_ID is the primary key in the customer_details table and this field is used as foreign key here so that any customer's record can be easily retrieved.

Right now we are keeping the table contents simple to get a better understanding of the concepts.

STEP 2: Let's create the script keeping the above information in mind.

Now, coming to customer_ID. customer_ID is a foreign key. Here is what you must know about this field. Consider this as a recap:

1. Since **customer_ID** is a foreign key.
2. It will link **customer_login** table with another table in which it exists as a primary key. In this case it is **customer_details** table.

3. Since **customer_login** table contains the foreign key, it is the child table and the table containing **customer_ID** as primary key i.e. **customer_details** becomes the parent table.

The format for defining a foreign key is:

FOREIGN KEY (customer_ID) REFERENCES customer_details(customer_ID)

Notice the table definition given below. We want one customer to have only one login details so, we have define **customer_id** as unique here. So, that there are no duplicate entries for one customer in this table.

So, writing the CREATE statement should be easy:

```
CREATE TABLE customer_login(
login_ID smallint NOT NULL AUTO_INCREMENT,
username varchar(35) NOT NULL,
password varchar(35) NOT NULL,
customer_ID smallint NOT NULL UNIQUE,
PRIMARY KEY (login_ID),
FOREIGN KEY (customer_ID) REFERENCES customer_details(customer_ID));
```

Step3: Login to the database and give the create command.

```
mysql> CREATE TABLE customer_login(
    -> login_ID smallint NOT NULL AUTO_INCREMENT,
    -> username varchar(35) NOT NULL,
    -> password varchar(35) NOT NULL,
    -> customer_ID smallint NOT NULL UNIQUE,
    -> PRIMARY KEY (login_ID),
    -> FOREIGN KEY (customer_ID) REFERENCES customer_details(customer_ID));
Query OK, 0 rows affected (0.03 sec)
```

Figure 1.18

Check table using:

desc customer_login;

```
mysql> desc customer_login;
+-------------+-------------+------+-----+---------+----------------+
| Field       | Type        | Null | Key | Default | Extra          |
+-------------+-------------+------+-----+---------+----------------+
| login_ID    | smallint    | NO   | PRI | NULL    | auto_increment |
| username    | varchar(35) | NO   |     | NULL    |                |
| password    | varchar(35) | NO   |     | NULL    |                |
| customer_ID | smallint    | NO   | UNI | NULL    |                |
+-------------+-------------+------+-----+---------+----------------+
4 rows in set (0.00 sec)
```

Figure 1.19

Look at the table description, the key value for customer_ID is unique. This means that each customer has only one customer_ID and one customer_ID can be assigned only one login. If we had not defined the foreign key as unique then the table description would have looked as follows:

```
mysql> desc customer_login;
+-------------+-------------+------+-----+---------+----------------+
| Field       | Type        | Null | Key | Default | Extra          |
+-------------+-------------+------+-----+---------+----------------+
| login_ID    | smallint    | NO   | PRI | NULL    | auto_increment |
| username    | varchar(35) | NO   |     | NULL    |                |
| password    | varchar(35) | NO   |     | NULL    |                |
| customer_ID | smallint    | NO   | MUL | NULL    |                |
+-------------+-------------+------+-----+---------+----------------+
4 rows in set (0.01 sec)
```

Figure 1.20

With this you are now ready to insert data into the tables.

1.9 Using 'INSERT' Statement for Populating Database

In this section we will insert records into the database so that we are able to use SQL queries. The data can be populated in a table with the help of 'INSERT' statement.

```
INSERT INTO table_name
(column1, column2, ... )
VALUES
(value1, value2, ... )
```

Now, let's have a look at the first table i.e., customer_details, we now try to get right values for all the fields.

```
Command Prompt - mysql -u meenu -p
Oracle is a registered trademark of Oracle Corporation and/or its
affiliates. Other names may be trademarks of their respective
owners.

Type 'help;' or '\h' for help. Type '\c' to clear the current input statement.

mysql> use my_first_database;
Database changed
mysql> show tables;
+-----------------------------+
| Tables_in_my_first_database |
+-----------------------------+
| customer_details            |
| customer_login              |
+-----------------------------+
2 rows in set (0.01 sec)

mysql> desc customer_details;
+------------------+--------------+------+-----+---------+----------------+
| Field            | Type         | Null | Key | Default | Extra          |
+------------------+--------------+------+-----+---------+----------------+
| customer_ID      | smallint     | NO   | PRI | NULL    | auto_increment |
| customer_FN      | varchar(35)  | NO   |     | NULL    |                |
| customer_SN      | varchar(35)  | NO   |     | NULL    |                |
| customer_contact | bigint       | NO   |     | NULL    |                |
| email_id         | varchar(255) | NO   |     | NULL    |                |
+------------------+--------------+------+-----+---------+----------------+
5 rows in set (0.01 sec)

mysql>
```

Figure 1.21

It is mandatory to provide values for fields that are not allowed to take not null values. In customer_details table it is mandatory to provide all the values.

Note that, the Primary Key for this table is customer_ID. It is an auto increment key. Since it is a customer ID, we would like to have all equal no. of digits in all the ID's. We have not set the starting value while creating the table. Let's set the first entry of the table to '10000' and from there onwards it will auto increment. We did not mention this in our table definition but we can alter the definition now. This can be achieved with the help of keyword 'ALTER'. Follow the steps given below:

Step 1: Login to database

1. `start the command prompt.`
2. `Type>mysql -u meenu -p`
3. `Enter password bpb`
4. `Type> use my_first_database;`

Step 2: Give the ALTER command for auto incredement primary key.

1. ALTER TABLE customer_details AUTO_INCREMENT=10000;
2. Hit 'Enter' key.

If all is ok then the following message will be displayed:

```
mysql> ALTER TABLE customer_details AUTO_INCREMENT=10000;
Query OK, 0 rows affected (0.06 sec)
Records: 0  Duplicates: 0  Warnings: 0
```

Figure 1.22

Now we start inserting records.

For the first record customer_id is already set to10000. Let's feed in values for rest of the field as shown below:

`customer_FN:Eric`

`customer_SN:Jackson`

`customer_contact:9898983434`

`email_id:ericjackson@yahoo.com`

So, we can insert data in the table as follows

INSERT into customer_details(customer_FN, customer_SN, customer_contact, email_id) VALUES('Eric', 'Jackson','9898983434','ericjackson@yahoo.com');

If the query is executed correctly the following message will be displayed :

Query OK, 1 row affected

If you want to see the data in the table, type the following statement in the command prompt:

Select * from customer_details;

We will learn about the SELECT statement in next chapter.

The output for this command will be as follows:

```
mysql> INSERT into customer_details(customer_FN, customer_SN, customer_contact, email) VALUES('Eric', 'Jackson','9898983
434','ericjackson@yahoo.com' );
ERROR 1054 (42S22): Unknown column 'email' in 'field list'
mysql> INSERT into customer_details(customer_FN, customer_SN, customer_contact, email_id) VALUES('Eric', 'Jackson','9898
983434','ericjackson@yahoo.com' );
Query OK, 1 row affected (0.01 sec)

mysql> select * from customer_details;
+-------------+-------------+-------------+------------------+-----------------------+
| customer_ID | customer_FN | customer_SN | customer_contact | email_id              |
+-------------+-------------+-------------+------------------+-----------------------+
|       10000 | Eric        | Jackson     |       9898983434 | ericjackson@yahoo.com |
+-------------+-------------+-------------+------------------+-----------------------+
1 row in set (0.00 sec)
```

Figure 1.23

Let's add two more records to see :

INSERT into customer_details(customer_FN, customer_SN, customer_contact, email_id) VALUES('George ', 'Mathews','9089376511','gm@yahoo.com');

INSERT into customer_details(customer_FN, customer_SN, customer_contact, email_id) VALUES('Riya', 'Pathak','9089346521','riya.patha2010@gmail.com');

INSERT into customer_details(customer_FN, customer_SN, customer_contact, email_id) VALUES('Aslam', 'Khan','9602346833','riya.patha2010@gmail.com');

```
mysql> INSERT into customer_details(customer_FN, customer_SN, customer_contact, email_id) VALUES('George ', ' Mathews','9089376511','gm@yahoo.com' );
Query OK, 1 row affected (0.01 sec)

mysql> INSERT into customer_details(customer_FN, customer_SN, customer_contact, email_id) VALUES('Riya', 'Pathak','9089346521','riya.patha2010@gmail.com' );
Query OK, 1 row affected (0.01 sec)

mysql> INSERT into customer_details(customer_FN, customer_SN, customer_contact, email_id) VALUES('Aslam', 'Khan','9602346833','riya.patha2010@gmail.com' );
Query OK, 1 row affected (0.01 sec)
```

Figure 1.24

You can now see how customer_ID is auto incrementing. With every record entry, the customer_ID increments by 1.

```
mysql> select * from customer_details;
+-------------+-------------+-------------+------------------+--------------------------+
| customer_ID | customer_FN | customer_SN | customer_contact | email_id                 |
+-------------+-------------+-------------+------------------+--------------------------+
|       10000 | Eric        | Jackson     |       9898983434 | ericjackson@yahoo.com    |
|       10001 | George      |  Mathews    |       9089376511 | gm@yahoo.com             |
|       10002 | Riya        | Pathak      |       9089346521 | riya.patha2010@gmail.com |
|       10003 | Aslam       | Khan        |       9602346833 | riya.patha2010@gmail.com |
+-------------+-------------+-------------+------------------+--------------------------+
4 rows in set (0.00 sec)
```

Figure 1.25

Now, let's come to populating the customer_login table.

Let's have a look at the table description once again:

```
mysql> desc customer_login;
+-------------+-------------+------+-----+---------+----------------+
| Field       | Type        | Null | Key | Default | Extra          |
+-------------+-------------+------+-----+---------+----------------+
| login_ID    | smallint    | NO   | PRI | NULL    | auto_increment |
| username    | varchar(35) | NO   |     | NULL    |                |
| password    | varchar(35) | NO   |     | NULL    |                |
| customer_ID | smallint    | NO   | MUL | NULL    |                |
+-------------+-------------+------+-----+---------+----------------+
4 rows in set (0.01 sec)
```

Figure 1.26

INSERT into customer_login(login_ID, username, password, customer_ID) VALUES('1', 'ejack','ejack@123','10000');

In this case we did not alter the table definition to start auto increment from a specific number, we have directly given a number. Now, while entering the next record let's not give a value for login_ID.

INSERT into customer_login(username, password, customer_ID)VALUES('gmathews', georgeforever','10001');

```
mysql> select * from customer_login;
+----------+----------+----------------+-------------+
| login_ID | username | password       | customer_ID |
+----------+----------+----------------+-------------+
|        1 | ejack    | ejack@123      |       10000 |
|        2 | gmathews | georgeforever  |       10001 |
+----------+----------+----------------+-------------+
2 rows in set (0.00 sec)
```

Figure 1.27

Let's try to create another record for customer_ID 10001

INSERT into customer_login(login_ID, username, password, customer_ID) VALUES('6', 'ripa','riya123','10003');

```
mysql> INSERT into customer_login(login_ID, username, password, customer_ID) VALUES('6', 'ripa','riya123','10001' );
ERROR 1062 (23000): Duplicate entry '10001' for key 'customer_login.customer_ID'
```

Figure 1.28

Let's insert one more value.

INSERT into customer_login(username, password, customer_ID) VALUES('akhan','ak@2021','10002');

```
mysql> select * from customer_login;
+----------+----------+----------------+-------------+
| login_ID | username | password       | customer_ID |
+----------+----------+----------------+-------------+
|        1 | ejack    | ejack@123      |       10000 |
|        2 | gmathews | georgeforever  |       10001 |
|        6 | ripa     | riya123        |       10003 |
|        7 | akhan    | ak@2021        |       10002 |
+----------+----------+----------------+-------------+
4 rows in set (0.00 sec)
```

Figure 1.29

Look at the login_ID values:

For the first and the third value, login_ID value of 1 an 6 was provided but for the second and fourth value since the login_ID value was not provided, it was autoincremented by 1 and assigned to the new set of data.

Now, let's try to explore what happens if we try to insert values for customer_id that does not exist in the customer_details table.

INSERT into customer_login(username, password, customer_ID) VALUES('azad','livelife','10004');

```
mysql> INSERT into customer_login(username, password, customer_ID) VALUES('azad','livelife','10004' );
ERROR 1452 (23000): Cannot add or update a child row: a foreign key constraint fails (`my_first_database`.`customer_login`, CONSTRAINT `customer_login_ibfk_1` FOREIGN KEY (`customer_ID`) REFERENCES `customer_details` (`customer_ID`))
mysql>
```

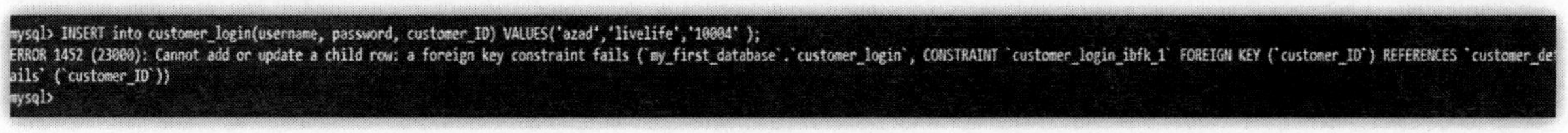

Figure 1.30

Look at the above statement carefully. The customer_ID of '10004'. However, this ID does not exists in the parent customer_details table. customer_ID is the primary key in the customer_details table and no records show **customer_ID** having a value of **'10004'** value. So, when you pass on the above INSERT statement following error will be shown:

ERROR 1452 (23000): Cannot add or update a child row: a foreign key constraint fails (`my_first_database`.`customer_login`, CONSTRAINT `customer_login_ibfk_1` FOREIGN KEY (`customer_ID`) REFERENCES `customer_details` (`customer_ID`))

Working with Queries

In this chapter, you will cover:

In the last chapter you have often used the SELECT statement to check records in the database. However, there is a lot more that can be achieved with the help of SELECT statement and this is what we are going to start this chapter with. Once you understand the concept of SELECT clause you will learn about other clauses that help in refining the SQL query.

2.1 The Query Clauses

You have used 'SELECT' clause several times in the last chapter to check table description and how records are stored the database. SELECT is just one of the 6 clauses. The full list of query clauses are given below:

- SELECT
- FROM
- WHERE
- GROUP BY
- HAVING
- ORDER BY

In this chapter we will learn about these Query clauses and how they can be used.

2.2 Determine Columns to Include with SELECT Clause

The SELECT clause is used to Select what data you want to retrieve from the database. The output is a result-set and the data is displayed in a result table. The interesting thing is that SELECT clause appears in the beginning of the query but it is the last clause to be evaluated by the database server before displaying the result set.

Syntax for SELECT clause

SELECT column_name1, column_name2, ...

FROM table_name;

If you want to select all the data from the table then write:

SELECT * FROM table_name;

So, when we wish to view the complete content of family_data we write:

SELECT * FROM customer_details;

The result is:

```
mysql> select * from customer_details;
+-------------+-------------+-------------+------------------+--------------------------+
| customer_ID | customer_FN | customer_SN | customer_contact | email_id                 |
+-------------+-------------+-------------+------------------+--------------------------+
|       10000 | Eric        | Jackson     |       9898983434 | ericjackson@yahoo.com    |
|       10001 | George      |  Mathews    |       9089376511 | gm@yahoo.com             |
|       10002 | Riya        | Pathak      |       9089346521 | riya.patha2010@gmail.com |
|       10003 | Aslam       | Khan        |       9602346833 | riya.patha2010@gmail.com |
+-------------+-------------+-------------+------------------+--------------------------+
4 rows in set (0.00 sec)
```

Figure 2.1

Now suppose we just want to send emails to all our customers, for that we want to select only three fields: Family ID number, customer's first name and email id. For that you need not display contents of all the columns of the table. For this we can make slight changes in the query and replace * with the column names i.e.,customer_ID, customer_FN and email_id. Look at the modified query given below:

SELECT customer_id, customer_FN, email_id FROM customer_details;

The result set will be as shown below:

```
mysql> SELECT customer_id, customer_FN, email_id  FROM customer_details;
+-------------+-------------+--------------------------+
| customer_id | customer_FN | email_id                 |
+-------------+-------------+--------------------------+
|       10000 | Eric        | ericjackson@yahoo.com    |
|       10001 | George      | gm@yahoo.com             |
|       10002 | Riya        | riya.patha2010@gmail.com |
|       10003 | Aslam       | riya.patha2010@gmail.com |
+-------------+-------------+--------------------------+
4 rows in set (0.00 sec)
```

Figure 2.2

SELECT clause can also be used along with built-in functions.

SELECT version(), user(), database();

```
mysql> SELECT version(), user(), database();
+-----------+-----------------+-------------------+
| version() | user()          | database()        |
+-----------+-----------------+-------------------+
| 8.0.25    | meenu@localhost | my_first_database |
+-----------+-----------------+-------------------+
1 row in set (0.00 sec)
```

Figure 2.3

2.2 Identify Tables using FROM clause

The **SELECT** clause is the first clause to be written in a query but it is the last one to be executed. The reason behind this is because in order to generate the result set it is important to first understand the conditions that are applied. It is therefore important to understand the importance of **FROM** clause at this point.

The **FROM** clause is mandatory clause in a **SELECT** statement. This clause indicates the names of the tables used to generate result.

So, SELECT and FROM clause work together to generate a result set. The SELECT statement tells which column data should be retrieved and the FROM clause indicates the table where the records would be available.

So, here are some examples.

First we will go with what we know best i.e., retrieving all data from **customer_details** table.

SELECT * FROM customer_details;

```
mysql> select * from customer_details;
+-------------+-------------+-------------+------------------+---------------------------+
| customer_ID | customer_FN | customer_SN | customer_contact | email_id                  |
+-------------+-------------+-------------+------------------+---------------------------+
|       10000 | Eric        | Jackson     |       9898983434 | ericjackson@yahoo.com     |
|       10001 | George      |  Mathews    |       9089376511 | gm@yahoo.com              |
|       10002 | Riya        | Pathak      |       9089346521 | riya.patha2010@gmail.com  |
|       10003 | Aslam       | Khan        |       9602346833 | riya.patha2010@gmail.com  |
+-------------+-------------+-------------+------------------+---------------------------+
4 rows in set (0.00 sec)
```

Figure 2.4

Now, we will retrieve selected columns(customer_FN, customer_SN and customer_contact) from customer_details table.

```
mysql> select customer_FN, customer_SN, customer_contact from customer_details;
+-------------+-------------+------------------+
| customer_FN | customer_SN | customer_contact |
+-------------+-------------+------------------+
| Eric        | Jackson     |       9898983434 |
| George      |  Mathews    |       9089376511 |
| Riya        | Pathak      |       9089346521 |
| Aslam       | Khan        |       9602346833 |
+-------------+-------------+------------------+
4 rows in set (0.00 sec)
```

Figure 2.5

We will now include user defined function calls in SELECT- FROM statement. Suppose, we want to see customer's first name and last name in the result set. The query for this will be as follows:

SELECT UPPER (customer_FN),UPPER(customer_SN), customer_contact FROMcustomer_details;

```
mysql> SELECT UPPER(customer_FN),UPPER( customer_SN), customer_contact FROM customer_details;
+--------------------+---------------------+------------------+
| UPPER(customer_FN) | UPPER( customer_SN) | customer_contact |
+--------------------+---------------------+------------------+
| ERIC               | JACKSON             |       9898983434 |
| GEORGE             |  MATHEWS            |       9089376511 |
| RIYA               | PATHAK              |       9089346521 |
| ASLAM              | KHAN                |       9602346833 |
+--------------------+---------------------+------------------+
4 rows in set (0.00 sec)
```

Figure 2.6

So as you can see in this table all the names are shown in upper case characters, also note the names of the columns - UPPER(student_FN) and UPPER(student_SN) .

You can also add column alias in the statement. For example instead of customer_FN and customer_SN you may want to see column names as FIRST_NAME and SURNAME. These are not the column names that we have defined, rather these are temporary name given to columns so that the result set is easy to understand and appears to be more readable. Alias name remains only for the duration of the query.

The syntax for alias name is as follows:

SELECT column_name AS alias_name

FROM table_name;

So, we can now rewrite the query as follows:

```
SELECTcustomer_ID,
UPPER(customer_FN) AS FIRST_NAME,
UPPER(customer_SN) AS SURNAME
 from customer_details;
```

Now, with this query the same result set will be displayed in more readable manner.

```
mysql> SELECT customer_ID,
    ->  UPPER(customer_FN) AS FIRST_NAME,
    -> UPPER( customer_SN) AS SURNAME
    ->  from customer_details;
+-------------+------------+----------+
| customer_ID | FIRST_NAME | SURNAME  |
+-------------+------------+----------+
|       10000 | ERIC       | JACKSON  |
|       10001 | GEORGE     |  MATHEWS |
|       10002 | RIYA       | PATHAK   |
|       10003 | ASLAM      | KHAN     |
+-------------+------------+----------+
4 rows in set (0.00 sec)
```

Figure 2.7

One interesting keyword that is often used with **SELECT** clause is **DISTINCT** keyword. To understand this clause we have created a table **customer_order** and inserted values in it as shown in the box below:

The customer_order table keeps an account of orders placed by the customers, the amount of the order, the name of the employee who took the order, the date or order and the date of supplying order. Try to create this table as an exercise.

```
CREATE TABLE customer_order (
order_ID smallint NOT NULL AUTO_INCREMENT,
customer_ID smallint NOT NULL,
login_ID smallint NOT NULL,
employee_name varchar(35) NOT NULL,
order_amount smallint NOT NULL,
customer_SN varchar(35) NOT NULL,
order_date date NOT NULL,
```

```
supply_date date NOT NULL,
    PRIMARY KEY (order_ID),
    FOREIGN KEY (customer_ID) REFERENCES customer_details(customer_ID),
    FOREIGN KEY (login_ID) REFERENCES customer_login(login_ID)
);
Insert into customer_order(order_ID,customer_ID,login_ID,employee_name,order_
amount,customer_SN,order_date,supply_date) values ('121','10000','1','Abhi-
manyu','250','Jackson','2020-01-03','2020-01-03');
Insert into customer_order(customer_ID,login_ID,employee_name,order_amount,-
customer_SN,order_date,supply_date) values ('10000','1','Abhimanyu','500','Jack-
son','2020-01-07','2020-01-07');
Insert into customer_order(customer_ID,login_ID,employee_name,order_amount,-
customer_SN,order_date,supply_date) values ('10002','7','Abhimanyu','250','Path
ak','2020-02-02','2020-02-02');
Insert into customer_order(customer_ID,login_ID,employee_name,order_amount,-
customer_SN,order_date,supply_date) values ('10002','7','Abhimanyu','65','Path
ak','2020-02-03','2020-02-03');
Insert into customer_order(customer_ID,login_ID,employee_name,order_amount,-
customer_SN,order_date,supply_date) values ('10001','2','Swamy','159','Geor
ge','2020-04-03','2020-04-03');
Insert into customer_order(customer_ID,login_ID,employee_name,order_amount,-
customer_SN,order_date,supply_date) values ('10000','1','Radha','1250','Jack-
son','2020-03-04','2020-03-04');
Insert into customer_order(customer_ID,login_ID,employee_name,order_amount,-
customer_SN,order_date,supply_date) values ('10000','1','Radha','2503','Jack-
son','2020-03-06','2020-03-06');
Insert into customer_order(customer_ID,login_ID,employee_name,order_amount,-
customer_SN,order_date,supply_date) values ('10002','7','Abhimanyu','550','Path
ak','2020-04-05','2020-04-05');
Insert into
customer_order(customer_ID,login_ID,employee_name,order_amount,cus-
tomer_SN,order_date,supply_date) values ('10001','2','Swamy','159','Geor
ge','2020-04-06','2020-04-06');
Insert into
```

```
customer_order(customer_ID,login_ID,employee_name,order_amount,custom-
er_SN,order_date,supply_date) values ('10000','1','Abhimanyu','138','Jack-
son','2020-05-06','2020-05-08');
Insert into customer_order(customer_ID,login_ID,employee_name,order_amount,-
customer_SN,order_date,supply_date) values ('10001','2','Abhimanyu','2000','Geor
ge','2020-06-02','2020-06-02');
Insert into customer_order(customer_ID,login_ID,employee_name,order_amount,-
customer_SN,order_date,supply_date) values ('10000','1','Abhimanyu','700','Jack-
son','2020-06-03','2020-06-03');
Insert into customer_order(customer_ID,login_ID,employee_name,order_amount,-
customer_SN,order_date,supply_date) values ('10002','7','Abhimanyu','150','Path
ak','2020-07-13','2020-07-13');
Insert into customer_order(customer_ID,login_ID,employee_name,order_amount,-
customer_SN,order_date,supply_date) values ('10001','2','Swamy','630','Geor
ge','2020-07-23','2020-07-23');
Insert into
customer_order(customer_ID,login_ID,employee_name,order_amount,cus-
tomer_SN,order_date,supply_date) values ('10000','1','Radha','180','Jack-
son','2020-08-10','2020-08-10');
Insert into customer_order(customer_ID,login_ID,employee_name,order_amount,-
customer_SN,order_date,supply_date) values ('10003','6','Swamy','250','Kh
an','2020-08-11','2020-08-11');
Insert into customer_order(customer_ID,login_ID,employee_name,order_amount,-
customer_SN,order_date,supply_date) values ('10000','1','Abhimanyu','5000','Jack-
son','2020-09-09','2020-09-09');
Insert into customer_order(customer_ID,login_ID,employee_name,order_
amount,customer_SN,order_date,supply_date) values ('10002','7','Rad-
ha','200','Pathak','2020-10-27','2020-10-29');
Insert into customer_order(customer_ID,login_ID,employee_name,order_amount,-
customer_SN,order_date,supply_date) values ('10000','1','Abhimanyu','3250','Jack-
son','2020-11-03','2020-11-03');
Insert into customer_order(customer_ID,login_ID,employee_name,order_amount,-
customer_SN,order_date,supply_date) values ('10000','1','swamy','1350','Jack-
son','2020-12-02','2020-12-03');
```

order_ID	customer_ID	login_ID	employee_name	order_amount	customer_SN	order_date	supply_date
121	10000	1	Abhimanyu	250	Jackson	2020-01-03	2020-01-03
122	10000	1	Abhimanyu	500	Jackson	2020-01-07	2020-01-07
123	10002	7	Abhimanyu	250	Pathak	2020-02-02	2020-02-02
124	10002	7	Abhimanyu	65	Pathak	2020-02-03	2020-02-03
125	10001	2	Swamy	159	George	2020-04-03	2020-04-03
126	10000	1	Radha	1250	Jackson	2020-03-04	2020-03-04
127	10000	1	Radha	2503	Jackson	2020-03-06	2020-03-06
128	10002	7	Abhimanyu	550	Pathak	2020-04-05	2020-04-05
129	10001	2	Swamy	159	George	2020-04-06	2020-04-06
130	10003	6	Abhimanyu	4000	Khan	2020-05-03	2020-05-03
131	10000	1	Abhimanyu	138	Jackson	2020-05-06	2020-05-08
132	10001	2	Abhimanyu	2000	George	2020-06-02	2020-06-02
133	10000	1	Abhimanyu	700	Jackson	2020-06-03	2020-06-03
134	10002	7	Abhimanyu	150	Pathak	2020-07-13	2020-07-13
135	10001	2	Swamy	630	George	2020-07-23	2020-07-23
136	10000	1	Radha	180	Jackson	2020-08-10	2020-08-10
137	10003	6	Swamy	250	Khan	2020-08-11	2020-08-11
138	10000	1	Abhimanyu	5000	Jackson	2020-09-09	2020-09-09
139	10002	7	Radha	200	Pathak	2020-10-27	2020-10-29
140	10000	1	Abhimanyu	3250	Jackson	2020-11-03	2020-11-03
141	10000	1	swamy	1350	Jackson	2020-12-02	2020-12-03

21 rows in set (0.00 sec)

Figure 2.8

SELECT DISTINCT statement is used when we do not any repeated values to be displayed and our interest is only in the distinct values. For example, try out the following statement:

SELECT customer_id FROM customer_order;

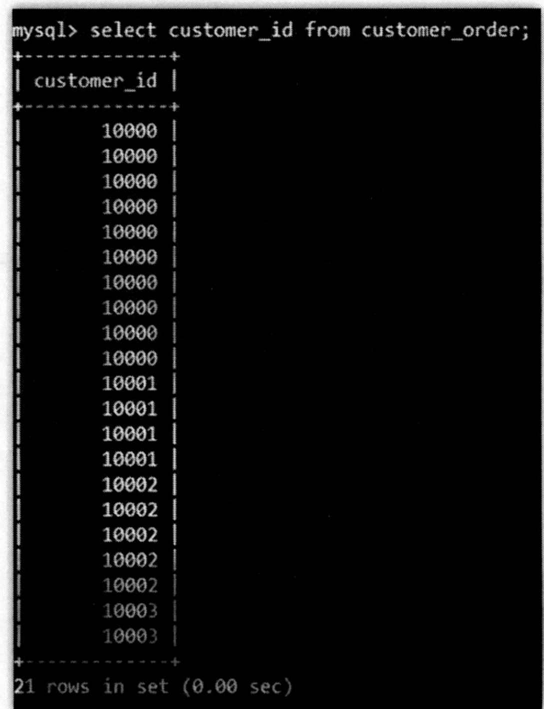

```
mysql> select customer_id from customer_order;
+-------------+
| customer_id |
+-------------+
|       10000 |
|       10000 |
|       10000 |
|       10000 |
|       10000 |
|       10000 |
|       10000 |
|       10000 |
|       10000 |
|       10000 |
|       10001 |
|       10001 |
|       10001 |
|       10001 |
|       10002 |
|       10002 |
|       10002 |
|       10002 |
|       10002 |
|       10003 |
|       10003 |
+-------------+
21 rows in set (0.00 sec)
```

Figure 2.9

The result set is very confusing, the **customer_id** is repeating and we want to know distinctly which all customers have placed an order for our services.

Now, add **DISTINCT** keyword to the above statement.

SELECT DISTINCT customer_id FROM customer_order;

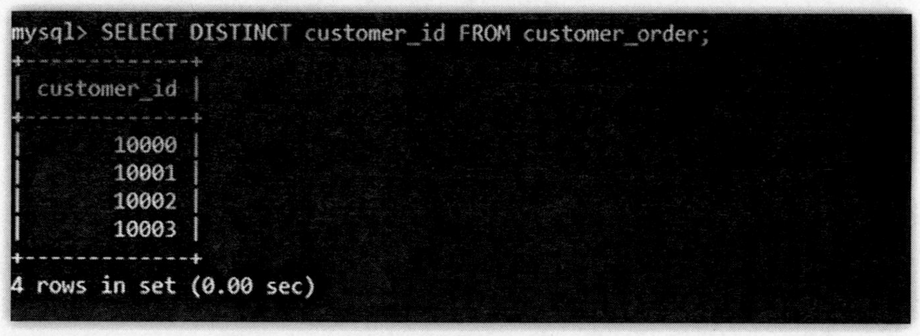

```
mysql> SELECT DISTINCT customer_id FROM customer_order;
+-------------+
| customer_id |
+-------------+
|       10000 |
|       10001 |
|       10002 |
|       10003 |
+-------------+
4 rows in set (0.00 sec)
```

Figure 2.10

Similarly, suppose a social networking site wants to know which all users have been actively playing various games it has to offer. All that needs to be done is the usage of DISTINCT clause on the table that stores information about games and its users and from data of millions of users the site will be able to retrieve the names of all the users who have used their games..

2.4 Filter Data using WHERE CLAUSE

When we are trying to retrieve data from any table we may not be interested in getting all the rows from the table. If you want to know the email id of customer having customer_FN = 'Eric' and customer_SN = 'Jackson', then you need not retrieve all the details of the table. This is where the WHERE clause is needed. The WHERE clause helps in filtering records. The syntax for using WHERE clause is as follows:

SELECT column_name1, column_name2, ...

FROM table_name

WHERE condition;

So, we can write:

SELECT email_id

FROM customer_details

WHERE customer_FN='Eric' AND customer_SN='Jackson';

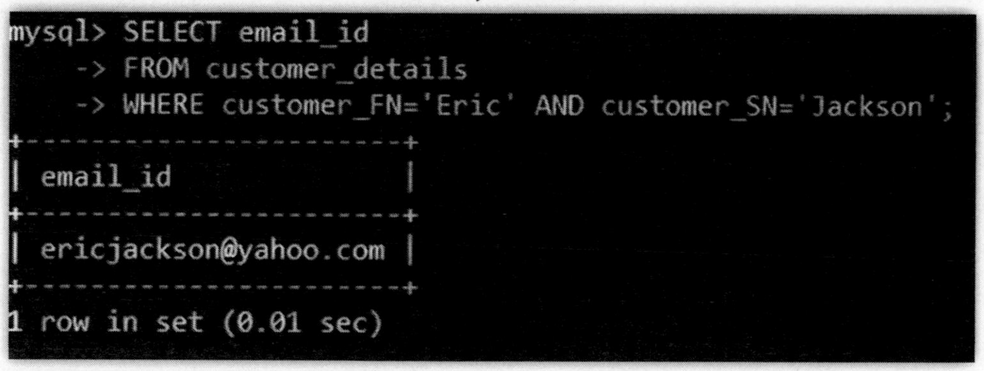

```
mysql> SELECT email_id
    -> FROM customer_details
    -> WHERE customer_FN='Eric' AND customer_SN='Jackson';
+-----------------------+
| email_id              |
+-----------------------+
| ericjackson@yahoo.com |
+-----------------------+
1 row in set (0.01 sec)
```

Figure 2.11

The above query tells us the email_ID assigned to Eric Jackson. Now we look for the login details for Eric Jackson. Remember, Eric Jackson is a common name and we should search on the basis of ID as it is unique.

Let us first retrieve **customer_id** of Eric Jackson from **customer_details**.

SELECT customer_ID FROM customer_details WHERE customer_FN = 'Eric'and customer_SN = 'Jackson';

```
mysql> SELECT customer_ID FROM customer_details WHERE customer_FN = 'Eric'and customer_SN = 'Jackson';
+-------------+
| customer_ID |
+-------------+
|       10000 |
+-------------+
1 row in set (0.00 sec)
```

Figure 2.12

We know the customer_ID of Eric Jackson is 10000. With this information we can now search for login information in the customer_login table.

SELECT username, password FROM customer_login WHERE customer_ID = '10000';

```
mysql> SELECT username, password FROM customer_login WHERE customer_ID = '10000';
+----------+-----------+
| username | password  |
+----------+-----------+
| ejack    | ejack@123 |
+----------+-----------+
1 row in set (0.01 sec)
```

Figure 2.13

So, the username for Eric Jackson is ejack and password is ejack@123.

In the above queries you may have noticed a new word **AND**. **AND** is used when there is more than one condition for filtering. In our data base there is only one student having the first name 'Eric' and we have created only four rows of data. So, we could have easily conducted a search using the first name. However, keeping the real scenario in mind, a website can have thousands of customers and there can be more than one customer having the First name Eric. So, it makes more sense to search using the customer's first name and the surname. Hence, the usage of AND is required to look for customer_ID on the basis of customer_FN and customer_SN.

So, AND operator is required when you want both the conditions to be true. Like AND operator there is another operator known as the 'OR' operator which is used for multiple conditions. However, OR is used if you want to any one of the multiple conditions to be true.

So, if you want to know the customer_ID and first name for customers having family_ID 10000 or customer_SN is Jackson.

SELECT customer_ID, customer_FN FROM customer_details

WHERE customer_ID='10000'

OR customer_SN='Jackson';

The output will be as follows:

```
mysql> SELECT customer_ID, customer_FN FROM customer_details
    -> WHERE customer_ID='10000'
    -> OR customer_SN='Jackson';
+-------------+-------------+
| customer_ID | customer_FN |
+-------------+-------------+
|       10000 | Eric        |
+-------------+-------------+
1 row in set (0.00 sec)
```

Figure 2.14

There is another operator called the **NOT** operator. As the name implies the NOT operator will display the result if the condition given is not true. Look at the following statement:
SELECT customer_ID, customer_FN FROM customer_details
WHERE NOT customer_ID = '10000';
Following result will be displayed:

```
mysql> SELECT customer_ID, customer_FN FROM customer_details
    -> WHERE  NOT customer_ID  = '10000';
+-------------+-------------+
| customer_ID | customer_FN |
+-------------+-------------+
|       10001 | George      |
|       10002 | Riya        |
|       10003 | Aslam       |
+-------------+-------------+
3 rows in set (0.00 sec)
```

Figure 2.15

2.5 Group rows together by common column values using GROUP BY CLAUSE

A SELECT statement can have a GROUP BY clause when there is a need to group the results on the basis of one or more columns. GROUP BY clause is often used when result has to be retrieved from multiple tables.

The syntax for GROUP BY clause is:

```
SELECT column_name1, column_name2..
FROM table_name
WHERE condition
GROUP BY column_names
```

```
mysql> select employee_name from customer_order group by employee_name;
+---------------+
| employee_name |
+---------------+
| Abhimanyu     |
| Swamy         |
| Radha         |
+---------------+
3 rows in set (0.00 sec)
```

Figure 2.16

The above results are grouped as per employee_name. Now let's see how many order Abhimanyu has taken.

```
mysql> select customer_id from customer_order where employee_name = 'Abhimanyu';
+-------------+
| customer_id |
+-------------+
|       10000 |
|       10000 |
|       10002 |
|       10002 |
|       10002 |
|       10003 |
|       10000 |
|       10001 |
|       10000 |
|       10002 |
|       10000 |
|       10000 |
+-------------+
12 rows in set (0.00 sec)
```

Figure 2.17

If we just wanted to know the count we could have simply said:

```
mysql> SELECT count('customer_id'), employee_name FROM customer_order GROUP BY employee_name;
+----------------------+---------------+
| count('customer_id') | employee_name |
+----------------------+---------------+
|                   12 | Abhimanyu     |
|                    5 | Swamy         |
|                    4 | Radha         |
+----------------------+---------------+
3 rows in set (0.00 sec)
```

Figure 2.18

The following example shows how many customer orders had an amount greater than 1000.

```
mysql> select * from customer_order where order_amount >1000 group by order_id;
+----------+-------------+----------+---------------+--------------+-------------+------------+-------------+
| order_ID | customer_ID | login_ID | employee_name | order_amount | customer_SN | order_date | supply_date |
+----------+-------------+----------+---------------+--------------+-------------+------------+-------------+
|      126 |       10000 |        1 | Radha         |         1250 | Jackson     | 2020-03-04 | 2020-03-04  |
|      127 |       10000 |        1 | Radha         |         2503 | Jackson     | 2020-03-06 | 2020-03-06  |
|      130 |       10003 |        6 | Abhimanyu     |         4000 | Khan        | 2020-05-03 | 2020-05-03  |
|      132 |       10001 |        2 | Abhimanyu     |         2000 | George      | 2020-06-02 | 2020-06-02  |
|      138 |       10000 |        1 | Abhimanyu     |         5000 | Jackson     | 2020-09-09 | 2020-09-09  |
|      140 |       10000 |        1 | Abhimanyu     |         3250 | Jackson     | 2020-11-03 | 2020-11-03  |
|      141 |       10000 |        1 | swamy         |         1350 | Jackson     | 2020-12-02 | 2020-12-03  |
+----------+-------------+----------+---------------+--------------+-------------+------------+-------------+
7 rows in set (0.00 sec)
```

Figure 2.19

2.6 Filter Unwanted Information using HAVING clause with GROUP BY clause

Having clause can be used along with **GROUP BY** clause to define a condition that will filter the unwanted information.

The syntax for HAVING clause is as follows:

```
SELECT column_name1, column_name2..
FROM table_name
GROUP BY column_names
HAVING condition
```

So, if we want to find out information about purchases of more than Rs. 1000 done by **customer_id** 10000, the query will be as follows.

```
select * from customer_order where order_amount > 1000 group by order_id
having customer_id = '10000'
```

mysql> select * from customer_order where order_amount >1000 group by order_id having customer_id ='10000';

order_ID	customer_ID	login_ID	employee_name	order_amount	customer_SN	order_date	supply_date
126	10000	1	Radha	1250	Jackson	2020-03-04	2020-03-04
127	10000	1	Radha	2503	Jackson	2020-03-06	2020-03-06
138	10000	1	Abhimanyu	5000	Jackson	2020-09-09	2020-09-09
140	10000	1	Abhimanyu	3250	Jackson	2020-11-03	2020-11-03
141	10000	1	swamy	1350	Jackson	2020-12-02	2020-12-03

5 rows in set (0.00 sec)

Figure 2.20

If you want to know information about the orders of more than rs 1000 place by customer_ID 10000 and executed by employee_name Abhimanyu, then the result would be:

```
select * from customer_order where order_amount > 1000 group by order_id
having customer_id = '10000' and employee_name = 'Abhimanyu'
```

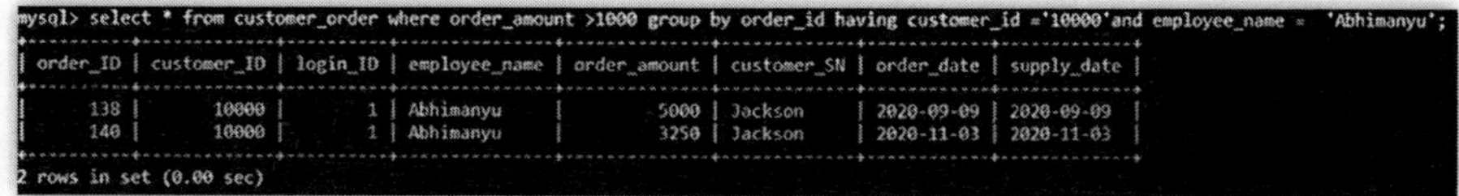

mysql> select * from customer_order where order_amount >1000 group by order_id having customer_id ='10000'and employee_name = 'Abhimanyu';

order_ID	customer_ID	login_ID	employee_name	order_amount	customer_SN	order_date	supply_date
138	10000	1	Abhimanyu	5000	Jackson	2020-09-09	2020-09-09
140	10000	1	Abhimanyu	3250	Jackson	2020-11-03	2020-11-03

2 rows in set (0.00 sec)

Figure 2.21

Sort the rows of the final result using ORDER BY CLAUSE

ORDER BY clause is used when you want the result set to display result in a certain order.

mysql> select * from customer_order order by employee_name;

order_ID	customer_ID	login_ID	employee_name	order_amount	customer_SN	order_date	supply_date
121	10000	1	Abhimanyu	250	Jackson	2020-01-03	2020-01-03
122	10000	1	Abhimanyu	500	Jackson	2020-01-07	2020-01-07
123	10002	7	Abhimanyu	250	Pathak	2020-02-02	2020-02-02
124	10002	7	Abhimanyu	65	Pathak	2020-02-03	2020-02-03
128	10002	7	Abhimanyu	550	Pathak	2020-04-05	2020-04-05
130	10003	6	Abhimanyu	4000	Khan	2020-05-03	2020-05-03
131	10000	1	Abhimanyu	138	Jackson	2020-05-06	2020-05-08
132	10001	2	Abhimanyu	2000	George	2020-06-02	2020-06-02
133	10000	1	Abhimanyu	700	Jackson	2020-06-03	2020-06-03
134	10002	7	Abhimanyu	150	Pathak	2020-07-13	2020-07-13
138	10000	1	Abhimanyu	5000	Jackson	2020-09-09	2020-09-09
140	10000	1	Abhimanyu	3250	Jackson	2020-11-03	2020-11-03
126	10000	1	Radha	1250	Jackson	2020-03-04	2020-03-04
127	10000	1	Radha	2503	Jackson	2020-03-06	2020-03-06
136	10000	1	Radha	180	Jackson	2020-08-10	2020-08-10
139	10002	7	Radha	200	Pathak	2020-10-27	2020-10-29
125	10001	2	Swamy	159	George	2020-04-03	2020-04-03
129	10001	2	Swamy	159	George	2020-04-06	2020-04-06
135	10001	2	Swamy	630	George	2020-07-23	2020-07-23
137	10003	6	Swamy	250	Khan	2020-08-11	2020-08-11
141	10000	1	swamy	1350	Jackson	2020-12-02	2020-12-03

21 rows in set (0.01 sec)

Figure 2.22

Now try this,

```
mysql> select * from customer_order order by customer_SN;
```

order_ID	customer_ID	login_ID	employee_name	order_amount	customer_SN	order_date	supply_date
125	10001	2	Swamy	159	George	2020-04-03	2020-04-03
129	10001	2	Swamy	159	George	2020-04-06	2020-04-06
132	10001	2	Abhimanyu	2000	George	2020-06-02	2020-06-02
135	10001	2	Swamy	630	George	2020-07-23	2020-07-23
121	10000	1	Abhimanyu	250	Jackson	2020-01-03	2020-01-03
122	10000	1	Abhimanyu	500	Jackson	2020-01-07	2020-01-07
126	10000	1	Radha	1250	Jackson	2020-03-04	2020-03-04
127	10000	1	Radha	2503	Jackson	2020-03-06	2020-03-06
131	10000	1	Abhimanyu	138	Jackson	2020-05-06	2020-05-08
133	10000	1	Abhimanyu	700	Jackson	2020-06-03	2020-06-03
136	10000	1	Radha	180	Jackson	2020-08-10	2020-08-10
138	10000	1	Abhimanyu	5000	Jackson	2020-09-09	2020-09-09
140	10000	1	Abhimanyu	3250	Jackson	2020-11-03	2020-11-03
141	10000	1	swamy	1350	Jackson	2020-12-02	2020-12-03
130	10003	6	Abhimanyu	4000	Khan	2020-05-03	2020-05-03
137	10003	6	Swamy	250	Khan	2020-08-11	2020-08-11
123	10002	7	Abhimanyu	250	Pathak	2020-02-02	2020-02-02
124	10002	7	Abhimanyu	65	Pathak	2020-02-03	2020-02-03
128	10002	7	Abhimanyu	550	Pathak	2020-04-05	2020-04-05
134	10002	7	Abhimanyu	150	Pathak	2020-07-13	2020-07-13
139	10002	7	Radha	200	Pathak	2020-10-27	2020-10-29

```
21 rows in set (0.00 sec)
```

Figure 2.23

To get a better understanding, try the following example in which we are trying to use order by clause along with group by clause:

Select * from customer_order where order_amount> 1000 group by order_id having customer_id = '10000' order by order_amount;

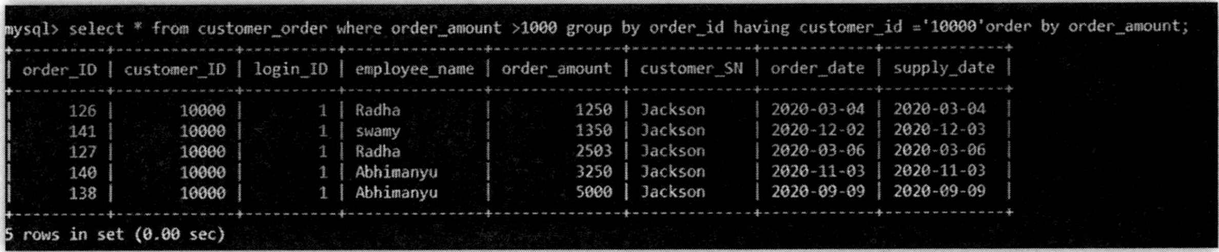

```
mysql> select * from customer_order where order_amount >1000 group by order_id having customer_id ='10000'order by order_amount;
```

order_ID	customer_ID	login_ID	employee_name	order_amount	customer_SN	order_date	supply_date
126	10000	1	Radha	1250	Jackson	2020-03-04	2020-03-04
141	10000	1	swamy	1350	Jackson	2020-12-02	2020-12-03
127	10000	1	Radha	2503	Jackson	2020-03-06	2020-03-06
140	10000	1	Abhimanyu	3250	Jackson	2020-11-03	2020-11-03
138	10000	1	Abhimanyu	5000	Jackson	2020-09-09	2020-09-09

```
5 rows in set (0.00 sec)
```

Figure 2.24

This query is used to retrieve records of customer_id '10000' which have done purchase of more than ₹ 1000. The order by clause is used to sort data based on order_amount.

2.7 Aggregate Functions

Aggregate functions can be performed on all the rows of a group. Following are the aggregate functions that can be used with all servers:

1. To get the maximum value within a set use Max() function
2. To get minimum value within a set use Min() function
3. To get average value across a set use Avg() function
4. To get sum of value across a set use Sum() function

5. To get the number of values in a set use count() function
6. Let's try out all these functions:

SELECT MAX(amount) FROM customer_orders;

```
mysql> select max(order_amount) from customer_order;
+-------------------+
| max(order_amount) |
+-------------------+
|              5000 |
+-------------------+
1 row in set (0.00 sec)
```

Figure 2.25

This displays the max order_amount in the table.

```
mysql> select order_amount from customer_order;
+--------------+
| order_amount |
+--------------+
|          250 |
|          500 |
|          250 |
|           65 |
|          159 |
|         1250 |
|         2503 |
|          550 |
|          159 |
|         4000 |
|          138 |
|         2000 |
|          700 |
|          150 |
|          630 |
|          180 |
|          250 |
|         5000 |
|          200 |
|         3250 |
|         1350 |
+--------------+
21 rows in set (0.00 sec)
```

Figure 2.26

Similarly you can use `min()`function to retrieve the minimum value of a field

`SELECT MIN(order_amount) FROM` customer_order;

```
+--------------------+
| min(order_amount)  |
+--------------------+
|                 65 |
+--------------------+
1 row in set (0.00 sec)
```

Figure 2.27

The Average value can be found using avg() function as shown below:

SELECT AVG(order_amount) FROM customer_order;

```
mysql> select avg(order_amount) from customer_order;
+-------------------+
| avg(order_amount) |
+-------------------+
|         1120.6667 |
+-------------------+
1 row in set (0.00 sec)
```

Figure 2.28

You can use the sum() function to calculate the total sum of amount in customer_order table.

SELECT SUM(order_amount) FROM customer_order;

```
mysql> SELECT SUM(order_amount) FROM customer_order;
+-------------------+
| SUM(order_amount) |
+-------------------+
|             23534 |
+-------------------+
1 row in set (0.00 sec)
```

Figure 2.29

We have already seen how the **count()** function works. Now, let's try to find out how many orders were taken by each employee.

select employee_name, count(*)order_amount from customer_order group by employee_name;

```
mysql> select employee_name, count(*)order_amount from customer_order group by employee_name;
+---------------+--------------+
| employee_name | order_amount |
+---------------+--------------+
| Abhimanyu     |           12 |
| Swamy         |            5 |
| Radha         |            4 |
+---------------+--------------+
3 rows in set (0.00 sec)
```

Figure 2.30

Check the output by counting the orders taken by each employee in the **customer_order** table.

```
mysql> select * from customer_order;
+----------+-------------+----------+---------------+--------------+-------------+------------+-------------+
| order_ID | customer_ID | login_ID | employee_name | order_amount | customer_SN | order_date | supply_date |
+----------+-------------+----------+---------------+--------------+-------------+------------+-------------+
|      121 |       10000 |        1 | Abhimanyu     |          250 | Jackson     | 2020-01-03 | 2020-01-03  |
|      122 |       10000 |        1 | Abhimanyu     |          500 | Jackson     | 2020-01-07 | 2020-01-07  |
|      123 |       10002 |        7 | Abhimanyu     |          250 | Pathak      | 2020-02-02 | 2020-02-02  |
|      124 |       10002 |        7 | Abhimanyu     |           65 | Pathak      | 2020-02-03 | 2020-02-03  |
|      125 |       10001 |        2 | Swamy         |          159 | George      | 2020-04-03 | 2020-04-03  |
|      126 |       10000 |        1 | Radha         |         1250 | Jackson     | 2020-03-04 | 2020-03-04  |
|      127 |       10000 |        1 | Radha         |         2503 | Jackson     | 2020-03-06 | 2020-03-06  |
|      128 |       10002 |        7 | Abhimanyu     |          550 | Pathak      | 2020-04-05 | 2020-04-05  |
|      129 |       10001 |        2 | Swamy         |          159 | George      | 2020-04-06 | 2020-04-06  |
|      130 |       10003 |        6 | Abhimanyu     |         4000 | Khan        | 2020-05-03 | 2020-05-03  |
|      131 |       10000 |        1 | Abhimanyu     |          138 | Jackson     | 2020-05-06 | 2020-05-08  |
|      132 |       10001 |        2 | Abhimanyu     |         2000 | George      | 2020-06-02 | 2020-06-02  |
|      133 |       10000 |        1 | Abhimanyu     |          700 | Jackson     | 2020-06-03 | 2020-06-03  |
|      134 |       10002 |        7 | Abhimanyu     |          150 | Pathak      | 2020-07-13 | 2020-07-13  |
|      135 |       10001 |        2 | Swamy         |          630 | George      | 2020-07-23 | 2020-07-23  |
|      136 |       10000 |        1 | Radha         |          180 | Jackson     | 2020-08-10 | 2020-08-10  |
|      137 |       10003 |        6 | Swamy         |          250 | Khan        | 2020-08-11 | 2020-08-11  |
|      138 |       10000 |        1 | Abhimanyu     |         5000 | Jackson     | 2020-09-09 | 2020-09-09  |
|      139 |       10002 |        7 | Radha         |          200 | Pathak      | 2020-10-27 | 2020-10-29  |
|      140 |       10000 |        1 | Abhimanyu     |         3250 | Jackson     | 2020-11-03 | 2020-11-03  |
|      141 |       10000 |        1 | swamy         |         1350 | Jackson     | 2020-12-02 | 2020-12-03  |
+----------+-------------+----------+---------------+--------------+-------------+------------+-------------+
21 rows in set (0.00 sec)
```

Figure 2.31

Now let's replace COUNT(*) BY COUNT(order_amount) and see what happens.

SELECT COUNT(order_amount) FROM customer_order;

```
mysql>  SELECT  COUNT(order_amount) FROM customer_order;
+---------------------+
| COUNT(order_amount) |
+---------------------+
|                  21 |
+---------------------+
1 row in set (0.01 sec)
```

Figure 2.32

The table has total 21 order_amount values.

Now let's count how many distinct employees are there in employee_name column.

SELECT COUNT(DISTINCT order_amount) FROM customer_order;

```
mysql> SELECT  COUNT(DISTINCT order_amount) FROM customer_order;
+------------------------------+
| COUNT(DISTINCT order_amount) |
+------------------------------+
|                           18 |
+------------------------------+
1 row in set (0.00 sec)
```

Figure 2.33

2.8 Evaluating a Condition

A WHERE clause can be used to evaluate more than one condition where every condition is separated by AND. Look at the statement given below:

SELECT a. customer_FN ,a.customer_SN, b.employee_name, b.supply_date FROMcustomer_detailsa, customer_orderb

WHERE b.order_amount > 500 AND

b.supply_date> "2020-08-30" AND

a.customer_ID = b.customer_ID;

It will display orders of amount greater thar s. 500 placed before 30 Aug 2020.

```
mysql> SELECT a. customer_FN ,a.customer_SN, b.employee_name, b.supply_date FROM  customer_details a, customer_order b
    -> WHERE b.order_amount > 500 AND
    -> b.supply_date > "2020-08-30" AND
    -> a.customer_ID = b.customer_ID;
+-------------+-------------+---------------+-------------+
| customer_FN | customer_SN | employee_name | supply_date |
+-------------+-------------+---------------+-------------+
| Eric        | Jackson     | Abhimanyu     | 2020-09-09  |
| Eric        | Jackson     | Abhimanyu     | 2020-11-03  |
| Eric        | Jackson     | swamy         | 2020-12-03  |
+-------------+-------------+---------------+-------------+
3 rows in set (0.01 sec)
```

Figure 2.34

Here you have to understand that while using WHERE clause a record is included in a result set only when all conditions become true for that row. The row will not be included in the record set even if one condition turns out to be false.

Let's say we need to find out for the same conditions only orders delivered by Radha or Swamy we can do that using OR or NOT condition. Have a look at the following statement:

SELECT a. customer_FN ,a.customer_SN, b.employee_name, b.supply_date FROMcustom-er_detailsa, customer_orderb

WHEREb.order_amount> 500 AND

b.supply_date> "2020-08-30" AND

(employee_name = "Swamy" or employee_name = "Radha") AND

a.customer_ID = b.customer_ID;

```
mysql> SELECT a. customer_FN ,a.customer_SN, b.employee_name, b.supply_date FROM  customer_details a, customer_order b
    -> WHERE b.order_amount > 500 AND
    -> b.supply_date > "2020-08-30" AND
    -> (employee_name = "Swamy" or employee_name = "Radha") AND
    -> a.customer_ID = b.customer_ID;
+-------------+-------------+---------------+-------------+
| customer_FN | customer_SN | employee_name | supply_date |
+-------------+-------------+---------------+-------------+
| Eric        | Jackson     | swamy         | 2020-12-03  |
+-------------+-------------+---------------+-------------+
1 row in set (0.00 sec)
```

Figure 2.35

Or we can also say:

SELECT a. customer_FN ,a.customer_SN, b.employee_name, b.supply_date FROMcustom-er_detailsa, customer_orderb

```
WHEREb.order_amount> 500 AND
b.supply_date> "2020-08-30" AND
NOT(employee_name = "Abhimanyu") AND
a.customer_ID = b.customer_ID;
```

```
mysql> SELECT a. customer_FN ,a.customer_SN, b.employee_name, b.supply_date FROM  customer_details a, customer_order b
    -> WHERE b.order_amount > 500 AND
    -> b.supply_date > "2020-08-30" AND
    -> NOT(employee_name = "Abhimanyu") AND
    -> a.customer_ID = b.customer_ID;
+-------------+-------------+---------------+-------------+
| customer_FN | customer_SN | employee_name | supply_date |
+-------------+-------------+---------------+-------------+
| Eric        | Jackson     | swamy         | 2020-12-03  |
+-------------+-------------+---------------+-------------+
1 row in set (0.00 sec)
```

Figure 2.36

In the above statement notice how the parentheses are placed. We should clearly define how AND and OR exists between two conditions. You will learn more about the usage of parentheses in the section coming up next. As of now, please understand how the outcome of AND and OR operator is evaluated.

You have learnt Boolean algebra in Class XI. The AND and OR operator work the same way as in Boolean algebra.

AND Operator

- True AND True = True
- False AND True = False
- True AND False = False
- False AND False = False

OR Operator

- Where True OR True = True
- Where False OR True = True
- Where True OR False = True
- Where False OR False = False

2.9 Usage of Parenthesis

In the last example we had three conditions and we put one condition in parentheses. If that is not done the results will be wrong and confusing. For a change let's try and see what happens if this is done.

We may want to give the following command if we want to find details of orders greater than 500 or orders placed before 30 August 2020

SELECT a. customer_FN ,a.customer_SN, b.employee_name, b.supply_date FROM customer_details a, customer_order b

```
    WHERE b.order_amount> 500 OR
b.supply_date> "2020-08-30" AND
```

```
a.customer_ID = b.customer_ID;
```

```
mysql> SELECT a. customer_FN ,a.customer_SN, b.employee_name, b.supply_date FROM  customer_details a, customer_order b
    ->      WHERE b.order_amount > 500 OR
    ->      b.supply_date > "2020-08-30" AND
    ->      a.customer_ID = b.customer_ID;
+-------------+-------------+---------------+-------------+
| customer_FN | customer_SN | employee_name | supply_date |
+-------------+-------------+---------------+-------------+
| Meenakshi   | Sinha       | Radha         | 2020-03-04  |
| Rakesh      | Verma       | Radha         | 2020-03-04  |
| Aslam       | Khan        | Radha         | 2020-03-04  |
| Riya        | Pathak      | Radha         | 2020-03-04  |
| George      |  Mathews    | Radha         | 2020-03-04  |
| Eric        | Jackson     | Radha         | 2020-03-04  |
| Meenakshi   | Sinha       | Radha         | 2020-03-06  |
| Rakesh      | Verma       | Radha         | 2020-03-06  |
| Aslam       | Khan        | Radha         | 2020-03-06  |
| Riya        | Pathak      | Radha         | 2020-03-06  |
| George      |  Mathews    | Radha         | 2020-03-06  |
| Eric        | Jackson     | Radha         | 2020-03-06  |
| Meenakshi   | Sinha       | Abhimanyu     | 2020-04-05  |
| Rakesh      | Verma       | Abhimanyu     | 2020-04-05  |
| Aslam       | Khan        | Abhimanyu     | 2020-04-05  |
| Riya        | Pathak      | Abhimanyu     | 2020-04-05  |
| George      |  Mathews    | Abhimanyu     | 2020-04-05  |
| Eric        | Jackson     | Abhimanyu     | 2020-04-05  |
| Meenakshi   | Sinha       | Abhimanyu     | 2020-05-03  |
| Rakesh      | Verma       | Abhimanyu     | 2020-05-03  |
| Aslam       | Khan        | Abhimanyu     | 2020-05-03  |
| Riya        | Pathak      | Abhimanyu     | 2020-05-03  |
| George      |  Mathews    | Abhimanyu     | 2020-05-03  |
| Eric        | Jackson     | Abhimanyu     | 2020-05-03  |
| Meenakshi   | Sinha       | Abhimanyu     | 2020-06-02  |
| Rakesh      | Verma       | Abhimanyu     | 2020-06-02  |
| Aslam       | Khan        | Abhimanyu     | 2020-06-02  |
| Riya        | Pathak      | Abhimanyu     | 2020-06-02  |
```

Figure 2.37

One look at the above result and you know it is all wrong and misleading. The reason behind this is that the instructions are not clear to the data server. Now think again what we want.

Our requirement is to find orders which are either greater than amount of ₹ 500 or have been placed before 30 Aug 2020.

```
mysql> SELECT a. customer_FN ,a.customer_SN, b.employee_name, b.supply_date, b.order_amount FROM  customer_details a, customer_order b
    -> WHERE (b.order_amount > 500 OR b.supply_date > "2020-08-30" )AND
    ->  a.customer_ID = b.customer_ID;
+-------------+-------------+---------------+-------------+--------------+
| customer_FN | customer_SN | employee_name | supply_date | order_amount |
+-------------+-------------+---------------+-------------+--------------+
| Eric        | Jackson     | Radha         | 2020-03-04  |         1250 |
| Eric        | Jackson     | Radha         | 2020-03-06  |         2503 |
| Riya        | Pathak      | Abhimanyu     | 2020-04-05  |          550 |
| Aslam       | Khan        | Abhimanyu     | 2020-05-03  |         4000 |
| George      |  Mathews    | Abhimanyu     | 2020-06-02  |         2000 |
| Eric        | Jackson     | Abhimanyu     | 2020-06-03  |          700 |
| George      |  Mathews    | Swamy         | 2020-07-23  |          630 |
| Eric        | Jackson     | Abhimanyu     | 2020-09-09  |         5000 |
| Riya        | Pathak      | Radha         | 2020-10-29  |          200 |
| Eric        | Jackson     | Abhimanyu     | 2020-11-03  |         3250 |
| Eric        | Jackson     | swamy         | 2020-12-03  |         1350 |
+-------------+-------------+---------------+-------------+--------------+
11 rows in set (0.00 sec)
```

Figure 2.38

2.10 Defining Your Condition

There is no doubt that a data server can handle lot of complications provided everything is defined clearly. Conditions are defined with the help of expressions which in turn may consists of numbers, strings, in built functions, sub queries etc. Further, conditions are always defined with the help of operators which may be comparison operators(=, !=, <,>,<>, Like,IN, BETWEEN, etc) or arithematic operator(+, -,*,/). So, all these things are used together to form a condition. Now let's have a look at Condition Types.

Types of Conditions

In order to remove unwanted data from our search we can use the following condition types.

Equality Condition

Conditions that use the sign '=' to equate one condition to the other are referred to as equality conditions. You have used this condition many times up till now.

We have been using the equality sign from the very beginning.

So, if we want to know the orders taken by employee_name 'Radha' we will give the following command:

Select * from customer_order where employee_name = "Radha";

mysql> Select * from customer_order where employee_name = "Radha";

order_ID	customer_ID	login_ID	employee_name	order_amount	customer_SN	order_date	supply_date
126	10000	1	Radha	1250	Jackson	2020-03-04	2020-03-04
127	10000	1	Radha	2503	Jackson	2020-03-06	2020-03-06
136	10000	1	Radha	180	Jackson	2020-08-10	2020-08-10
139	10002	7	Radha	200	Pathak	2020-10-27	2020-10-29

4 rows in set (0.00 sec)

Figure 2.39

Inequality Condition

The inequality condition is the opposite of equality condition and is expressed by '!=' and '<>' symbol.

Select * from customer_order where employee_name != "Radha";

mysql> Select * from customer_order where employee_name != "Radha";

order_ID	customer_ID	login_ID	employee_name	order_amount	customer_SN	order_date	supply_date
121	10000	1	Abhimanyu	250	Jackson	2020-01-03	2020-01-03
122	10000	1	Abhimanyu	500	Jackson	2020-01-07	2020-01-07
123	10002	7	Abhimanyu	250	Pathak	2020-02-02	2020-02-02
124	10002	7	Abhimanyu	65	Pathak	2020-02-03	2020-02-03
125	10001	2	Swamy	159	George	2020-04-03	2020-04-03
128	10002	7	Abhimanyu	550	Pathak	2020-04-05	2020-04-05
129	10001	2	Swamy	159	George	2020-04-06	2020-04-06
130	10003	6	Abhimanyu	4000	Khan	2020-05-03	2020-05-03
131	10000	1	Abhimanyu	138	Jackson	2020-05-06	2020-05-08
132	10001	2	Abhimanyu	2000	George	2020-06-02	2020-06-02
133	10000	1	Abhimanyu	700	Jackson	2020-06-03	2020-06-03
134	10002	7	Abhimanyu	150	Pathak	2020-07-13	2020-07-13
135	10001	2	Swamy	630	George	2020-07-23	2020-07-23
137	10003	6	Swamy	250	Khan	2020-08-11	2020-08-11
138	10000	1	Abhimanyu	5000	Jackson	2020-09-09	2020-09-09
140	10000	1	Abhimanyu	3250	Jackson	2020-11-03	2020-11-03
141	10000	1	swamy	1350	Jackson	2020-12-02	2020-12-03

17 rows in set (0.00 sec)

Figure 2.40

Now try the following:

Select * from customer_order where employee_name<> "Radha";

Conditions used to define range

We have seen examples of range before, but for a better understanding here we go once again. When we try to find if an expression falls within a range or not we write queries to define a range.

SELECT * FROM customer_details WHERE customer_ID>10000;

```
mysql>  SELECT * FROM customer_details WHERE customer_ID >10000;
+-------------+-------------+-------------+------------------+----------------------------+
| customer_ID | customer_FN | customer_SN | customer_contact | email_id                   |
+-------------+-------------+-------------+------------------+----------------------------+
|       10001 | George      |  Mathews    |       9089376511 | gm@yahoo.com               |
|       10002 | Riya        | Pathak      |       9089346521 | riya.patha2010@gmail.com   |
|       10003 | Aslam       | Khan        |       9602346833 | riya.patha2010@gmail.com   |
|       10004 | Rakesh      | Verma       |       7089676523 | rakesh.verma@gmail.com     |
|       10005 | Meenakshi   | Sinha       |       9989645523 | msinha@gmail.com           |
+-------------+-------------+-------------+------------------+----------------------------+
5 rows in set (0.01 sec)
```

Figure 2.41

Now, we will define the same query using BETWEEN operator. While defining a range using BETWEEN operator, specify the lesser value first and the higher value later.

SELECT * FROM customer_details WHERE customer_ID BETWEEN 10001 AND10009;

```
mysql> SELECT * FROM customer_details WHERE customer_ID BETWEEN 10001 AND 10009;
+-------------+-------------+-------------+------------------+----------------------------+
| customer_ID | customer_FN | customer_SN | customer_contact | email_id                   |
+-------------+-------------+-------------+------------------+----------------------------+
|       10001 | George      |  Mathews    |       9089376511 | gm@yahoo.com               |
|       10002 | Riya        | Pathak      |       9089346521 | riya.patha2010@gmail.com   |
|       10003 | Aslam       | Khan        |       9602346833 | riya.patha2010@gmail.com   |
|       10004 | Rakesh      | Verma       |       7089676523 | rakesh.verma@gmail.com     |
|       10005 | Meenakshi   | Sinha       |       9989645523 | msinha@gmail.com           |
+-------------+-------------+-------------+------------------+----------------------------+
5 rows in set (0.00 sec)
```

Figure 2.42

Membership Conditions

Sometimes the requirement is not for looking values in a range but in a set of certain values. To give you a better idea let's suppose that you need to find out the details for 'Radha' or 'Swamy'.

Select * from customer_order where employee_name = "Radha" or employee_name = "Swamy";

```
mysql> Select * from customer_order where employee_name = "Radha" or employee_name = "Swamy";
+----------+-------------+----------+---------------+--------------+-------------+------------+-------------+
| order_ID | customer_ID | login_ID | employee_name | order_amount | customer_SN | order_date | supply_date |
+----------+-------------+----------+---------------+--------------+-------------+------------+-------------+
|      125 |       10001 |        2 | Swamy         |          159 | George      | 2020-04-03 | 2020-04-03  |
|      126 |       10000 |        1 | Radha         |         1250 | Jackson     | 2020-03-04 | 2020-03-04  |
|      127 |       10000 |        1 | Radha         |         2503 | Jackson     | 2020-03-06 | 2020-03-06  |
|      129 |       10001 |        2 | Swamy         |          159 | George      | 2020-04-06 | 2020-04-06  |
|      135 |       10001 |        2 | Swamy         |          630 | George      | 2020-07-23 | 2020-07-23  |
|      136 |       10000 |        1 | Radha         |          180 | Jackson     | 2020-08-10 | 2020-08-10  |
|      137 |       10003 |        6 | Swamy         |          250 | Khan        | 2020-08-11 | 2020-08-11  |
|      139 |       10002 |        7 | Radha         |          200 | Pathak      | 2020-10-27 | 2020-10-29  |
|      141 |       10000 |        1 | swamy         |         1350 | Jackson     | 2020-12-02 | 2020-12-03  |
+----------+-------------+----------+---------------+--------------+-------------+------------+-------------+
9 rows in set (0.00 sec)
```

Figure 2.43

We can simplify the above query and get the right result sets using operator IN.

Select * from customer_order where employee_name in ("Radha" ,"Swamy");

```
mysql> Select * from customer_order where employee_name in ("Radha" ,"Swamy");
+----------+-------------+----------+---------------+--------------+-------------+------------+-------------+
| order_ID | customer_ID | login_ID | employee_name | order_amount | customer_SN | order_date | supply_date |
+----------+-------------+----------+---------------+--------------+-------------+------------+-------------+
|      125 |       10001 |        2 | Swamy         |          159 | George      | 2020-04-03 | 2020-04-03  |
|      126 |       10000 |        1 | Radha         |         1250 | Jackson     | 2020-03-04 | 2020-03-04  |
|      127 |       10000 |        1 | Radha         |         2503 | Jackson     | 2020-03-06 | 2020-03-06  |
|      129 |       10001 |        2 | Swamy         |          159 | George      | 2020-04-06 | 2020-04-06  |
|      135 |       10001 |        2 | Swamy         |          630 | George      | 2020-07-23 | 2020-07-23  |
|      136 |       10000 |        1 | Radha         |          180 | Jackson     | 2020-08-10 | 2020-08-10  |
|      137 |       10003 |        6 | Swamy         |          250 | Khan        | 2020-08-11 | 2020-08-11  |
|      139 |       10002 |        7 | Radha         |          200 | Pathak      | 2020-10-27 | 2020-10-29  |
|      141 |       10000 |        1 | swamy         |         1350 | Jackson     | 2020-12-02 | 2020-12-03  |
+----------+-------------+----------+---------------+--------------+-------------+------------+-------------+
9 rows in set (0.00 sec)
```

Figure 2.44

Pattern Matching

Pattern matching in another interesting feature that you will enjoy working with and would probably use a lot as a developer. The concept is very simple. It allows you to use an underscore (_) to match any single character and percentage sign(%) to match 0, 1 or more characters. Before we go ahead with pattern matching you need to know that in case of pattern matching you use two comparison operators: **LIKE** and **NOT LIKE**.

So, now let's get started with some exercises:

We, go ahead with the same example. Let's try to find out the email id having the name starting with 'e'.

SELECT email_id from customer_details WHERE email_id LIKE 'e%';

```
mysql> SELECT email_id from customer_details WHERE email_id LIKE 'e%';
+-----------------------+
| email_id              |
+-----------------------+
| ericjackson@yahoo.com |
+-----------------------+
1 row in set (0.00 sec)
```

Figure 2.45

Similarly, to look for surname having name ending with 'ma':

Select * from customer_details where customer_SN like '%ma';

Now let's see if we can find gmail accounts by looking for email ids containing the string '@gmail'.

SELECT * from customer_details WHERE email_id LIKE '%@gmail%';

```
mysql> SELECT * from customer_details WHERE email_id LIKE '%@gmail%';
+-------------+-------------+-------------+------------------+--------------------------+
| customer_ID | customer_FN | customer_SN | customer_contact | email_id                 |
+-------------+-------------+-------------+------------------+--------------------------+
|       10002 | Riya        | Pathak      |       9089346521 | riya.patha2010@gmail.com |
|       10003 | Aslam       | Khan        |       9602346833 | riya.patha2010@gmail.com |
|       10004 | Rakesh      | Verma       |       7089676523 | rakesh.verma@gmail.com   |
|       10005 | Meenakshi   | Sinha       |       9989645523 | msinha@gmail.com         |
+-------------+-------------+-------------+------------------+--------------------------+
4 rows in set (0.00 sec)
```

Figure 2.46

The next example shows how to look for a five letter word with 'h' being the second letter of the surname.

SELECT * from customer_details WHERE customer_SN LIKE '_h_';

```
mysql> SELECT * from customer_details WHERE customer_SN LIKE '_h__';
+-------------+-------------+-------------+------------------+--------------------------+
| customer_ID | customer_FN | customer_SN | customer_contact | email_id                 |
+-------------+-------------+-------------+------------------+--------------------------+
|       10003 | Aslam       | Khan        |       9602346833 | riya.patha2010@gmail.com |
+-------------+-------------+-------------+------------------+--------------------------+
1 row in set (0.00 sec)
```

Figure 2.47

3 Joins

In this chapter, you will cover:

- Joins and its type
- Cartesian product

3.1 Introduction

It is easy to work with one table but in the real time scenario you will deal with multiple tables and often there will be need to display combined results. We use **Joins** when we want to retrieve data from two or more tables in the same query.

SQL Join clause is used to combine the information of more than one table in the database. A Join is achieved with the help of a field that is common in tables.

3.2 Cartesian product

Let's try to retrieve data from the two tables **customer_details** and **customer_login** using a simple **FROM** clause.

Let's have a look at the table definition for both the tables.

The table customer_details looks something like this:

```
mysql> select * from customer_details;
+-------------+-------------+-------------+------------------+---------------------------+
| customer_ID | customer_FN | customer_SN | customer_contact | email_id                  |
+-------------+-------------+-------------+------------------+---------------------------+
|       10000 | Eric        | Jackson     |       9898983434 | ericjackson@yahoo.com     |
|       10001 | George      |  Mathews    |       9089376511 | gm@yahoo.com              |
|       10002 | Riya        | Pathak      |       9089346521 | riya.patha2010@gmail.com  |
|       10003 | Aslam       | Khan        |       9602346833 | riya.patha2010@gmail.com  |
|       10004 | Rakesh      | Verma       |       7089676523 | rakesh.verma@gmail.com    |
|       10005 | Meenakshi   | Sinha       |       9989645523 | msinha@gmail.com          |
+-------------+-------------+-------------+------------------+---------------------------+
6 rows in set (0.00 sec)
```

Figure 3.1

And the table customer_login is as follows:

```
mysql> select * from customer_details;
+-------------+-------------+-------------+------------------+---------------------------+
| customer_ID | customer_FN | customer_SN | customer_contact | email_id                  |
+-------------+-------------+-------------+------------------+---------------------------+
|       10000 | Eric        | Jackson     |       9898983434 | ericjackson@yahoo.com     |
|       10001 | George      |  Mathews    |       9089376511 | gm@yahoo.com              |
|       10002 | Riya        | Pathak      |       9089346521 | riya.patha2010@gmail.com  |
|       10003 | Aslam       | Khan        |       9602346833 | riya.patha2010@gmail.com  |
|       10004 | Rakesh      | Verma       |       7089676523 | rakesh.verma@gmail.com    |
|       10005 | Meenakshi   | Sinha       |       9989645523 | msinha@gmail.com          |
+-------------+-------------+-------------+------------------+---------------------------+
6 rows in set (0.00 sec)
```

Figure 3.2

Now, let's try to retrieve the customer_FN, customer_SN and username using a simple FROM clause.

SELECT a.customer_FN, a.customer_SN, b.username

FROM customer_details a JOIN customer_login b;

```
mysql> SELECT a.customer_FN, a.customer_SN, b.username
    -> FROM customer_details a JOIN customer_login b;
+-------------+-------------+----------+
| customer_FN | customer_SN | username |
+-------------+-------------+----------+
| Eric        | Jackson     | akhan    |
| Eric        | Jackson     | ripa     |
| Eric        | Jackson     | gmathews |
| Eric        | Jackson     | ejack    |
| George      |  Mathews    | akhan    |
| George      |  Mathews    | ripa     |
| George      |  Mathews    | gmathews |
| George      |  Mathews    | ejack    |
| Riya        | Pathak      | akhan    |
| Riya        | Pathak      | ripa     |
| Riya        | Pathak      | gmathews |
| Riya        | Pathak      | ejack    |
| Aslam       | Khan        | akhan    |
| Aslam       | Khan        | ripa     |
| Aslam       | Khan        | gmathews |
| Aslam       | Khan        | ejack    |
| Rakesh      | Verma       | akhan    |
| Rakesh      | Verma       | ripa     |
| Rakesh      | Verma       | gmathews |
| Rakesh      | Verma       | ejack    |
| Meenakshi   | Sinha       | akhan    |
| Meenakshi   | Sinha       | ripa     |
| Meenakshi   | Sinha       | gmathews |
| Meenakshi   | Sinha       | ejack    |
+-------------+-------------+----------+
24 rows in set (0.00 sec)
```

Figure 3.3

Both the tables customer_details has 6 rows of data and customer_login has 4 rows of data, but the result set has 24 rows!! What exactly has gone wrong here? Here each customer name is repeated 4 times. Clearly this is a case where the developer has not given clear instructions. Since we have not told the database server how we want to join the two tables, it has created a **CROSS JOIN**. Cross join is a Cartesian product which is every permutation of tables customer_details and customer_login. 6 rows of customer_details x 4 rows of customer_login makes 24 rows that you get in this result set.

But we are not interested in the cross join. We are interested in related data. To get related data we have to define the relation between the two tables. We can define the relation with the help of ON subclause.

```
SELECT a.customer_FN,a.customer_SN,b.username FROM
customer_details a JOIN customer_login b ON
a.customer_ID = b.customer_ID;
```

```
mysql> SELECT a.customer_FN, a.customer_SN, b.username FROM
    -> customer_details a JOIN customer_login b ON
    ->  a.customer_ID = b.customer_ID;
+-------------+-------------+----------+
| customer_FN | customer_SN | username |
+-------------+-------------+----------+
| Eric        | Jackson     | ejack    |
| George      |  Mathews    | gmathews |
| Aslam       | Khan        | ripa     |
| Riya        | Pathak      | akhan    |
+-------------+-------------+----------+
4 rows in set (0.00 sec)
```

Figure 3.4

We have defined the relation between the two tables with the help of **customer_ID. customer_ID** is a primary key in **customer_details** and it is foreign key for **customer_login**. Server, will get the value of customer_ID from customer_details and then match it with customer_ID value in customer_login and then retrieves the corresponding values from the customer_login table.

So, basically joins are used to compare and actually join tables and return rows of data from two or more tables. There are two types of Joins:

1. INNER JOIN
2. OUTER JOIN

The INNER JOIN will provide you with matching results from tables whereas the OUTER JOIN will provide you some dissimilar data along with matched data.

3.2.1 Inner Join

Let's have a look at the content of customer_details table. The table data is shown below:

SELECT * from customer_details;

```
mysql> select * from customer_details;
+-------------+-------------+-------------+------------------+---------------------------+
| customer_ID | customer_FN | customer_SN | customer_contact | email_id                  |
+-------------+-------------+-------------+------------------+---------------------------+
|       10000 | Eric        | Jackson     |       9898983434 | ericjackson@yahoo.com     |
|       10001 | George      |  Mathews    |       9089376511 | gm@yahoo.com              |
|       10002 | Riya        | Pathak      |       9089346521 | riya.patha2010@gmail.com  |
|       10003 | Aslam       | Khan        |       9602346833 | riya.patha2010@gmail.com  |
+-------------+-------------+-------------+------------------+---------------------------+
4 rows in set (0.00 sec)
```

Figure 3.5

The table has a primary key **customer_ID**.

Now, let's retrieve all records of **customer_login**

Select * from customer_login;

```
mysql> select * from customer_login;
+----------+----------+---------------+-------------+
| login_ID | username | password      | customer_ID |
+----------+----------+---------------+-------------+
|        1 | ejack    | ejack@123     |       10000 |
|        2 | gmathews | georgeforever |       10001 |
|        6 | ripa     | riya123       |       10003 |
|        7 | akhan    | ak@2021       |       10002 |
+----------+----------+---------------+-------------+
4 rows in set (0.00 sec)
```

Figure 3.6

Customer login has login_ID as primary key and a foreign key customer_ID which is related to the customer_details table.

We will now join the two tables based on customer_ID and no other filtering condition to get a result set that displays customer_FN, customer_SN ,customer_ID and username.

select a.customer_FN, a.customer_SN, a.customer_ID, b.username from customer_details a inner join customer_login b on a.customer_ID = b.customer_ID;

```
mysql> select a.customer_FN, a.customer_SN, a.customer_ID, b.username from customer_details a inner join customer_login
b on a.customer_ID = b.customer_ID;
+-------------+-------------+-------------+----------+
| customer_FN | customer_SN | customer_ID | username |
+-------------+-------------+-------------+----------+
| Eric        | Jackson     |       10000 | ejack    |
| George      |  Mathews    |       10001 | gmathews |
| Riya        | Pathak      |       10002 | akhan    |
| Aslam       | Khan        |       10003 | ripa     |
+-------------+-------------+-------------+----------+
4 rows in set (0.00 sec)
```

Figure 3.7

In case of inner join if there is no attribute in common between the tables then it will return nothing. to understand this let's insert two more records of customer in customer_details for which there is no corresponding records in customer_login.

```
mysql> select * from customer_details;
+-------------+-------------+-------------+------------------+---------------------------+
| customer_ID | customer_FN | customer_SN | customer_contact | email_id                  |
+-------------+-------------+-------------+------------------+---------------------------+
|       10000 | Eric        | Jackson     |       9898983434 | ericjackson@yahoo.com     |
|       10001 | George      |  Mathews    |       9089376511 | gm@yahoo.com              |
|       10002 | Riya        | Pathak      |       9089346521 | riya.patha2010@gmail.com  |
|       10003 | Aslam       | Khan        |       9602346833 | riya.patha2010@gmail.com  |
|       10004 | Rakesh      | Verma       |       7089676523 | rakesh.verma@gmail.com    |
|       10005 | Meenakshi   | Sinha       |       9989645523 | msinha@gmail.com          |
+-------------+-------------+-------------+------------------+---------------------------+
```

Figure 3.8

Now, let's again use the same query.

select a.customer_FN, a.customer_SN, a.customer_ID, b.username from customer_detailsa inner join customer_login b on a.customer_ID = b.customer_ID;

```
mysql> select a.customer_FN, a.customer_SN, a.customer_ID, b.username from customer_details a inner join customer_login
b on a.customer_ID = b.customer_ID;
+-------------+-------------+-------------+----------+
| customer_FN | customer_SN | customer_ID | username |
+-------------+-------------+-------------+----------+
| Eric        | Jackson     |       10000 | ejack    |
| George      |  Mathews    |       10001 | gmathews |
| Aslam       | Khan        |       10003 | ripa     |
| Riya        | Pathak      |       10002 | akhan    |
+-------------+-------------+-------------+----------+
4 rows in set (0.00 sec)
```

Figure 3.9

The result is the same.

However, there would be times when you want the result data to display all the rows of both the tables so that you can see which rows are related and which are not. In such cases we can make use of outer join.

3.2.2 Outer join

Outer joins on the other hand return results of inner join along with records that have no corresponding match in the other table. Outer join can be of three types.

1. **LEFT OUTER JOIN / LEFT JOIN:** It will get all data from the first table but only corresponding data from the second table.
2. **RIGHT OUTER JOIN/ RIGHT JOIN:** In case of RIGHT OUTER JOIN the result set will include the result from inner join and also rows from the table in the right for which no match exists in the left table.
3. **FULL OUTER JOIN/ FULL JOIN:** Returns all matched and unmatched data from both the tables. However, it is not supported by MySQL.

Have a look at the query given below:

select a.customer_FN, a.customer_SN, a.customer_ID, b.username from customer_details a left outer join customer_login b on a.customer_ID = b.customer_ID;

```
mysql> select a.customer_FN, a.customer_SN, a.customer_ID, b.username from customer_details a left outer join customer_login b on a.customer_ID = b.customer_ID;
+-------------+-------------+-------------+-----------+
| customer_FN | customer_SN | customer_ID | username  |
+-------------+-------------+-------------+-----------+
| Eric        | Jackson     |       10000 | ejack     |
| George      |  Mathews    |       10001 | gmathews  |
| Riya        | Pathak      |       10002 | akhan     |
| Aslam       | Khan        |       10003 | ripa      |
| Rakesh      | Verma       |       10004 | NULL      |
| Meenakshi   | Sinha       |       10005 | NULL      |
+-------------+-------------+-------------+-----------+
6 rows in set (0.00 sec)
```

Figure 3.10

The above result set has 6 rows of data. As you can see, for customer_ID 10004 and 10005 there is no data available in the **customer_login** table. Hence, for these three values of login_ID, the corresponding data from customer_login(i.e. username) is displayed as NULL.

All six rows are displayed when we use Left outer join. Now, let's see what happens if we use Right outer join.

select a.customer_FN, a.customer_SN, a.customer_ID, b.username from customer_details a right outer join customer_login b on a.customer_ID = b.customer_ID;

```
mysql> select a.customer_FN, a.customer_SN, a.customer_ID, b.username from customer_details a right outer join customer_login b on a.customer_ID = b.customer_ID;
+-------------+-------------+-------------+-----------+
| customer_FN | customer_SN | customer_ID | username  |
+-------------+-------------+-------------+-----------+
| Eric        | Jackson     |       10000 | ejack     |
| George      |  Mathews    |       10001 | gmathews  |
| Aslam       | Khan        |       10003 | ripa      |
| Riya        | Pathak      |       10002 | akhan     |
+-------------+-------------+-------------+-----------+
4 rows in set (0.00 sec)
```

Figure 3.11

As you can see only 4 rows of data is displayed if we use Right outer join.

Explanation

When you use a left outer join, the table on the left side of the join determines how many rows the result set will have. The table on the right provides result if a match is found or else NULL is displayed in the result set. The same way in right outer join the table on the right determines the number of rows in the result set.

So, now try this:

select a.username, b.customer_FN, b.customer_SN, b.customer_ID from customer_login a right outer join customer_details b on a.customer_ID = b.customer_ID;

```
mysql> select a.username, b.customer_FN, b.customer_SN, b.customer_ID from customer_login a right outer join customer_details b on a.customer_ID = b.customer_ID;
+----------+-------------+-------------+-------------+
| username | customer_FN | customer_SN | customer_ID |
+----------+-------------+-------------+-------------+
| ejack    | Eric        | Jackson     |       10000 |
| gmathews | George      |  Mathews    |       10001 |
| akhan    | Riya        | Pathak      |       10002 |
| ripa     | Aslam       | Khan        |       10003 |
| NULL     | Rakesh      | Verma       |       10004 |
| NULL     | Meenakshi   | Sinha       |       10005 |
+----------+-------------+-------------+-------------+
6 rows in set (0.00 sec)
```

Figure 3.12

3.2.3 Cross Join

Cross Join can join two or more unrelated tables. Each row of the first table is joined with all the rows of the second table. Cross join is not used to establish relationship like inner join and outer join

select customer_details.customer_FN, customer_login.username from customer_details, customer_login;

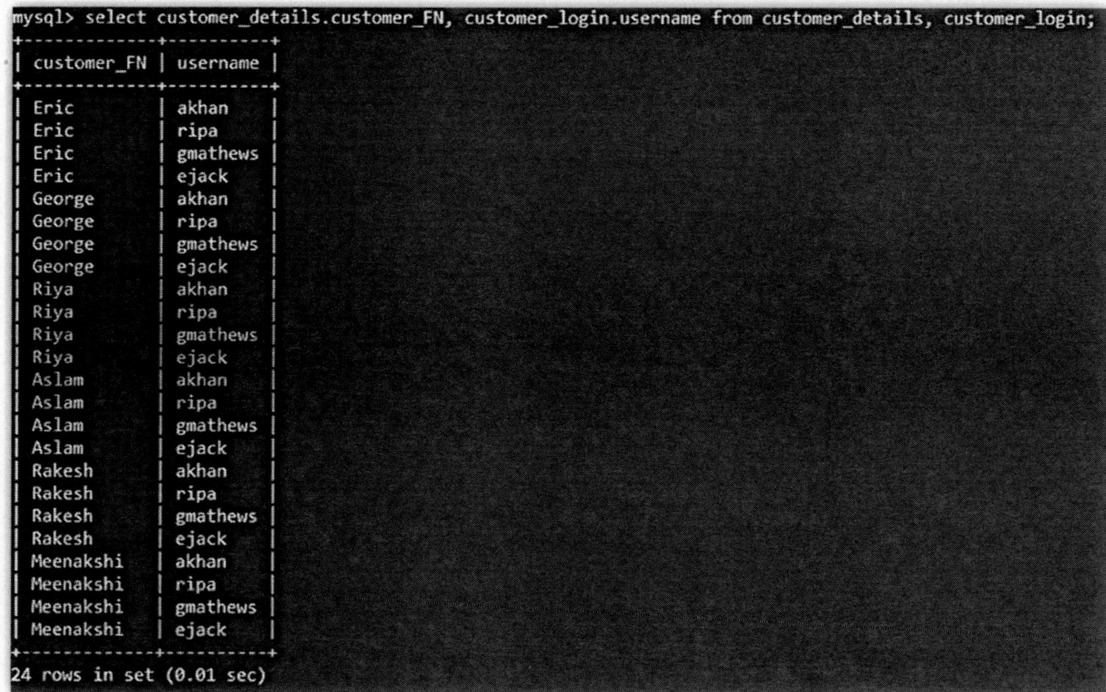

```
mysql> select customer_details.customer_FN, customer_login.username from customer_details, customer_login;
+-------------+----------+
| customer_FN | username |
+-------------+----------+
| Eric        | akhan    |
| Eric        | ripa     |
| Eric        | gmathews |
| Eric        | ejack    |
| George      | akhan    |
| George      | ripa     |
| George      | gmathews |
| George      | ejack    |
| Riya        | akhan    |
| Riya        | ripa     |
| Riya        | gmathews |
| Riya        | ejack    |
| Aslam       | akhan    |
| Aslam       | ripa     |
| Aslam       | gmathews |
| Aslam       | ejack    |
| Rakesh      | akhan    |
| Rakesh      | ripa     |
| Rakesh      | gmathews |
| Rakesh      | ejack    |
| Meenakshi   | akhan    |
| Meenakshi   | ripa     |
| Meenakshi   | gmathews |
| Meenakshi   | ejack    |
+-------------+----------+
24 rows in set (0.01 sec)
```

Figure 3.13

3.2.4 Equi Join

Equi join is a join created by matching the values of specific columns if the tables.

select * from customer_details join customer_login on customer_details.customer_ID = customer_login.customer_ID;

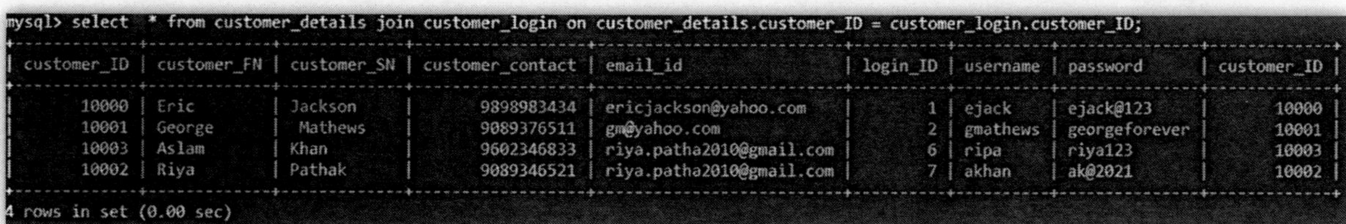

```
mysql> select  * from customer_details join customer_login on customer_details.customer_ID = customer_login.customer_ID;
+-------------+-------------+-------------+------------------+---------------------------+----------+----------+---------------+-------------+
| customer_ID | customer_FN | customer_SN | customer_contact | email_id                  | login_ID | username | password      | customer_ID |
+-------------+-------------+-------------+------------------+---------------------------+----------+----------+---------------+-------------+
|       10000 | Eric        | Jackson     |       9898983434 | ericjackson@yahoo.com     |        1 | ejack    | ejack@123     |       10000 |
|       10001 | George      |  Mathews    |       9089376511 | gm@yahoo.com              |        2 | gmathews | georgeforever |       10001 |
|       10003 | Aslam       | Khan        |       9602346833 | riya.patha2010@gmail.com  |        6 | ripa     | riya123       |       10003 |
|       10002 | Riya        | Pathak      |       9089346521 | riya.patha2010@gmail.com  |        7 | akhan    | ak@2021       |       10002 |
+-------------+-------------+-------------+------------------+---------------------------+----------+----------+---------------+-------------+
4 rows in set (0.00 sec)
```

Figure 3.14

Using a Sub query as table

Suppose in customer_order table we want to see records of customers who have not placed order with employee "Abhimanyu".

select * from customer_order where employee_name NOT IN('Abhimanyu');

mysql> select * from customer_order where employee_name NOT IN('Abhimanyu');

order_ID	customer_ID	login_ID	employee_name	order_amount	customer_SN	order_date	supply_date
125	10001	2	Swamy	159	George	2020-04-03	2020-04-03
126	10000	1	Radha	1250	Jackson	2020-03-04	2020-03-04
127	10000	1	Radha	2503	Jackson	2020-03-06	2020-03-06
129	10001	2	Swamy	159	George	2020-04-06	2020-04-06
135	10001	2	Swamy	630	George	2020-07-23	2020-07-23
136	10000	1	Radha	180	Jackson	2020-08-10	2020-08-10
137	10003	6	Swamy	250	Khan	2020-08-11	2020-08-11
139	10002	7	Radha	200	Pathak	2020-10-27	2020-10-29
141	10000	1	swamy	1350	Jackson	2020-12-02	2020-12-03

9 rows in set (0.00 sec)

Figure 3.15

Now let's learn how to substitute the value in the real query.

Updating table

To update records of the table you can use UPDATE statement as shown below:

UPDATE table_name

SET column_name1 = value1, column_name2 = value2, ...

WHERE condition;

For example,

If you look at customer_details and customer_login table you will notice a mistake in records.

mysql> select * from customer_details;

customer_ID	customer_FN	customer_SN	customer_contact	email_id
10000	Eric	Jackson	9898983434	ericjackson@yahoo.com
10001	George	Mathews	9089376511	gm@yahoo.com
10002	Riya	Pathak	9089346521	riya.patha2010@gmail.com
10003	Aslam	Khan	9602346833	riya.patha2010@gmail.com
10004	Rakesh	Verma	7089676523	rakesh.verma@gmail.com
10005	Meenakshi	Sinha	9989645523	msinha@gmail.com

6 rows in set (0.09 sec)

mysql> select * from customer_login;

login_ID	username	password	customer_ID
1	ejack	ejack@123	10000
2	gmathews	georgeforever	10001
6	ripa	riya123	10003
7	akhan	ak@2021	10002

4 rows in set (0.05 sec)

Figure 3.16

The login details of customer_id 10003 and 10002 have got exchanged. We can use the update statement to change these values.

1. **update customer_login**

Set username = 'akhan', password = 'ak@2021' where customer_ID = '10003';

```
mysql> update customer_login
    -> Set username = ' akhan ', password = ' ak@2021 ' where customer_ID = ' 10003 '
    -> ;
Query OK, 1 row affected (0.04 sec)
Rows matched: 1  Changed: 1  Warnings: 0

mysql> select * from customer_login;
+----------+----------+---------------+-------------+
| login_ID | username | password      | customer_ID |
+----------+----------+---------------+-------------+
|        1 | ejack    | ejack@123     |       10000 |
|        2 | gmathews | georgeforever |       10001 |
|        6 |  akhan   |  ak@2021      |       10003 |
|        7 | akhan    | ak@2021       |       10002 |
+----------+----------+---------------+-------------+
4 rows in set (0.00 sec)
```

Figure 3.17

2. **update customer_login**

Set username = 'ripa', password = 'riya123' where customer_ID = '10002';

```
mysql> update customer_login
    -> Set username = ' ripa ', password = ' riya123 ' where customer_ID = ' 10002 ';
Query OK, 1 row affected (0.02 sec)
Rows matched: 1  Changed: 1  Warnings: 0

mysql> select * from customer_login;
+----------+----------+---------------+-------------+
| login_ID | username | password      | customer_ID |
+----------+----------+---------------+-------------+
|        1 | ejack    | ejack@123     |       10000 |
|        2 | gmathews | georgeforever |       10001 |
|        6 |  akhan   |  ak@2021      |       10003 |
|        7 |  ripa    |  riya123      |       10002 |
+----------+----------+---------------+-------------+
4 rows in set (0.00 sec)
```

Figure 3.18

Dropping a table

If there is a need to drop a table we can use the DROP Statement to remove it permanently from the database.

`DROP TABLE table_name;`

If you try to delete a table that does not exist then MySQL will generate an error.

You can also use DROP statement to drop Multiple Tables

DROP TABLE IF EXISTS table_name1, table_name2 , table_name3;

The IF EXISTS option shows one warning as table1 does not exist.

Dropping a database

If you plan to drop a database be assured that this will lead to complete loss of information stored in that database. Hence you should be very sure about executing this command. The command for dropping a database is very simple:

DROP database_name;

4 MySQL for Python

In this chapter, you will cover:

- Basic Rules for Writing SQL Queries
- Connect MySQL database to Python using MySQL Connector
- Create a database in Mysql using Python
- Retrieve records from database using Python
- Creating a Database

Introduction

Now that you are clear about how python works it is time to dive into some more advance topics. This chapter will take you on a different journey. Often a software application is associated with a database for storing information. In this chapter you will learn how to install MySQL database, how to configure it with Python and how to use Python to interact with MySQL.

As a revision we will create a new database using command prompt for making MYSQL work with Python.

Now that you have configured MySQL, open your command prompt and type the command given in the box below:

```
mysql -u root -p
```

You will now be prompted to provide your password. Enter your password and your command prompt should look like this:

```
Command Prompt - mysql -u root -p
Microsoft Windows [Version 6.3.9600]
(c) 2013 Microsoft Corporation. All rights reserved.

C:\Users\MYPC>mysql -u root -p
Enter password: *****
Welcome to the MySQL monitor.  Commands end with ; or \g.
Your MySQL connection id is 8
Server version: 6.0.0-alpha-community-nt-debug MySQL Community Server (GPL)

Type 'help;' or '\h' for help. Type '\c' to clear the buffer.

mysql>
```

Figure 4.1

To start off with SQL we have to first create a database. For this please follow the steps given below:

Step1: Start your command prompt window

Go to start > Run and type cmd. Or go to start and just search for cmd. Your command prompt window will open.

Step2:Log into your account

Give the following command:

```
mysql -u root -p
```

Now, press **enter**. The command prompt window will now show "**Enter password:**"

1. Type the root password that you had set at the time of configuration.
2. We will now create a database for managing our work. The name of this database would be PYMYSQL.
3. Type the following instructions:

Syntax:

```
CREATE DATABASE DATABASE_NAME;
```

So, let's say we create a MySQL database for Python Programs by the name PYMYSQL. So theCommand for Creating database PYMYSQL will be as follows:

```
CREATE DATABASE PYMYSQL;
```

4.1 Basic Rules for Writing SQL Queries

Here are few things that you need to know:

- SQL commands are not case sensitive. You can use upper or lower case it does not matter.
- The database name cannot have spaces.
- All MySQL commands end with a semicolon(**;**). If you forget to enter semicolon then in the next line enter ';' and press enter so that the command can be executed.

If the database is created you will see the following message:

Query OK, 1 row affected

4.2 Connect MySQL database to Python using MySQL Connector

The standard interface for Python database access modules is defined by the python Database API. All the Python database module adhere to this interface. The DB-API encourages similarity between modules that would be used by Python to access database. This helps in achieving consistency. It becomes easy to work with different databases as the process involved is similar. These are some basic steps that must be followed to work with any database. Working with the API involves:

1. Importing the API module
2. Getting connected to the database

3. Execute SQL queries
4. Close the connection.

You can install mysql connector by giving ***pip installmysql-connector-python*** command.

```
Command Prompt
C:\Users\MYPC>cd C:\Users\MYPC\AppData\Local\Programs\Python\Python38-32\Scripts

C:\Users\MYPC\AppData\Local\Programs\Python\Python38-32\Scripts>pip install mysq
l-connector-python
Collecting mysql-connector-python
  Downloading mysql_connector_python-8.0.19-py2.py3-none-any.whl (355 kB)
     |████████████████████████████████| 355 kB 504 kB/s
Collecting protobuf==3.6.1
  Downloading protobuf-3.6.1-py2.py3-none-any.whl (390 kB)
     |████████████████████████████████| 390 kB 3.3 MB/s
Collecting dnspython==1.16.0
  Downloading dnspython-1.16.0-py2.py3-none-any.whl (188 kB)
     |████████████████████████████████| 188 kB 3.3 MB/s
Requirement already satisfied: six>=1.9 in c:\users\mypc\appdata\local\programs\
python\python38-32\lib\site-packages (from protobuf==3.6.1->mysql-connector-pyth
on) (1.14.0)
Requirement already satisfied: setuptools in c:\users\mypc\appdata\local\program
s\python\python38-32\lib\site-packages (from protobuf==3.6.1->mysql-connector-py
thon) (41.2.0)
Installing collected packages: protobuf, dnspython, mysql-connector-python
Successfully installed dnspython-1.16.0 mysql-connector-python-8.0.19 protobuf-3
.6.1

C:\Users\MYPC\AppData\Local\Programs\Python\Python38-32\Scripts>
```

Figure 4.2

4.3 Create a database in Mysql using Python

Give the following command:

```
Show databases;
```

```
C:\Users\MYPC>mysql -u root -p
Enter password: *****
Welcome to the MySQL monitor.  Commands end with ; or \g.
Your MySQL connection id is 17
Server version: 6.0.0-alpha-community-nt-debug MySQL Community Server (GPL)

Type 'help;' or '\h' for help. Type '\c' to clear the buffer.

mysql> SHOW DATABASES;
+--------------------+
| Database           |
+--------------------+
| information_schema |
| mysql              |
| pymysql            |
| test               |
+--------------------+
4 rows in set (0.00 sec)
```

Figure 4.3: *Displaying Databases*

Next step is to grant privileges to your database. You can now create a user that will have complete privilege over this database.

```
GRANT ALL PRIVILEGES ON pymysql.* TO 'pymysqladmin'@'localhost' IDENTIFIED BY
'pymysql123';
```

Please Note:

1. In this case the name of the **user** that has full privileges on **PYMYSQL database** is '**pymysqladmin**'.
2. The password is '**pymysql123**'.

Now to connect to the database you will have to follow two simple steps:

Step 1: Import mysql.connector

```
>>> import mysql.connector as msql
```

Step 2: Open connection to database

It is important to connect to MySQL using **connect()** method which returns a **connection object**.

Syntax:

```
your_connection_name = msql.connect(host=host_name,user=user_name,passwd=-database_password,charset='utf8', database= database_name)
```

In our case we create a connection object **pycon** using **connect()** method.

```
>>>pycon = msql.connect(host = 'localhost',user='pymysqladmin',passwd='pymysql123',charset='utf8',database='pymysql')
```

For higher version of MySQL you need not provide **charset='utf8'** parameter, this is a requirement for MySQL 6.0. Figure 4.4 shows how this code will look in Python shell.

```
>>> import mysql.connector as msql
>>> pycon = msql.connect(host = 'localhost',user='pymysqladmin',passwd='pymysql1
23',charset='utf8',database='pymysql')
```

Figure 4.4

Connecting to MySQL using mysql.connector

> Note: You can check if the connection has been established with the MySQL database or not with the help of is_connected( ) function.
>
> ```
> >>>pycon.is_connected()
> True
> >>>
> ```

Step 3: Creating cursor object:

```
>>>mycursor = pycon.cursor()
```

Creating a cursor is very important because whenever you pass on a query to database it will return a result set. This result must be stored somewhere and a cursor is used for this purpose.

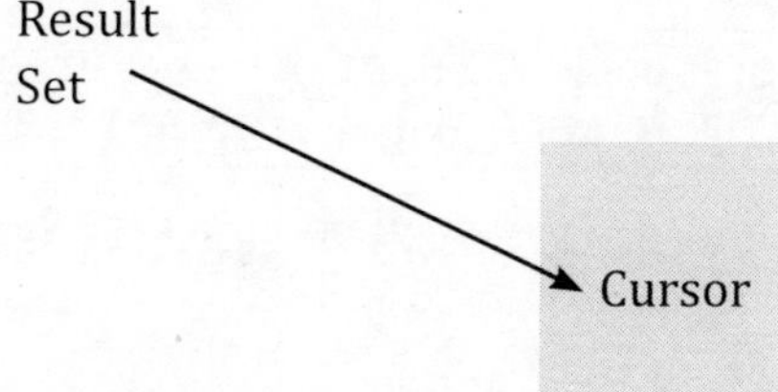

***Figure 4.5:** Storing Result set in Cursor*

However, there are some constraints imposed on this cursor. The most important one is that a cursor is **Read-only** in nature. This means that you cannot update a table in your database using cursor.

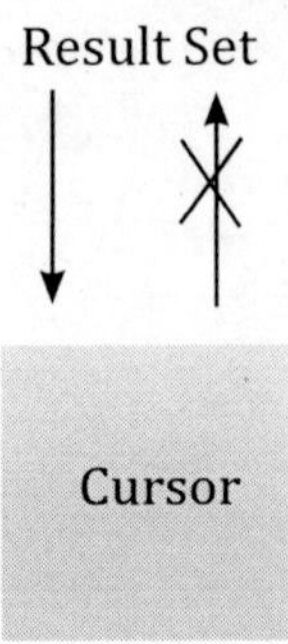

Figure 4.6

So, this is how one can work, assign the cursor to a variable.

mycursor = pycon.cursor()

mycursor = Result set

Figure 4.7

Assigning cursor to a variable

So, you now have a variable **mycursor** which can be used to manage the cursor.

The cursor uses the **execute()** method to execute the SQL queries using Python.

It is important to close the cursor object, once you have completed the task. This can be done using cursor.close() method()

Step 4: Create a Table

We will now create a table by the name **book** with the following 3 fields:

1. chapter_num which is auto increment and the primary key.
2. The second field is the **chapter** (for the name of the chapter), it is a text field and is not null.
3. There is another not null field by the name **pages**.

The mysql statement for create table is:

```
CREATE TABLE book ( chapter_num INT UNSIGNED PRIMARY KEY AUTO_INCREMENT, chapter
TEXT NOT NULL,pages INT NOT  NULL )
```

In Python this statement will be executed with the help of cursor as shown below:

```
mycursor.execute("CREATE TABLE book ( chapter_num INT UNSIGNED PRIMARY KEY
AUTO_INCREMENT, chapter TEXT NOT NULL,pages INT NOT  NULL )")
```

You can use your command prompt to check directly if the table has been successfully created.

Login using the privilieges:

```
mysql -u pymysqladmin -p
Enter Password: pymysql123
```

So, that you are able to work on the table give the following command:

```
use pymysql;
```

Now to check if the table has been created type:

```
show columns from book;
```

```
mysql> show columns from book;
+-------------+------------------+------+-----+---------+----------------+
| Field       | Type             | Null | Key | Default | Extra          |
+-------------+------------------+------+-----+---------+----------------+
| chapter_num | int(10) unsigned | NO   | PRI | NULL    | auto_increment |
| chapter     | text             | NO   |     |         |                |
| pages       | int(11)          | NO   |     |         |                |
+-------------+------------------+------+-----+---------+----------------+
3 rows in set (0.06 sec)
```

Figure 4.8

Now, as an exercise let's just add one record directly from command prompt using MySQL query and then check try to retrieve that record using Python.

On your command prompt type:

```
insert into book values(1,'Introduction',12);
```

Now, check if the record has been added to the table:

```
select * from book;
```

```
+-------------+--------------+-------+
| chapter_num | chapter      | pages |
+-------------+--------------+-------+
|           1 | Introduction |    12 |
+-------------+--------------+-------+
1 row in set (0.00 sec)
```

Figure 4.9

4.4 Retrieve records from database using Python

Now, we know that there is one record in the **book** table.

From your Python Idle you can check the records in the book table using the syntax given below:

Syntax:

```
cursor_name.fetchall()
```

Figure 4.10 displays how you can connect to MySQL server using Python

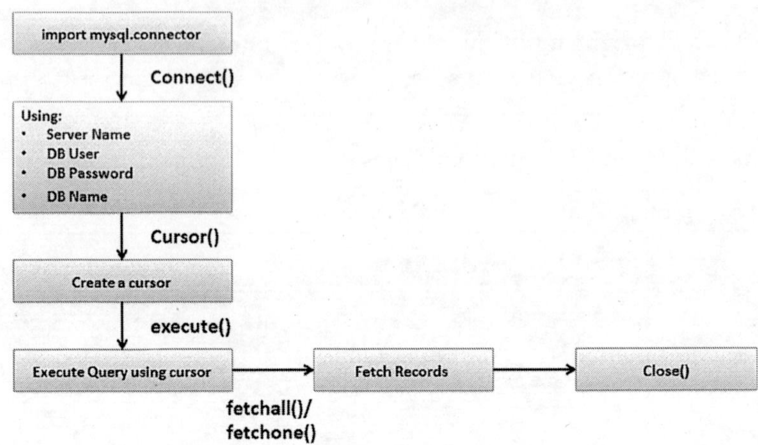

Figure 4.10

Steps involved in retrieving the records are as follows:

Step 1:Import the API Module.

```
>>>import mysql.connector as msql
```

Step 2:Acquire a connection with the database.

```
>>>pycon = msql.connect(host = 'localhost',user='pymysqladmin',passwd='py-
mysql123',charset='utf8',database='pymysql')
```

Step 3:Use the connection object to create a cursor

```
mycursor = pycon.cursor()
```

Step 4: Execute the MySQL function using the SQL statements

```
>>> statement = 'select * from pymysql.book;'
>>>mycursor.execute(statement)
```

Step 5: Fetch data

```
>>>mycursor.fetchall()
```

So, we can retrieve the records using mycursor as shown below:

```
>>>import mysql.connector as msql
>>>pycon = msql.connect(host = 'localhost',user='pymysqladmin',passwd='py-
mysql123',charset='utf8',database='pymysql')
>>>mycursor = pycon.cursor()
>>> statement = 'select * from pymysql.book;'
>>>mycursor.execute(statement)
>>>mycursor.fetchall()
[(1, 'Introduction', 12)]
```

Step 6:Closing connection()

Though this step is not followed in the above example, it is a mandatory step.

```
>>>mycursor.close()
```

We would be following it in the coming examples.

You can match the records with records obtained by mySQL directly.

Now Let's try to insert record through python shell.

Go to Python shell and give the following commands:

```
>>>mycursor.execute("""INSERT INTO book(chapter, pages) VALUES("Basics",
"15");""")
>>>pycon.commit()
>>> statement = 'select * from book;'
>>>mycursor.execute(statement)
>>>mycursor.fetchall()
[(1, 'Introduction', 12), (6, 'Basics', 15)]
```

So, you can see that the second record has been added. You can recheck directly using the command prompt

```
mysql> select * from book;
+-------------+--------------+-------+
| chapter_num | chapter      | pages |
+-------------+--------------+-------+
|           1 | Introduction |    12 |
|           6 | Basics       |    15 |
+-------------+--------------+-------+
2 rows in set (0.00 sec)
```

Figure 4.11

We have broadly explored how things work. Now in the coming sections you will learn about how basic MySQL queries are executed on the MySQL bash and how the same queries are executed in Python.

4.5 Creating a Database

To understand how to create a database using Python it is important to know how database is actually created using direct MySQL queries this is explained in Section 12.4.1. Section 12.4.2 explains how to create MySQL database using Python.

4.5.1 Creating Database directly using MySQL

Follow the steps given below to create a MySQL database using SQL.

Step 1: Type the following command:

```
mysql -u root -p
```

Step 2: Enter Password

You will be prompted to enter the password for working with MySQL. You have set this password at the time of installation. In this case it was "bpb12"

```
Command Prompt - mysql -u root -p
Microsoft Windows [Version 6.3.9600]
(c) 2013 Microsoft Corporation. All rights reserved.

C:\Users\MYPC>mysql -u root -p
Enter password: *****
Welcome to the MySQL monitor.  Commands end with ; or \g.
Your MySQL connection id is 26
Server version: 6.0.0-alpha-community-nt-debug MySQL Community Server (GPL)

Type 'help;' or '\h' for help. Type '\c' to clear the buffer.

mysql> _
```

Figure 4.12

Entering Password to connect to MySQL

Step 3: provide the command to create a database.

```
mysql> CREATE DATABASE SCHOOL;
```

Type the following command to see if the database you just created is present in the list or not:

```
Command Prompt - mysql -u root -p
C:\Users\MYPC>mysql -u root -p
Enter password: *****
Welcome to the MySQL monitor.  Commands end with ; or \g.
Your MySQL connection id is 26
Server version: 6.0.0-alpha-community-nt-debug MySQL Community Server (GPL)

Type 'help;' or '\h' for help. Type '\c' to clear the buffer.

mysql> CREATE DATABASE SCHOOL;
Query OK, 1 row affected (0.08 sec)

mysql> SHOW DATABASES;
+--------------------+
| Database           |
+--------------------+
| information_schema |
| mysql              |
| pymysql            |
| school             |
| test               |
+--------------------+
5 rows in set (0.22 sec)

mysql>
```

Figure 4.13

Use 'SHOW DATABASES' command to check if your database is showing

Now we will attempt to do the same through Python interface. In order to do that let's first drop the database and check if it has been deleted

```
DROP DATABASE SCHOOL;
```

Now, type SHOW DATABASES; again to check if it has been removed as shown in Figure

```
mysql> SHOW DATABASES;
+--------------------+
| Database           |
+--------------------+
| information_schema |
| mysql              |
| pymysql            |
| test               |
+--------------------+
4 rows in set (0.00 sec)
```

Figure 4.14

4.5.2 Creating Database using Python

In this section you will learn to create the same database using Python. You are already familiar with the steps involved. You know that for creating a database by the name 'SCHOOL' you must give 'CREATE database SCHOOL;' command. We use **mycursor.execute()** to pass on the same command to the database.

```
import mysql.connector as msql
pycon = msql.connect(host = 'localhost',user='root',passwd='bpb12',charset='utf8')
mycursor = pycon.cursor()
statement = 'CREATE database SCHOOL;'
mycursor.execute(statement)
cursor.execute("SHOW DATABASES;")
mycursor.execute("SHOW DATABASES;")
mycursor.fetchall()
```

Compare the previous output with the output displayed below.

```
>>> import mysql.connector as msql
>>> pycon = msql.connect(host = 'localhost',user='root',passwd='bpb12',charset='utf8')
>>> mycursor = pycon.cursor()
>>> statement = 'CREATE database SCHOOL;'
>>> mycursor.execute(statement)
>>> mycursor.execute("SHOW DATABASES;")
>>> mycursor.fetchall()
[('information_schema',), ('mysql',), ('pymysql',), ('school',), ('test',)]
```

Figure 4.15

Now excute the command "SHOW DATABASES;"for MySQL and check the output. This is displayed in the following figure.

```
mysql> SHOW DATABASES;
+--------------------+
| Database           |
+--------------------+
| information_schema |
| mysql              |
| pymysql            |
| school             |
| test               |
+--------------------+
5 rows in set (0.00 sec)
```

Figure 4.16

You can drop the database using Python in the same manner:

```
#drop the database
statement = 'DROP DATABASE SCHOOL;'
mycursor.execute(statement)
mycursor.execute("SHOW DATABASES;")
mycursor.fetchall()
```

Following figure displays how you can check the information related to databases in Python shell as well as in MySQL Bash.

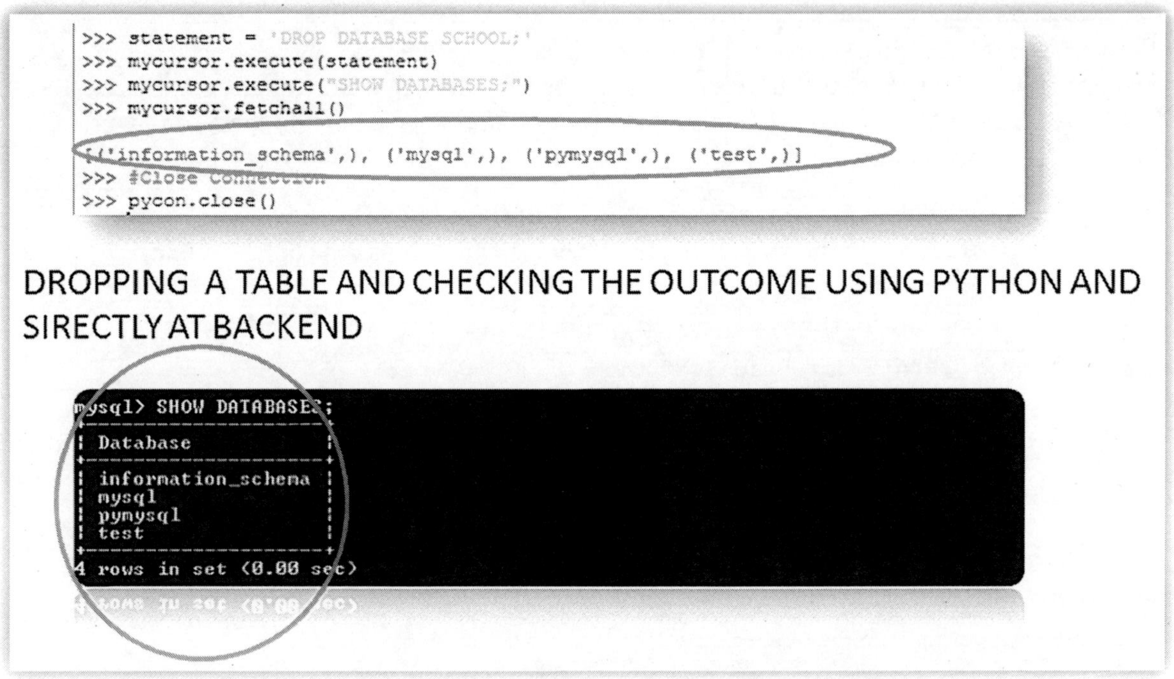

```
>>> statement = 'DROP DATABASE SCHOOL;'
>>> mycursor.execute(statement)
>>> mycursor.execute("SHOW DATABASES;")
>>> mycursor.fetchall()

[('information_schema',), ('mysql',), ('pymysql',), ('test',)]
>>> #Close Connection
>>> pycon.close()
```

DROPPING A TABLE AND CHECKING THE OUTCOME USING PYTHON AND SIRECTLY AT BACKEND

```
mysql> SHOW DATABASES;
+--------------------+
| Database           |
+--------------------+
| information_schema |
| mysql              |
| pymysql            |
| test               |
+--------------------+
4 rows in set (0.00 sec)
```

Figure 4.17

Comparison of output when checked using Python shell and MySQL Bash

Example 1:

Create a Table – Book Library using Python

> **Note:**
>
> We will now work on our pymysql database that we had initially created in this chapter. We created a table by the name book in it. Now, in the same database we will create another table by the name **book_library**.

You may recall that after configuring MySQL we had created privileges for **pymysql** database. The **username** for the database was: **pymysqladmin**and the **Password: pymysql123**.

```
Microsoft Windows [Version 6.3.9600]
(c) 2013 Microsoft Corporation. All rights reserved.

C:\Users\MYPC>mysql -u pymysqladmin -p
Enter password: **********
Welcome to the MySQL monitor.  Commands end with ; or \g.
Your MySQL connection id is 33
Server version: 6.0.0-alpha-community-nt-debug MySQL Community Server (GPL)

Type 'help;' or '\h' for help. Type '\c' to clear the buffer.

mysql> use pymysql;
Database changed
mysql>
```

Figure 4.18

Now, let's first see how we can create a table by the name BOOK_LIBRARY directly on MySQL.

```
CREATE TABLE BOOK_LIBRARY(
    BOOK_ID SMALLINT NOT NULL AUTO_INCREMENT,
    BOOK_NAME CHAR(20) NOT NULL,
    AUTHOR_NAME CHAR(20) NOT NULL,
    PAGES SMALLINT NOT NULL,
    COST SMALLINT NOT NULL,
    PRIMARY KEY (BOOK_ID)
);
```

Figure 4 shows how this would look at MySQL Bash

```
mysql> CREATE TABLE BOOK_LIBRARY(
    ->     BOOK_ID SMALLINT NOT NULL AUTO_INCREMENT,
    ->     BOOK_NAME CHAR(20) NOT NULL,
    ->     AUTHOR_NAME CHAR(20) NOT NULL,
    ->     PAGES SMALLINT NOT NULL,
    ->     COST SMALLINT NOT NULL,
    ->     PRIMARY KEY (BOOK_ID)
    -> );
Query OK, 0 rows affected (0.27 sec)
```

Figure 4.19

Now Check the table. Type "SHOW COLUMNS FROM BOOK_LIBRARY"

```
mysql> SHOW COLUMNS FROM BOOK_LIBRARY;
+-------------+-------------+------+-----+---------+----------------+
| Field       | Type        | Null | Key | Default | Extra          |
+-------------+-------------+------+-----+---------+----------------+
| BOOK_ID     | smallint(6) | NO   | PRI | NULL    | auto_increment |
| BOOK_NAME   | char(20)    | NO   |     |         |                |
| AUTHOR_NAME | char(20)    | NO   |     |         |                |
| PAGES       | smallint(6) | NO   |     |         |                |
| COST        | smallint(6) | NO   |     |         |                |
```

Figure 4.20

We will now try to accomplish the same task using Python, but before that let's drop the table from the database('DROP TABLE BOOK_LIBRARY').

```
mysql> DROP TABLE BOOK_LIBRARY;
Query OK, 0 rows affected (0.27 sec)

mysql> SHOW COLUMNS FROM BOOK_LIBRARY;
ERROR 1146 (42S02): Table 'pymysql.book_library' doesn't exist
```

Figure 4.21

Creating a table using Python

The code given below explains how the table can be created using Python.

```
import mysql.connector as msql

pycon = msql.connect(host = 'localhost',user='pymysqladmin',passwd='py-
mysql123',charset='utf8',database='pymysql')

mycursor = pycon.cursor()

statement = """CREATE TABLE BOOK_LIBRARY(BOOK_ID SMALLINT UNSIGNED PRIMARY
KEY AUTO_INCREMENT, BOOK_NAME CHAR(20) NOT NULL,AUTHOR_NAME CHAR(20) NOT
NULL, PAGES SMALLINT NOT NULL,COST SMALLINT NOT NULL )"""

mycursor.execute(statement)

statement = 'SHOW COLUMNS FROM BOOK_LIBRARY;'

mycursor.execute(statement)

mycursor.fetchall()

pycon.close()
```

Following shows the output on Python shell and the MySQL bash

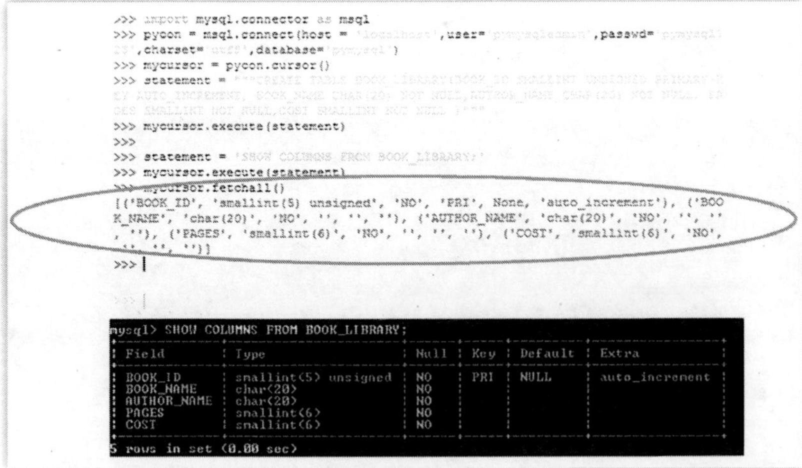

Figure 4.22

We will now work on this table for inserting and updating records.

4.6 Working with Database Using Python

In this section you will learn how to use Python to:

1. Insert Records in Database
2. Select Records
3. Fetch selected records using 'WHERE' Clause
4. Delete records from database and
5. Update records in Database

4.6.1 Inserting Records

Records can be inserted into a table using the "INSERT" statement. Figure 4.23 expalins how INSERT is used to insert statementsdirectly in the MySQL database

MySQL Insert statement:

```
INSERT INTO BOOK_LIBRARY(BOOK_NAME,AUTHOR_NAME,PAGES,COST) VALUES ('The
Secret','Rhonda Byrne',198,3);
```

```
mysql> INSERT INTO BOOK_LIBRARY(BOOK_NAME,AUTHOR_NAME,PAGES,COST) VALUES ('The S
ecret','Rhonda Byrne',198,3);
Query OK, 1 row affected (0.06 sec)

mysql> SELECT * FROM BOOK_LIBRARY;
+---------+------------+--------------+-------+------+
| BOOK_ID | BOOK_NAME  | AUTHOR_NAME  | PAGES | COST |
+---------+------------+--------------+-------+------+
|       1 | The Secret | Rhonda Byrne |   198 |    3 |
+---------+------------+--------------+-------+------+
1 row in set (0.00 sec)
```

Figure 4.23

Following figure displays how the records can be inserted in a database using Python.

Insert Records Using Python

```
>>> import mysql.connector as msql
>>> pycon = msql.connect(host = 'localhost',user='pymysqladmin',passwd='pymysql1
23',charset='utf8',database='pymysql')
>>> mycursor = pycon.cursor()
>>> statement = """INSERT INTO BOOK_LIBRARY(BOOK_NAME,AUTHOR_NAME,PAGES,COST) VA
LUES ('The Power','Rhonda Byrne',272,6);"""
>>> mycursor.execute(statement)
>>> pycon.commit()
```

Figure 4.24

> **Note:**
>
> **pycon.commit()** reflects changes in the database.

It is time to check results. Following figure displays how it should look in Python shell and MySQL Bash.

```
>>> mycursor.execute(statement)
>>> mycursor.fetchall()
[(1, 'The Secret', 'Rhonda Byrne', 198, 3), (3, 'The Power', 'Rhonda Byrne', 272
, 6)]
```

```
mysql> SELECT * FROM BOOK_LIBRARY;
+---------+------------+--------------+-------+------+
| BOOK_ID | BOOK_NAME  | AUTHOR_NAME  | PAGES | COST |
+---------+------------+--------------+-------+------+
|       1 | The Secret | Rhonda Byrne |   198 |    3 |
|       3 | The Power  | Rhonda Byrne |   272 |    6 |
+---------+------------+--------------+-------+------+
2 rows in set (0.00 sec)
```

Figure 4.25

Example 2:

Inserting Values Dynamically in table BOOK_LIBRARY

Code:

```
import mysql.connector as msql
data =[]
pycon = msql.connect(host = 'localhost',user='pymysqladmin',passwd='py-
mysql123',charset='utf8',database='pymysql')
mycursor = pycon.cursor()
statement = """INSERT INTO BOOK_LIBRARY(BOOK_NAME,AUTHOR_NAME,PAGES,COST)
VALUES (%s,%s,%s,%s);"""
#Get Name of the Book
val1 = input("Enter Book Name : ")

#Append value to list
data.append(val1)
#Get Name of the Author
val2 = input("Enter Author Name : ")

#Append value to list
data.append(val2)

#Get value of number of pages and convert to int
val3 = int(input("Enter Number of Pages: "))
#Append value to list
data.append(val3)

#Get value of cost and convert to int
val4 = int(input("Enter Cost in $: "))

#Append value to list
data.append(val4)
```

```
#Convert list to tuple
data2 = tuple(data)

print(data2)
mycursor.execute(statement,data2)
pycon.commit()
pycon.close()
```

Output:

```
Enter Book Name : The Magic
Enter Author Name : Rhonda Byrne
Enter Number of Pages: 272
Enter Cost in $: 6
('The Magic', 'Rhonda Byrne', 272, 6)
```

You must now check if the new recotd is showing in the database

```
mysql> SELECT * FROM BOOK_LIBRARY;
+---------+------------+--------------+-------+------+
| BOOK_ID | BOOK_NAME  | AUTHOR_NAME  | PAGES | COST |
+---------+------------+--------------+-------+------+
|       1 | The Secret | Rhonda Byrne |   198 |    3 |
|       3 | The Power  | Rhonda Byrne |   272 |    6 |
|       4 | The Magic  | Rhonda Byrne |   272 |    6 |
+---------+------------+--------------+-------+------+
3 rows in set (0.00 sec)
```

Figure 4.26

Note:

The above code can also be written using format() function instead of using % formatting. You can see what suits you more.

Code:

```
import mysql.connector as msql
pycon = msql.connect(host = 'localhost',user='pymysqladmin',passwd='py-
mysql123',charset='utf8',database='pymysql')
mycursor = pycon.cursor()
statement = """INSERT INTO BOOK_LIBRARY(BOOK_NAME,AUTHOR_NAME,PAGES,COST) VAL-
UES ('{0}','{1}',{2},{3});"""
val1 = input("Enter Book Name : ")
val2 = input("Enter Author Name : ")
val3 = int(input("Enter Number of Pages: "))
val4 = int(input("Enter Cost in $: "))
mycursor.execute(statement.format(val1,val2,val3,val4))
pycon.commit()
pycon.close()
```

Output:

```
Enter Book Name : The Hero
Enter Author Name : Rhonda Byrne
Enter Number of Pages: 240
Enter Cost in $: 6
```

```
Microsoft Windows [Version 6.3.9600]
(c) 2013 Microsoft Corporation. All rights reserved.

C:\Users\MYPC>mysql -u pymysqladmin -p
Enter password: **********
Welcome to the MySQL monitor.  Commands end with ; or \g.
Your MySQL connection id is 7
Server version: 6.0.0-alpha-community-nt-debug MySQL Community Server (GPL)

Type 'help;' or '\h' for help. Type '\c' to clear the buffer.

mysql> use pymysql;
Database changed
mysql> SELECT * FROM BOOK_LIBRARY;
+---------+------------+--------------+-------+------+
| BOOK_ID | BOOK_NAME  | AUTHOR_NAME  | PAGES | COST |
+---------+------------+--------------+-------+------+
|       1 | The Secret | Rhonda Byrne |   198 |    3 |
|       3 | The Power  | Rhonda Byrne |   272 |    6 |
|       4 | The Magic  | Rhonda Byrne |   272 |    6 |
|       5 | The Hero   | Rhonda Byrne |   240 |    6 |
+---------+------------+--------------+-------+------+
4 rows in set (0.00 sec)

mysql>
```

Figure 4.27

Sometimes while working with a database you may require to add multiple records together. For that you can use execute many. Let's see how this is done. Suppose. There is a requirement for adding following 5 records in the book_library table:

Table 4.1

BOOK_NAME	AUTHOR_NAME	PAGES	COST
I AM Magic	Maria Robins	63	13
One Truth, One Law	Erin Werley	87	6
Mind Magic	Merlin Starlight	265	19
Advanced Manifesting	Linda West	172	4
The Frequency	Linda West	180	4

Step1: Put each record in brackets.

```
('I AM Magic','Maria Robins',63,13)
('One Truth, One Law','Erin Werley',87,6)
('Mind Magic ','Merlin Starlight',265,19)
('Advanced Manifesting','Linda West',172,4)
('The Frequency','Linda West',180,4)
```

Step2: Prepare a list of these records.

```
values =[('I AM Magic','Maria Robins',63,13), ('One Truth, One Law','Erin Wer-
ley',87,6), ('Mind Magic for Beginners','Merlin Starlight',265,19), ('Advanced
Manifesting','Linda West',172,4), ('The Frequency','Linda West',180,4)]
```

Step3: Execute the code

We will now use this list to add values as shown below:

```
import mysql.connector as msql

pycon = msql.connect(host = 'localhost',user='pymysqladmin',passwd='py-
mysql123',charset='utf8',database='pymysql')

mycursor = pycon.cursor()

statement = """INSERT INTO BOOK_LIBRARY(BOOK_NAME,AUTHOR_NAME,PAGES,COST) VAL-
UES (%s,%s,%s,%s);"""

values =[('I AM Magic','Maria Robins',63,13), ('One Truth, One Law','Erin Wer-
ley',87,6), ('Mind Magic','Merlin Starlight',265,19), ('Advanced Manifest-
ing','Linda West',172,4), ('The Frequency','Linda West',180,4)]

mycursor.executemany(statement,values)

pycon.commit()

pycon.close()

print("Records Inserted!!")
```

Output:

```
Records Inserted!!
```

```
mysql> SELECT * FROM BOOK_LIBRARY;
+---------+-----------------------+------------------+-------+------+
| BOOK_ID | BOOK_NAME             | AUTHOR_NAME      | PAGES | COST |
+---------+-----------------------+------------------+-------+------+
|       1 | The Secret            | Rhonda Byrne     |   198 |    3 |
|       3 | The Power             | Rhonda Byrne     |   272 |    6 |
|       4 | The Magic             | Rhonda Byrne     |   272 |    6 |
|       5 | The Hero              | Rhonda Byrne     |   240 |    6 |
|       8 | I AM Magic            | Maria Robins     |    63 |   13 |
|       9 | One Truth, One Law    | Erin Werley      |    87 |    6 |
|      10 | Mind Magic            | Merlin Starlight |   265 |   19 |
|      11 | Advanced Manifesting  | Linda West       |   172 |    4 |
|      12 | The Frequency         | Linda West       |   180 |    4 |
+---------+-----------------------+------------------+-------+------+
9 rows in set (0.00 sec)
```

Figure 4.28

4.6.2 Select Records

Lead in required

Fetching all records from a table

Look at the illustration given above. The SELECT * FROM BOOK_LIBRARY ; query displayed all the records present in the BOOK_LIBRARY TABLE. In the next section we will retrieve all records using Python.

4.6.2.1 Fetching all records from a table in Python using fetchall()

The following code illustrates how to retrieve all records from a table.

Code:

```
import mysql.connector as msql
pycon = msql.connect(host = 'localhost',user='pymysqladmin',passwd='py-mysql123',charset='utf8',database='pymysql')
mycursor = pycon.cursor()
statement = """SELECT * FROM BOOK_LIBRARY;"""
mycursor.execute(statement)
result_set = mycursor.fetchall()
print("The Results are as follows: ")
for result in result_set:
    print(result)
pycon.close()
print("Done!!")
```

Output:

```
The Results are as follows:
(1, 'The Secret', 'Rhonda Byrne', 198, 3)
(3, 'The Power', 'Rhonda Byrne', 272, 6)
(4, 'The Magic', 'Rhonda Byrne', 272, 6)
(5, 'The Hero', 'Rhonda Byrne', 240, 6)
(8, 'I AM Magic', 'Maria Robins', 63, 13)
(9, 'One Truth, One Law', 'Erin Werley', 87, 6)
(10, 'Mind Magic', 'Merlin Starlight', 265, 19)
(11, 'Advanced Manifesting', 'Linda West', 172, 4)
(12, 'The Frequency', 'Linda West', 180, 4)
Done!!
```

Figure 4.29

4.6.2.2 Fetching one record from a table in Python using fetchone()

In python you can use fetchone() function to retrieve only the first record of the table.

Code:

```
import mysql.connector as msql

pycon = msql.connect(host = 'localhost',user='pymysqladmin',passwd='py-
mysql123',charset='utf8',database='pymysql')

mycursor = pycon.cursor()

statement = """SELECT * FROM BOOK_LIBRARY;"""

mycursor.execute(statement)

result_set = mycursor.fetchone()

print(result_set)

pycon.close()

print("Done!!")
```

Output:

```
(1, 'The Secret', 'Rhonda Byrne', 198, 3)

Done!!
```

Example 3:

Retrieving selected columns from a table

Figure 4.30 displays how selected records can be retrieved directly from MySQL using SQL.

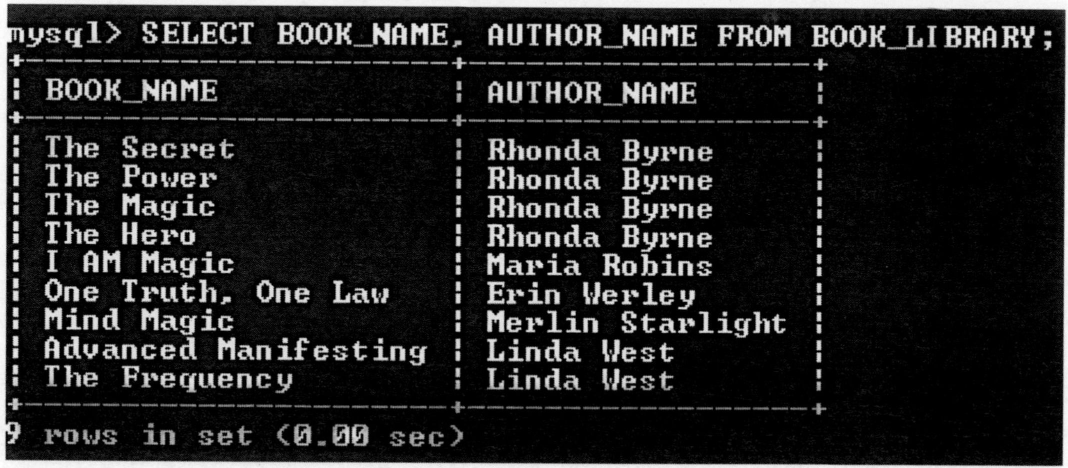

Figure 4.30

Retrieving columns using Python

```
import mysql.connector as msql
pycon = msql.connect(host = 'localhost',user='pymysqladmin',passwd='py-
mysql123',charset='utf8',database='pymysql')
mycursor = pycon.cursor()
statement = """SELECT BOOK_NAME, AUTHOR_NAME FROM BOOK_LIBRARY;"""
mycursor.execute(statement)
result_set = mycursor.fetchall()
print("The Results are as follows: ")
for result in result_set:
    print(result)
pycon.close()
print("Done!!")
```

Output:

```
The Results are as follows:
('The Secret', 'Rhonda Byrne')
('The Power', 'Rhonda Byrne')
('The Magic', 'Rhonda Byrne')
('The Hero', 'Rhonda Byrne')
('I AM Magic', 'Maria Robins')
('One Truth, One Law', 'Erin Werley')
('Mind Magic', 'Merlin Starlight')
('Advanced Manifesting', 'Linda West')
('The Frequency', 'Linda West')
Done!!
```

Figure 4.31

Retrieving selected columns of first row using fetchone()

Code:

```
import mysql.connector as msql
pycon = msql.connect(host = 'localhost',user='pymysqladmin',passwd='py-
mysql123',charset='utf8',database='pymysql')
mycursor = pycon.cursor()
statement = """SELECT BOOK_NAME, AUTHOR_NAME FROM BOOK_LIBRARY;"""
mycursor.execute(statement)
result_set = mycursor.fetchone()
print(result_set)
pycon.close()
print("Done!!")
```

Output

```
('The Secret', 'Rhonda Byrne')
Done!!
```

4.6.3 Fetching selected records from a table in Python using 'WHERE' clause

The **'WHERE'** clause is used to filter records on the basis of a condition. Let's say we want to know all information of books having cost greater or equal to $7. We would give the following command:

```
SELECT * FROM BOOK_LIBRARY WHERE COST >= 7;
```

```
mysql> SELECT * FROM BOOK_LIBRARY WHERE COST>=7;
+---------+-------------+------------------+-------+------+
| BOOK_ID | BOOK_NAME   | AUTHOR_NAME      | PAGES | COST |
+---------+-------------+------------------+-------+------+
|       8 | I AM Magic  | Maria Robins     |    63 |   13 |
|      10 | Mind Magic  | Merlin Starlight |   265 |   19 |
+---------+-------------+------------------+-------+------+
2 rows in set (0.04 sec)
```

Figure 4.32

Using 'WHERE' clause with Python

The following code displays how to used "WHERE" clause using Python.

```
import mysql.connector as msql
pycon = msql.connect(host = 'localhost',user='pymysqladmin',passwd='py-
mysql123',charset='utf8',database='pymysql')
mycursor = pycon.cursor()
statement = """SELECT * FROM BOOK_LIBRARY WHERE COST>=7;"""
mycursor.execute(statement)
result_set = mycursor.fetchall()
for result in result_set:
    print(result)
pycon.close()
print("Done!!")
```

To, display the data retrieved from the database **mycursor** is used to fetch all the records out of the cursor and these records are assigned to another variable by the name **result_set.**Youo can then iterate through **result_set** to display data or to do any other work or to update underlying data.

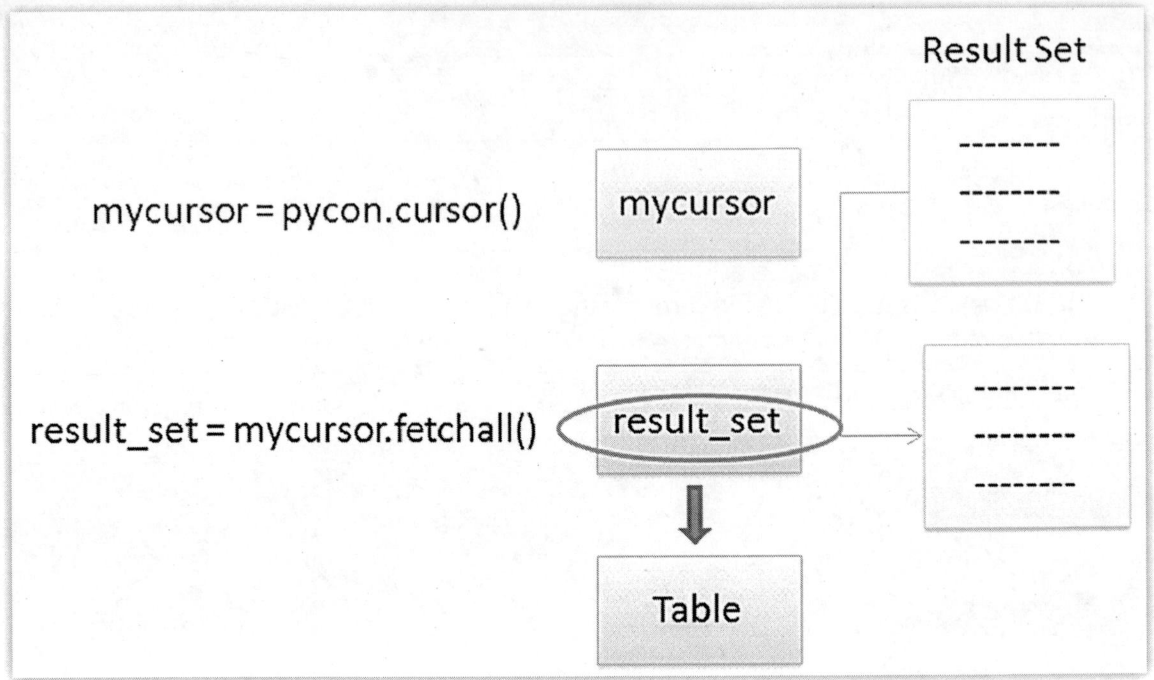

Figure 4.33

Output

```
(8, 'I AM Magic', 'Maria Robins', 63, 13)

(10, 'Mind Magic', 'Merlin Starlight', 265, 19)

Done!!
```

Select all records from BOOK_LIBRARY table where the author name has "Rhon" in it.

```
mysql> SELECT * FROM BOOK_LIBRARY WHERE AUTHOR_NAME LIKE '%Rhon%';
+---------+------------+--------------+-------+------+
| BOOK_ID | BOOK_NAME  | AUTHOR_NAME  | PAGES | COST |
+---------+------------+--------------+-------+------+
|       1 | The Secret | Rhonda Byrne |   198 |    3 |
|       3 | The Power  | Rhonda Byrne |   272 |    6 |
|       4 | The Magic  | Rhonda Byrne |   272 |    6 |
|       5 | The Hero   | Rhonda Byrne |   240 |    6 |
+---------+------------+--------------+-------+------+
4 rows in set (0.00 sec)
```

Figure 4.34

Code:

```
import mysql.connector as msql
pycon = msql.connect(host = 'localhost',user='pymysqladmin',passwd='py-
mysql123',charset='utf8',database='pymysql')
mycursor = pycon.cursor()
statement = """SELECT * FROM BOOK_LIBRARY WHERE AUTHOR_NAME LIKE '%Rhon%';"""
mycursor.execute(statement)
result_set = mycursor.fetchall()
for result in result_set:
    print(result)
pycon.close()
print("Done!!")
```

Output

```
(1, 'The Secret', 'Rhonda Byrne', 198, 3)
(3, 'The Power', 'Rhonda Byrne', 272, 6)
(4, 'The Magic', 'Rhonda Byrne', 272, 6)
(5, 'The Hero', 'Rhonda Byrne', 240, 6)
Done!!
```

Escape query values by using the placholder %s method:

Code:

```
import mysql.connector as msql
pycon = msql.connect(host = 'localhost',user='pymysqladmin',passwd='py-
mysql123',charset='utf8',database='pymysql')
mycursor = pycon.cursor()
statement = """SELECT * FROM BOOK_LIBRARY WHERE AUTHOR_NAME = %s;"""
author = ("Rhonda Byrne",)
mycursor.execute(statement,author)
result_set = mycursor.fetchall()
for result in result_set:
    print(result)
pycon.close()
print("Done!!")
```

Output

```
(1, 'The Secret', 'Rhonda Byrne', 198, 3)
(3, 'The Power', 'Rhonda Byrne', 272, 6)
(4, 'The Magic', 'Rhonda Byrne', 272, 6)
(5, 'The Hero', 'Rhonda Byrne', 240, 6)
Done!!
```

4.6.4 Using ORDER BY Clause

```
mysql> SELECT * FROM BOOK_LIBRARY ORDER BY BOOK_NAME;
+---------+-----------------------+------------------+-------+------+
| BOOK_ID | BOOK_NAME             | AUTHOR_NAME      | PAGES | COST |
+---------+-----------------------+------------------+-------+------+
|      11 | Advanced Manifesting  | Linda West       |   172 |    4 |
|       8 | I AM Magic            | Maria Robins     |    63 |   13 |
|      10 | Mind Magic            | Merlin Starlight |   265 |   19 |
|       9 | One Truth, One Law    | Erin Werley      |    87 |    6 |
|      12 | The Frequency         | Linda West       |   180 |    4 |
|       5 | The Hero              | Rhonda Byrne     |   240 |    6 |
|       4 | The Magic             | Rhonda Byrne     |   272 |    6 |
|       3 | The Power             | Rhonda Byrne     |   272 |    6 |
|       1 | The Secret            | Rhonda Byrne     |   198 |    3 |
+---------+-----------------------+------------------+-------+------+
9 rows in set (0.00 sec)
```

Figure 4.35

Code:

```
import mysql.connector as msql
pycon = msql.connect(host = 'localhost',user='pymysqladmin',passwd='py-
mysql123',charset='utf8',database='pymysql')
mycursor = pycon.cursor()
statement = """SELECT * FROM BOOK_LIBRARY WHERE AUTHOR_NAME = %s;"""
author = ("Rhonda Byrne",)
mycursor.execute(statement,author)
result_set = mycursor.fetchall()
for result in result_set:
    print(result)
pycon.close()
print("Done!!")
```

Output:

```
(11, 'Advanced Manifesting', 'Linda West', 172, 4)
(8, 'I AM Magic', 'Maria Robins', 63, 13)
(10, 'Mind Magic', 'Merlin Starlight', 265, 19)
(9, 'One Truth, One Law', 'Erin Werley', 87, 6)
(12, 'The Frequency', 'Linda West', 180, 4)
(5, 'The Hero', 'Rhonda Byrne', 240, 6)
(4, 'The Magic', 'Rhonda Byrne', 272, 6)
(3, 'The Power', 'Rhonda Byrne', 272, 6)
(1, 'The Secret', 'Rhonda Byrne', 198, 3)
Done!!
```

4.6.5 Deleting records using DELETE command

You have learnt how to insert and retrieve records from the database. In this section you will learn-how to delete records from the database.

```
import mysql.connector as msql

pycon = msql.connect(host = 'localhost',user='pymysqladmin',passwd='py-
mysql123',charset='utf8',database='pymysql')

mycursor = pycon.cursor()

statement = """DELETE FROM BOOK_LIBRARY WHERE BOOK_ID = 8"""

mycursor.execute(statement)

pycon.commit()

pycon.close()

print("Done!!")
```

Output

```
mysql> SELECT * FROM BOOK_LIBRARY;
+---------+----------------------+------------------+-------+------+
| BOOK_ID | BOOK_NAME            | AUTHOR_NAME      | PAGES | COST |
+---------+----------------------+------------------+-------+------+
|       1 | The Secret           | Rhonda Byrne     |   198 |    3 |
|       3 | The Power            | Rhonda Byrne     |   272 |    6 |
|       4 | The Magic            | Rhonda Byrne     |   272 |    6 |
|       5 | The Hero             | Rhonda Byrne     |   240 |    6 |
|       9 | One Truth, One Law   | Erin Werley      |    87 |    6 |
|      10 | Mind Magic           | Merlin Starlight |   265 |   19 |
|      11 | Advanced Manifesting | Linda West       |   172 |    4 |
|      12 | The Frequency        | Linda West       |   180 |    4 |
+---------+----------------------+------------------+-------+------+
8 rows in set (0.00 sec)
```

Figure 4.36

4.6.6 Update Clause

Code:

```
import mysql.connector as msql
pycon = msql.connect(host = 'localhost',user='pymysqladmin',passwd='py-
mysql123',charset='utf8',database='pymysql')
mycursor = pycon.cursor()
statement = """UPDATE BOOK_LIBRARY SET BOOK_ID = 2 WHERE BOOK_ID = 12;"""
mycursor.execute(statement)
pycon.commit()
pycon.close()
print("Done!!")
```

Output:

```
mysql> SELECT * FROM BOOK_LIBRARY;
+---------+---------------------+-------------------+-------+------+
| BOOK_ID | BOOK_NAME           | AUTHOR_NAME       | PAGES | COST |
+---------+---------------------+-------------------+-------+------+
|       1 | The Secret          | Rhonda Byrne      |   198 |    3 |
|       2 | The Frequency       | Linda West        |   180 |    4 |
|       3 | The Power           | Rhonda Byrne      |   272 |    6 |
|       4 | The Magic           | Rhonda Byrne      |   272 |    6 |
|       5 | The Hero            | Rhonda Byrne      |   240 |    6 |
|       9 | One Truth, One Law  | Erin Werley       |    87 |    6 |
|      10 | Mind Magic          | Merlin Starlight  |   265 |   19 |
|      11 | Advanced Manifesting| Linda West        |   172 |    4 |
+---------+---------------------+-------------------+-------+------+
8 rows in set (0.00 sec)
```

Figure 4.37

You now know how Python can be used to interact with the database. You can execute any kind of SQL query with the help of Python. Interaction with database with the help of Python is very easy as it involves standard steps. Once you understand how to implement these steps you can easily code any type of application that interacts with the database.

Short questions and answers

1. Write the Python code create a database having the name TEXTILE.

Answer:

The following code shows how a database name 'TEXTILE' can be created using Python.

```
>>> import mysql.connector as msql
>>>pycon = msql.connect(host = 'localhost',user='root',passwd='bpb12',char-
set='utf8')
>>>mycursor = pycon.cursor()
>>> statement = 'CREATE database TEXTILE;'
>>>mycursor.execute(statement)
>>>pycon.commit()
>>>pycon.close()
```

You can verify results in the database

```
mysql> SHOW DATABASES;
+--------------------+
| Database           |
+--------------------+
| information_schema |
| mysql              |
| pymysql            |
| test               |
| textile            |
+--------------------+
5 rows in set (0.05 sec)
```

Figure 4.38

2. Given a database by the name textile, has user id – shopkeeper, password – shoptoday. Write the python code to connect to the textile database.

```
mysql> GRANT ALL PRIVILEGES ON TEXTILE.* TO 'shopkeeper'@'localhost' IDENTIFIED
BY  'shoptoday';
Query OK, 0 rows affected (0.34 sec)

mysql> quit
Bye

C:\Users\MYPC>mysql -u shopkeeper -p
Enter password: *********
Welcome to the MySQL monitor.  Commands end with ; or \g.
Your MySQL connection id is 36
Server version: 6.0.0-alpha-community-nt-debug MySQL Community Server (GPL)

Type 'help;' or '\h' for help. Type '\c' to clear the buffer.

mysql> use textile;
Database changed
mysql> _
```

Figure 4.39

Answer:

```
import mysql.connector as msql

pycon = msql.connect(host = 'localhost',user='shopkeeper',passwd='shoptoday',data-
base='textile')
```

3. A company has created a new database to keep a track of its employees. The following table shows the employee records. A new employee Karan has joined the firm as project manager. His Employee Number is 7980, Salary of 10 Lacs. Insert his record in the table taking system date as the hire date. Explain the steps involved

EmpNo	EmpName	Job	Hiredate	Sal
7110	Rai	Director	2013-08-11	2500000
7123	Rishab	Software Developer	2020-01-01	500000
7128	Lee	Software Developer	2018-03-01	500000
7801	Ray	Temp	2020-07-01	60000

Figure 4.40

Answer:

```
import mysql.connector as msql
from datetime import datetime
pycon = msql.connect(host = 'localhost',user='root',passwd='password',char-
set='utf8',database = 'database_name')
mycursor = pycon.cursor()
now = datetime.now()
formatted_date = now.strftime(‘%Y-%m-%d’)
statement = "INSERT INTO emp VALUES(7980,'Karan','Project Manag-
er','{}',1000000);".format(formatted_date)
mycursor.execute(statement)
pycon.commit()
pycon.close()
```

Verify Results

EmpNo	EmpName	Job	Hiredate	Sal
7110	Rai	Director	2013-08-11	2500000
7123	Rishab	Software Developer	2020-01-01	500000
7128	Lee	Software Developer	2018-03-01	500000
7801	Ray	Temp	2020-07-01	60000
7980	Karan	Project Manager	2020-07-15	1000000

5 rows in set (0.00 sec)

Figure 4.41

4. In view of Lockdown the company decides to reduce the salary of all its employees by 10000. How will you update the table? Work on the emp table from the previous example.

Answer:

```
import mysql.connector as msql
pycon = msql.connect(host = 'localhost',user='root',passwd='password',char-
set='utf8',database = 'database_name')
mycursor = pycon.cursor()
statement = 'UPDATE emp SET Sal = Sal - 10000;'
mycursor.execute(statement)
pycon.commit()
pycon.close()
```

Output:

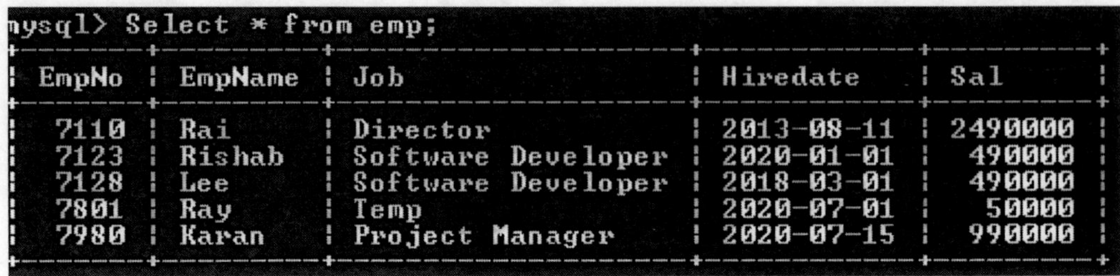

mysql> Select * from emp;

EmpNo	EmpName	Job	Hiredate	Sal
7110	Rai	Director	2013-08-11	2490000
7123	Rishab	Software Developer	2020-01-01	490000
7128	Lee	Software Developer	2018-03-01	490000
7801	Ray	Temp	2020-07-01	50000
7980	Karan	Project Manager	2020-07-15	990000

Figure 4.42

5. Modern Fashion sells various types of fashionable clothes for men and women on all leading online stores. In view of COVID-19 pandemic, the store decides to give 50% discount on women clothing and 25% discount on men clothing. Explain step by step how you would reflect these changes on MySQL database using Python interface.

```
mysql> select * from modernFashions;
+----------+-----------+---------+------+
| item_num | item_name | for_who | cost |
+----------+-----------+---------+------+
|      101 | maxi      | women   | 2500 |
|      102 | jackets   | women   | 4500 |
|      103 | jackets   | men     | 6000 |
|      104 | patiala   | women   |  900 |
|      105 | pyjamas   | men     |  999 |
|      106 | scarfs    | women   | 3900 |
|      107 | skirts    | women   | 5900 |
|      109 | Jeans     | men     | 3999 |
+----------+-----------+---------+------+
8 rows in set (0.00 sec)
```

Figure 4.43

Answer:

```
import mysql.connector as msql
pycon = msql.connect(host = 'localhost',user='root',passwd='password',char-
set='utf8',database = 'database_name')
mycursor = pycon.cursor()
statement = "UPDATE modernFashions SET cost = cost - 0.5*cost where for_who
= '{}';".format('women')
mycursor.execute(statement)
pycon.commit()
pycon.close()
```

Output:

```
mysql> select * from modernFashions;
+----------+-----------+---------+------+
| item_num | item_name | for_who | cost |
+----------+-----------+---------+------+
|      101 | maxi      | women   | 2500 |
|      102 | jackets   | women   | 4500 |
|      103 | jackets   | men     | 6000 |
|      104 | patiala   | women   |  900 |
|      105 | pyjamas   | men     |  999 |
|      106 | scarfs    | women   | 3900 |
|      107 | skirts    | women   | 5900 |
|      109 | Jeans     | men     | 3999 |
+----------+-----------+---------+------+
8 rows in set (0.00 sec)
```

Figure 4.44

6. For the **emp** table shown below:

EmpNo	EmpName	Job	Hiredate	Sal
7110	Rai	Director	2013-08-11	2540000
7123	Rishab	Software Developer	2020-01-01	540000
7128	Lee	Software Developer	2018-03-01	540000
7801	Ray	Temp	2020-07-01	100000
7980	Karan	Project Manager	2020-07-15	1040000

5 rows in set (0.02 sec)

Figure 4.45

Increment the salary of all the employees by 50000 who have been working in the firm before the year 2015 started.

Answer:

```
import mysql.connector as msql

pycon = msql.connect(host = 'localhost',user='root',passwd='password',char-
set='utf8',database = 'database_name')

mycursor = pycon.cursor()

statement = "UPDATE emp SET sal = sal + 50000 where hiredate<='2015-01-01';".
format('2015-01-01')

mycursor.execute(statement)

pycon.commit()

pycon.close()
```

Output:

EmpNo	EmpName	Job	Hiredate	Sal
7110	Rai	Director	2013-08-11	2590000
7123	Rishab	Software Developer	2020-01-01	540000
7128	Lee	Software Developer	2018-03-01	540000
7801	Ray	Temp	2020-07-01	100000
7980	Karan	Project Manager	2020-07-15	1040000

Figure 4.46

7. Define the following Database Object methods:

   a. `close()`

   b. `cursor()`

   c. `rollback()`

Answer:

a. `close()` method is used to close the cursor

b. `cursor()` method is used to return a database cursor object that can be used to execute the SQL queries.

c. `rollback()` method is used to roll back pending transaction to the state that existed before the transaction began.